SNAPPING

SNAPPING

America's Epidemic of
Sudden Personality Change

FLO CONWAY and JIM SIEGELMAN

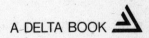
A DELTA BOOK

A DELTA BOOK
Published by
Dell Publishing Co., Inc.
1 Dag Hammarskjold Plaza
New York, New York 10017

For Hal Conway

9

Contents

PART ONE
A New Phenomenon

1 Snapping

> *Lo! I tell you a mystery.*
> *We shall not all sleep, but we shall all be changed,*
> *in a moment,*
> *in the twinkling of an eye . . .*
>
> *—1 Corinthians 15:51 (RSV)*

SINCE THE EARLY seventies, America has been gripped by an epidemic of sudden personality change.

On the surface, it appears that a new age of enlightenment is at hand. People of all ages are discovering new faiths, beliefs, and practices that are changing them in ways they never dreamed of. Around the country, college students are finding meaning and purpose in new forms of worship and religious devotion. Upwardly mobile young couples and working singles are taking part in new therapies that root out painful episodes from their past. Businessmen and housewives are learning simple self-help techniques that eliminate stress and tension from their daily lives.

Has mankind crossed the threshold of a great new era of human fulfillment? Many people think so. Vast numbers of individuals who have experienced these profound changes in their lives talk of "big breakthroughs," moments of spiritual "rebirth" and "revelation," and of "getting it," "finding it," or suddenly "becoming clear." Or they describe soaring "peak experiences," "ecstasies," and levels of awareness they call "transcendence," "bliss," and "cosmic consciousness." There are those who boast miracle cures for lifelong physical ailments and inconsolable fits of depression, while even more report rich new supplies of "inner energy" and creativity. Since the sixties, millions of Americans have set out in search of experiences such as these, exploring new pathways to spiritual fulfillment and participating in the nearly eight thousand techniques for expanding human awareness that have been introduced into our culture. At last count, six million alone had taken up some form of meditation, and over three million young Americans had joined the one thousand religious cults active in the United States.

No doubt in the course of their explorations a great many people have in fact had powerful new experiences that were the cause or catalyst of some profound improvement in their lives.

But there is another side to this epidemic of personality change, a side that has been largely dismissed, downplayed, or altogether ignored. It is the dark side of the experience, the side that cannot rightly be described in any of these glowing terms, one that has not been illuminated until now. Yet its signs are personally familiar to a large and growing number of Americans, and its effects have already been dramatically reflected in the headlines.

The news of the decade contains appalling tragedies: the Manson family murders, the Symbionese Liberation Army's kidnapping of Patricia Hearst, and the wave of random killings in New York City allegedly committed by a young postal worker, David Berkowitz, who renamed himself "Son of Sam." What turned the former high school cheerleaders and homecoming queens of the Manson Family into obedient mass murderers? Why didn't Patty Hearst flee her captors when she had more than ample opportunity? What change could have come over Berkowitz, a young man who was almost court-martialed in the army for refusing to carry a weapon, that would prompt him to prowl the streets of New York with a .44-caliber handgun?

What, if anything, have these transformations in common with the rebirth in Jesus Christ of two men as dissimilar as former Nixon aide Charles Colson and one-time black revolutionary Eldridge Cleaver, and what elements do they share with the mysteries of sudden personality change that abound in modern life? Beyond the headlines, countless paradoxes arise in the many popular group therapies and self-help techniques that have come out of the "consciousness explosion" of the sixties, in the mushroom growth of Evangelical Christianity in the seventies, and in the mounting controversy over America's rich and powerful religious cults.

The college student leaves school without warning and is discovered by his parents selling flowers on a street corner. The wealthy executive, taking full responsibility for his fate, quits his job at a moment's notice to sit on the beach and play the flute. A young mother abandons her children after having a "personal encounter with the Holy Spirit." A middle-aged housewife runs away from home to take a month-long course in levitation. A former Yippie leader gives up political activism to follow a fourteen-year-old guru, then embarks on a career as a life insurance salesman. These stories raise even larger and more perplexing questions. Are these changes good or bad? Are they permanent? What's really behind them? Who's susceptible? Me? My kids? Everyone?

For many Americans, the quest for personal growth or spiritual fulfillment culminates in an experience that is unmistakably traumatic, an experience that has negative, and perhaps disastrous, effects on their personalities and their lives. In contrast to the reported pleasures and benefits of the "big breakthrough," for many individuals sudden change comes in a moment of intense experience that is not so much a "peak" as a precipice, an unforeseen break in the continuity of awareness that may leave them detached, withdrawn, disoriented—or utterly confused. The experience itself may produce hallucinations or delusions or render the individual extremely vulnerable to suggestion. It may lead to changes that alter lifelong habits, values, and beliefs, disrupt friendships, marriages, and family relationships; and, in extreme instances, excite self-destructive, violent, or criminal behavior.

Former members of religious cults and veterans of mass-marketed group therapies and self-help techniques provide vivid confirmation of the existence of this phenomenon when they speak of what they have experienced in the process of some cult ritual or therapeutic technique. For the most part, these individuals are at a loss to explain what happened to them. Many, however, describe it in one graphic, almost visible term. "Something *snapped* inside me," they report, or, "I just *snapped*"—as if their awareness were a piece of brittle plastic or a drawn-out rubber band. And, indeed, this is often the impression of those people who are closest to them: their parents, spouses, friends, and colleagues. To these observers, it appears as if the individual's entire personality has "snapped," that there is a new person inside the old one, someone completely different and unrecognizable.

Because this exceptional transformation has not been looked at on its own —although countless Americans have struggled in vain to understand their experience or gone to great lengths to rationalize it—in this book we investigate the phenomenon we call *snapping*, a term which designates the sudden, drastic alteration of personality in all its many forms. We chose this word not only because we have heard it so often from other people but because, to us, it depicts the way in which intense experience may affect fundamental information-processing capacities of the brain. Our research has confirmed that snapping is not merely an alteration of behavior or belief. It can bring about a much deeper and more comprehensive change in individual awareness and personality. And, as we have discovered, it poses an even more pervasive threat to our society as a whole, one that challenges psychiatric, legal, and social interpretation.

———

As co-authors we come to this investigation from different vantage points. My colleague, Flo Conway, traversed the West Coast in the sixties, observing in the course of her academic and professional work the heyday of America's newborn human potential movement. Out of that glorious consciousness explosion came a flood of group techniques and radical therapies, among them encounter, psychodrama, Gestalt, primal therapy, and guided fantasy, some of which had been used professionally for years. Once popularized, however, elements of these techniques spread quickly throughout the West Coast and into psychotherapy, counseling and rehabilitation, and crisis centers around the country.

In her doctoral research in communication, Flo studied these new techniques and observed their effects in a number of therapeutic and clinical settings. She was struck by the proliferation of such powerful tools in the hands of many therapists and group leaders who had little or no understanding of their immediate or long-range effects, and she saw the need for new theory, research, and follow-up studies. Throughout those years, her larger commitment, both professionally and personally, was to reach a new understanding of human development that would go beyond the conventional view that human activity can be wholly explained by drawing analogies to animals and machines. In her effort to validate those aspects of experience that are uniquely human, she developed new methods of interpretation; and before national and international forums, she presented new ways of looking at the profound changes taking place among people and cultures, changes which psychiatry and the traditional social sciences have been unable to explain. Choosing as the foundation of her theory the basic principles of the communication sciences, she offered steps toward a comprehensive view of the human mind as a system of interacting communication processes. This system contained within its framework the essential elements of traditional theories of personality as well as more recent discoveries concerning both animal and human behavior.

At the same time, I was taking quite a different tack back east. In my studies of philosophy, psychology, and literature at Harvard University and later at Trinity College, Cambridge, I kept bumping into prevailing doctrines which proclaimed that the human "spirit," the human "mind," and even the human "imagination" didn't exist. Like Flo, I was startled to find that, because they were "subjective" and could not be "verified" or "reliably reproduced," vital human processes had been declared categorically off limits by both Western science and philosophy.

From an academic point of view, I was drawn to those mysteries of consciousness that were all around me in the early seventies: the still-rampant use of psychedelics, the growing interest in Eastern philosophy and meditation, and the curious rise of the "new religion." However, I did not try to crack these riddles so much as humor them in a number of articles I wrote for national magazines and newspapers. I wrote about college classmates who returned from retreats speaking in "tongues," their eyes on fire, and otherwise "blissed out." I told of the public gathering I had attended to see a film that would reveal how anyone could attain a state of "perfect knowledge." (The presentation was delayed two hours because no one in the sponsoring organization knew how to run a movie projector.) But that was before anyone had begun to question what went on in America's religious cults.

By 1974, the situation wasn't funny any longer. The Children of God, the first cult of "Jesus Freaks," was being investigated by the Attorney General of New York. The Hare Krishna and the Moonies had taken to the streets, and people were being jailed around the country for attempting to "deprogram" cult members who had allegedly been "brainwashed." To add to the confusion, a new breed of entrepreneurs had begun marketing human awareness on a nationwide scale, like fast food, in slick, prepackaged mass-group therapies and self-help techniques.

That year, Flo and I joined forces in New York while working for a new national magazine. There we compared notes and personal experiences and immediately noticed some disturbing common patterns in what we'd been seeing all around us. The closer we looked, the more some of these profound breakthroughs people were talking about appeared quite different from what they were being called. Moreover, when we viewed our findings through the lens of Flo's perspective in communication, it became clear that at a much deeper level many of the techniques being used to create intense personal and spiritual experiences posed a hidden threat to fundamental processes of the mind. In the months that followed, I, too, became a serious student of communication, immersing myself in the major texts and seminal works of the diverse field in search of the key concepts and the plain language needed to convey Flo's intricate system of the mind in everyday terms. Then, together, we forged a joint framework for further exploration.

For the past four years, we have focused our investigation on America's religious cults and mass-marketed therapies, threading our way through their various doctrines, rituals, procedures, philosophies, and private jargons to reach what we now believe to be their common threat to human development. In the course of our research, we came to the conclusion that America's cults and mass therapies should be viewed together because they use nearly identical techniques of manipulating the mind and because, in this decade, many of them have become impossible to categorize. Some use sophisticated therapeutic methods yet call themselves religions and claim tax exemptions. Others invoke the names of Hindu deities yet advertise their medical and scientific credibility. For many, refined techniques of marketing and persuasion reap huge sums of money on a national—and even international—scale. Nearly all rely on the impenetrable legal sanctions of the First Amendment and defy both government regulation and consumer protection through the establishment of charitable trusts, foundations, or nonprofit institutions.

We traveled to dozens of cities and towns across the country in the course of our research, in an effort to get an extensive cross-section of opinion and experience. Like most cultural trends, America's cults and mass therapies began in the major centers of media and population on both coasts and then moved quickly inland to the heart of America, where popular religions have always found fertile soil. Today the largest religious cults, such as the Unification Church, the Hare Krishna, the Divine Light Mission, and the Way, have centers and temples in every major city, in many smaller towns, and on most college campuses. The most popular mass therapies, Transcendental Meditation and Scientology's Dianetics, for instance, have dozens of outlets from coast to coast; and many of the newer ones, such as est and its latest outgrowth, Lifespring, are expanding into regional markets and spawning local imitators.

In our travels, we talked with hundreds of individuals and heard innumerable testimonials about wonder cures and instant renewals and revelations; as we probed, many of these accounts broke down in nonsense or contradiction. More often, we were told vivid—and surprisingly similar—stories about individual quests for personal growth and spiritual fulfillment that culminated in what we call snapping. Time after time, we heard about people who were transformed "in a moment, in the twinkling of an eye," people who, at the time, had no idea what had happened to them except that somewhere something inside them had "snapped." We heard, as well, about individuals whose transformations were only relatively sudden and slightly less dramatic, people who slid not instantly but in the course of a weekend or a month into states of mind that were equally baffling and, on occasion, even more bizarre.

In this book, the people who have undergone these sudden changes speak for themselves. Our attempt to understand the depth of their experiences has led us to a new perspective on the nature of personality—what it consists of, how it is formed, and how it can be transformed. Here we use the term "personality" in the largest sense of the word: the living system of the human mind in its combined individual and social nature, which finds its outward expression in the unique qualities observable in every human being. On this basis, we range freely through the various levels of this system, and whether we refer to the organic process of "awareness" in terms of the more philosophical notion of "consciousness" or use the general term "mind" in place of "personality," our concern always is to deal with the larger system of personality as most readers commonly use the term in its everyday sense.

We offer our new perspective with one immediate goal in mind: to point out what we consider to be the hidden dangers in the techniques currently employed by many of America's religious cults and mass therapies. Given a comprehensive picture of these dangers, the reader may better determine the difference between a cult and a legitimate religion and may find some criteria for establishing when a worthwhile therapeutic method is being put to potentially harmful use.

On a broader level, however, this investigation of snapping addresses questions that touch the whole of American society. Each American is vulnerable to snapping, even if he or she has never considered participating in a religious cult or mass therapy. The techniques used by America's cults and therapies permeate every level of American society, from government and business to our daily social interactions. Yet most of us have little understanding of the extent to which we ourselves—not only our beliefs and opinions but our individual personalities—may be shaped and changed by those around us and by things we experience every day.

In the course of our work, Flo and I have encountered only one objection to the method of our investigation. "Why," some people have asked, "don't you participate in these cult rituals and therapies yourselves? You can't possibly understand them unless you have actually *experienced* them on your own."

To that charge, we take no stand in defense of "objectivity" or of maintaining our professional "detachment." Obviously, we would be unable to gain any perspective at all if we subjected ourselves to each of the cult rituals and therapeutic techniques described in this book. Even if we did, it wouldn't work. No investigator—whether journalistic or scientific—who heads into a group in search of "the experience" can possibly capture the experience of those who have made a personal commitment to that group.

In another sense, however, each of us has already experienced these cults and therapies in ways no cult member or group participant ever could. We have known close friends and colleagues to return from cult retreats and marathon encounter groups as complete strangers. We have been personally confronted on the streets, where our donations were solicited and our beliefs assaulted. We have attended private dinners and intimate gatherings at which we were matter-of-factly condemned to hell and told that we were agents of "Satan's world." And for over a decade, we have watched with special concern the use and what we consider abuse of our fundamental American freedoms, especially those expressed in the First Amendment to the Constitution.

The phenomenon of snapping has changed the news, the law, the meaning of religion, and the people we live with and work around every day. In the pages that follow, we will explore this extraordinary phenomenon in detail: the attitudes it grew out of, the techniques those attitudes gave rise to, the experiences produced by those techniques, and the effects of those experiences upon the mind. We turn first to the search for self, America's legacy from the sixties, which has been transformed into something very different in the seventies.

2 The Search

The office of those who seek new worlds is to stumble upon those they never expected to find.

—*Cervantes*

IN THE EARLY SIXTIES, with the increase in leisure and affluence, the advent of psychedelic drugs, and the rediscovery of Eastern thought, Americans set out to explore the underused, often dormant capacities of thought, feeling, imagination, self-expression, and relationship that have come to be known as their human potential. In the process, they crossed new thresholds of sensation and discovered the "high," the privileged domain of peak experience attainable through drugs, encounter groups, and meditation. For the first time, many people recognized this experience as a missing link in their development and were drawn to it. The search was on: for the highest high, the tallest peak, the deepest reach of experience.

In addition to the immediate physical and emotional rewards, the tools and techniques of the new movement held an even greater promise of release: from childhood traumas, lifelong undesirable habits, conditioned roles, and traditional social expectations. Inevitably, however, this rich new world of personal growth became subject to exploitation and abuse as unlearned, uncommitted amateurs moved in to till the field. Without warnings or guidelines, America's searchers, in their earnest longing to find something higher and their sincere desire for self-improvement, had no way of interpreting their experiences, of separating the truly spiritual from the sham, or of distinguishing genuine personal growth from artificially induced sensation.

And, not surprisingly, people started getting hurt, set back both financially and personally.

It's not easy to locate the ones who have been hurt, for they rarely want to talk about it. The gains to be derived from the search are by nature a personal matter, and so its losses too become a torturous private ordeal. Very often, people are reluctant to admit that their best efforts yielded something less than the stunning breakthrough they were seeking. Many remain deeply embarrassed at what they consider to be a personal shortcoming or insurmountable flaw in their own capacity for growth, while others may be unable to overcome the fear and confusion that lingers for months, even years, following the traumatic climax of their quest. And some who have sought psychiatric care, even briefly, are obscured forever within the confidentiality of the doctor-patient relationship.

As we began our investigation of snapping, we quickly learned that the traditional channels of communication would be virtually useless for our purposes. But when we passed a quiet word along the grapevine of the human potential movement, a large network of contacts opened up to us, revealing beneath the jubilant surface of the movement a substratum teeming with shocking, often tragic tales of snapping.

A woman we will call Jean Turner is only one of an inestimable number of individuals of all ages who have wandered into this shadow world of human potential. The man who told us about her is a respected psychologist who had been active in the movement from its beginning, but recently he had become troubled by some of the paths down which it had strayed. He had known Jean Turner for several years. When he gave us her name, he explained that she had had an "extreme reaction" to one of the mass therapies we discussed, but he said that he did not want to prejudice our conversation in any way. He just told us to call her, which we did. She offered to come out to the small house we had rented for this particular round of interviews on the West Coast.

When she appeared at noon the next day, our first impression was of a tall, attractive, middle-aged woman whom we might have met anywhere. Her shyness, even apprehensiveness, as she sat down with us seemed quite normal under the unusual circumstances of our meeting. After brief amenities we told her something about our project and our backgrounds. She nodded, smiled, and said she would try to help us in whatever way she could. She told us she was fifty-two, a college-educated mother of three, now divorced, just visiting the West Coast from her home in a city some distance away.

She had read a recent newspaper article which provided her with a term for her current social status. "Displaced Homemaker," she said. "There are so many of us and nobody has paid much attention to this group of women who, after years of raising children and husbands, come out middle-aged and without a skill. What do you do then? You have no money, no security, nothing. Who are you?"

She smiled again, but her eyes were glistening with tears.

"I had raised my children through every kind of crisis imaginable," she said. "When they were grown and healthy I felt pretty good about it, but it was as though the most important part of my life was over. I had to find meaning. That's when I started to search."

Her search for meaning first led her into a new experience she was hearing about in the media and from her friends: Transcendental Meditation. The invention of the Indian guru Maharishi Mahesh Yogi, TM is the largest and most widely known of America's mass-marketed self-help techniques. It has been hailed as a nonchemical means of relieving nervous tension, and its relatively low cost makes it an ideal point of embarkation for the practical-minded or casual seeker.

Its initial impact on Jean Turner was profound.

"TM gave me glimpses of what it was like to be living on a different level. After a four-day residence course, I came back home and for two weeks my body and mind were completely one. I was just working and going about things, but every day would seem to fly by. I would look back and say, *What an incredible experience to be moving on this level.* That was the beginning; it really opened me up to the search."

Through TM, Jean told us, she found relief from stress, as the technique promised. She experienced enjoyable physical sensations of relaxation and bliss. These initial moments of fulfillment spurred the expansion of her search. For a while, she continued to pursue the Maharishi's path of exploration, attending several TM weekend retreats and enrolling in a TM "Science of Creative Intelligence" course. Then a friend invited her to participate in another new experience, a small-group encounter session.

"I didn't even know what an encounter group was. I had no idea—" She smiled. "I even stopped and bought a notebook thinking I was going to hear a lecture." Then she turned serious. "At first it was too much for me. I saw all this closeness and touching. I'd had no exposure to anything like that before, and at one point I just ran out of the room. Then a lovely young woman took me aside and we talked for an hour. I had never known what it was like to be close with another woman."

After she got over her initial fear, Jean's first encounter-group experience turned out to be a pleasant one. There was nothing mystical about it, she explained, no overwhelming effects; but the experience of "sharing" touched something in her and prompted her to investigate other encounter groups.

In the next one, she found a form of transcendence that surpassed anything she had become acquainted with in TM.

"I thought I must be getting in touch with my psychic energy. How else could you explain it? It was all mind, nobody was doing anything or saying anything, and I just got high. I got so high I didn't know what to do with it. It was a beautiful feeling of well-being, warmth, and loving. It was so strange, at first, because nobody seemed to be making it happen to me. I went home and all night long these warm feelings kept coming up in my body. I didn't know what to do with them. I felt that I either wanted to have fantastic sex or be a four-year-old child."

The "encounter high," as it has been called, the first great revelation of the consciousness explosion, not only gave Jean Turner new sensations of warmth and inner peace; it opened her up to whole new dimensions of experience through intimate encounters with other people in later groups and in her daily life during the next few years. When she first heard about the mass-group therapy called est, she explained, she was far from naïve about the powerful effects of both meditation and encounter.

Erhard Seminars Training, est, is the most successful mass-group therapy offered to Americans in the seventies. Described as "sixty hours that transform your life," the est "training" services 250 people at a time in four marathon sessions, usually held over two consecutive weekends. Est trainees gather in a hotel ballroom or other large meeting area, signing an agreement not to leave their seats without permission or to speak unless called upon. No eating, smoking, drinking, or use of drugs is permitted during the training. Bathroom breaks, which came every twelve hours in the early days, have since been increased because of frequent accidents.

As our conversation turned to est that day, Jean Turner stiffened. Up to that point she had answered our questions with relative ease. Now she became guarded and oddly remote, as if suddenly threatened and wondering whether or not she could trust us.

She hesitated, then recited a phrase we had heard frequently from others: "Let me say first that I feel est was one of the most positive things I've ever done."

We said nothing. She looked back and forth between us, appeared to change her mind, and began again.

"Est was extremely different from anything I had ever been in," she said, her voice low and shaky. "I say that because I was personally encountered by the trainer and taken through a lot of trauma. I'm still afraid to talk about it, because I haven't found people to be very understanding."

We assured her that she was not the first person we had talked to who had expressed reservations about est. This seemed to help, and gradually her story emerged. It came out in jumbled sequence, in rushes of words interspersed with emotionally charged pauses and, occasionally, tears. It was as if her est experience still lay in fragments in her memory. Now and again we asked gently for clarification, but we did not try to force the pace or confront her with our own conclusions. Ultimately we got a chronological picture of her story.

Est, she said, had been for her a grueling physical ordeal. "During the first body process—it was a meditation technique—I experienced a great deal of pain in my legs," she said. "After that first full day of training, we left very late, and I had this terrible pain from my knees down. The next day I was scared. If I hadn't paid two hundred and fifty dollars I wouldn't have gone back. I was tired. I was on the verge of tears, but I made myself go back. The first thing I did was tell the trainer how I felt. I said, 'I'm scared. I have some idea of what this is all about, getting things up from my past, but do I have to experience my whole life here?' That was when the trainer came over to me and encountered me, taking me back through the first time I ever experienced pain in my legs. Of course, it went back to when I had rheumatic fever as a child. I've always had weak legs; there were days when I couldn't walk to the bus stop because of the pain in my legs. I had been treated for arthritis over the years and I was in pretty bad physical condition when I started the training. The doctors had said they couldn't do anything for it. They said I had to live with it."

She told us that her est trainer had wasted no time in excavating buried experiences and emotions from her past.

Then—"I had a healing," she said. "When the trainer focused on all that, it was indescribable. It was too much; the pain in my legs was so intense. Then I felt waves of heat come over me, and all the pain went away. I wouldn't choose to go through that pain again, but since that day I haven't had a single pain in my legs."

Presumably, the intensity of that confrontation broke through something very deep and painful that had plagued her all her life. The resulting cure was real and dramatic, and it left Jean Turner in a state of physical ecstasy that kept up throughout the following week. Toward the end of her next est weekend, however, she said she experienced a second overwhelming—but very different—emotional reaction.

"It came up in me like a ball," she told us, her voice rising. "I thought I was going to be sick. At the same time I experienced a release from my body as though somebody had pulled a ripcord in me. It just shot up and unraveled out of my body. That whole day I hadn't known where I was. Then suddenly I found myself screaming at the trainer. I was calling him a son of a bitch. It came out at him, I don't know why, except that the sound of his voice was getting to me. He was encountering someone else when it came up and I let go. When I sat down, my body was just flooded with feeling. I think the fact that all this anger had come up in front of two hundred and fifty people must have had some effect. I was so humiliated. It just kept coming and coming in great waves. I felt all this heat in my wrists and I felt like I couldn't move my arms. But I sat there with it because I knew there was going to be a break soon, and I said to myself, *I'm getting out of here.* And I did. I managed to leave the training at that point."

Here was the phenomenon we call snapping in its most extreme physical form.

"I walked out of est," she continued, "and I walked about a mile home and just went to bed. When I woke up the next morning, I was disoriented and scared to death. I didn't want any part of est. I called the city's mental health service and they sent out a crew. They stayed with me for about an hour. They seemed to understand what I was going through. One of them asked me if I had blown my mind and I said, 'Yes, I don't know what that means, but it sounds like what's happened.' I was afraid. I felt very shaky. My son was coming in that night and I didn't think I could drive out to meet him. After the first weekend of the training, I had sent him this incredible note: *Get your ass over here! I have to clean up my shit!* He'd never heard any of this language. It was est jargon and I was full of it."

Later that day, she told us, she did decide to make contact with est.

"I called their office. I never talked to the trainer, but the manager told me this had happened because I hadn't gone to the very end of the training. Something was unfinished. So I agreed to do the second weekend over again in the next training, which was a month away."

During the intervening month, she experienced "the most marvelous body feelings I had ever known," she told us. "I had never felt so good. Something was going on that I didn't want to interrupt. I was just high all the time."

Then finally, overtaken by the urge to share her feelings, she went to the est office.

"I walked in and shouted, IF YOU DON'T GET IT, THEN YOU AIN'T GOT IT! The secretary looked at me as if to say, What's going on with you? I walked into the manager's office and he hugged me."

When the month's wait was over, Jean Turner completed her est training without further incident. Afterward, her physical high continued and spilled over into other realms.

"After seven more days of experiencing these body things, I began fantasizing," she recalled. "It was beautiful. I was out of touch with reality; it was as though I could see on a different dimension. I experienced an intense joy the whole time."

Then her state of mind took an even more startling upturn.

"I reached a point where the fantasies became real," she said. "It was poetical. I was speaking in biblical languages. At times I couldn't open my mouth, but when I did it came out in verse. I was alone in my apartment for a week, and I felt like I was getting a whole new body, a renewal. I was extremely active. I couldn't stop dancing. I didn't want to stop, it was too good. My body just felt so powerful."

Then her high topped out and veered sharply downward.

"I can't explain it except that I became afraid," she told us. "Somewhere I knew this behavior wasn't right and I started feeling fear. So I called the est office and the manager asked me where I was and I told him. He said, 'We can't help you, but we can *assist* you.' He told me to come to a seminar that night, but I needed help right then."

In panic, she called a friend—the man who later put us in touch with her—who arranged for her to go into a psychiatric hospital. She spent two weeks there and then was released at her own request without further medication or professional care. Not long afterward, however, her delusions returned and she was readmitted to the hospital. The second time she was released on thorazine, a powerful tranquilizer. For the next ten months she underwent weekly psychiatric care and was put on antidepressant drugs.

Est is, without a doubt, the most controversial of America's mass therapies. It has been the subject of countless magazine articles, several best-selling books, and endless hours of talk-show discussion. Celebrities who are among est's roughly 100,000 graduates include Valerie Harper, Cher, Cloris Leachman, John Denver, Buzz Aldrin, Marion Javits, and John Dean.

The est package was put together in 1971 by Werner Erhard, a man whose personal background has assumed mythic proportions. Born Jack Rosenberg in Philadelphia, Werner Erhard started his career as a used-car salesman. In 1960 he left his job, his wife, and four children and headed west to California. On his way out, as legend has it, he read an article in *Esquire*, "The Men Who Made the New Germany," and pieced together a new identity for himself from biographical threads of Werner Heisenberg, the formulator of the Uncertainty Principle of modern physics, and Ludwig Erhard, who served as West Germany's economics minister. As Erhard, he arrived in California, where he spent some time training encyclopedia salesmen and began experimenting with the various techniques emerging from the explosion of human awareness there. Eventually, he began working for Mind Dynamics, one of the first consumer products to package the discoveries being made in the still-experimental stages of the human potential movement. Then, in 1971, Erhard fused all his newly acquired knowledge into est, a conglomeration of techniques and principles from such scattered sources as encounter, psychodrama, Gestalt therapy, Scientology, Zen Buddhism, Dale Carnegie—and marine boot camp.

The actual title of est is reputed to come from a science-fiction novel, *est: The Steersman Handbook,* by a now untraceable author named L. Clark Stevens. Stevens's est stood for *electronic social transformation.* His book foretold the rise of the "est people," a generation of postliterate men who would bring about the transformation of society. Not long after he formulated est, Erhard is said to have had his own great catalytic experience while driving in his Mustang. Somewhere along the highway, he "got it"—est's term for its own brand of enlightenment—in a moment of insight that informed him that "What is, is," and "What isn't, isn't." This experience led Erhard to further revelations. He has said, "What I recognized is that you can't put it together. It's already together, and what you have to do is experience it being together."

For the most part, the est training consists of endless hours of lectures on the nature of reality, perception, and belief systems. The lectures are intertwined with a series of est "processes," mental exercises aimed at erasing the trainee's "tapes" (est jargon for patterns of thought and feeling that, est says, prevent one from fully experiencing life). The course of the training is laced with direct verbal assaults in which trainees are dubbed "turkeys" and "assholes" and drawn into "personal encounters" with the est trainer. During the course of the weekend, many trainees cry, faint, vomit, or lose sphincter control. At the end of the training, for his $350 (currently; the price has doubled since est began), each trainee is supposed to "get it" in a moment of sudden realization that he alone is responsible for creating everything that happens to him.

Like many graduates, Jean Turner failed to "get it" in the est fashion. The pain in her legs disappeared as a result of the intense physical outpouring she had experienced, and for this she could be grateful. For a brief time, too, she had had a taste of est's often-stated goal: "To transform your ability to experience living so that the situations you have been putting up with clear up in the process of life itself." But the fulfillment she sought in est never came about. When we met her, almost two years after the training, Jean seemed confused and vulnerable.

Jean's story naturally raises two important questions: Might she have been unusually vulnerable or, as some might claim, predisposed to a severe episode in the aftermath of the est training? Was her painful experience a rare exception among est graduates? We cannot say with certainty that Jean's est training was solely responsible for what happened to her. Inevitably, in today's world, questions of vulnerability arise. To date, there are no statistics available on either the immediate or later lives of est graduates. There is, however, documented evidence which shows that Jean Turner is not the only est trainee to have undergone an emotional disturbance extreme enough to require psychiatric treatment.

Not long after our conversation with her, we read an article in the March,

1977, issue of *American Journal of Psychiatry* titled "Psychiatric Disturbances Associated with Erhard Seminars Training: I. A Report of Cases," the first such report in the professional literature. Here three psychiatrists describe five cases that "represent a segment of est trainees who came to our attention in a variety of emergency psychiatric settings." Each of these experienced reactions very similar to, or even more extreme than, Jean Turner's in connection with their est training; four of the five cases had no record of previous psychiatric disorder.

At the end of our interview, Jean Turner admitted that she was still anxious—and still searching.

"Lately I've been experiencing some discomfort and tension in my body," she said, "and I've been waking up with feelings of anger. But I don't want to go back on the drugs they gave me at the hospital. I want to deal with it.

"I went to see this doctor who does acupuncture," she said as we escorted her to her car. "He gave me a book and I'm reading it now. It sounds like something I will pursue."

3 The Fall

Theseus and his comrade Pirithous in their descent to Hades to bring back the goddess of the underworld . . . sat down to rest for a while, only to find that they had grown to the rocks and could not rise.

—Carl Jung,
Modern Man in Search of a Soul

THE CHILDREN of the seventies have set out on a different kind of search. The great cultural upheaval has subsided, and in lieu of self-realization their goal is spiritual fulfillment, a headier destination and one with even deeper pitfalls along the road.

Several years ago, as the smoke from the sixties, Vietnam, and Watergate began to clear, those pitfalls became apparent with the emergence of a new group of Americans. These were the early cult members, young people who had left home and school in pursuit of those rare moments of insight and revelation sought by us all. What they found were organizations such as the Unification Church, the Children of God, the International Society for Krishna Consciousness, the Divine Light Mission, the Forever Family, the Church of Scientology, the Love Family, the Assembly, the Body, the Way, the Farm, and the Tony and Susan Alamo Foundation. In the beginning, the cults gave little cause for concern. Their disciples were few in number, and whether they went barefoot, shaved their heads, and chanted or wore dark suits and ties and passed out leaflets, they were all simply variations on a familiar American theme: law-abiding citizens exercising their constitutional right to freedom of religion. If those citizens seemed a little strange, at least they didn't get in anyone's way. At worst, the early cult members were mere loose threads in America's colorful social fabric.

As they became more numerous, however, their various faiths and practices began to blur in the public eye. The question of whether someone was a follower of the Swami, the Reverend, the Perfect Master, the Guru, the Yogi, His Holiness, Krishna, or even Jesus became much less important to those the disciple approached than the flowers, incense, books, peanut brittle, cookies—and in some cases vacuum cleaners—that he or she was selling. For in addition to their earnest looks and tireless proselytizing, many of America's young cult members had taken up fund raising in a big way. They had learned to solicit door-to-door in residential neighborhoods, set up folding tables outside suburban shopping malls, and make intensely personal approaches in bus and train stations and airport terminals coast to coast.

Yet this industrious and charitable public image bore no relation whatsoever to the bizarre stories being told reporters, judges, doctors, and anyone else who would lend an ear to a distraught parent or jilted lover. These stories told of people who had changed completely, almost overnight. While they claimed to have found true happiness and fulfillment, many seemed to have lost their spontaneity and humor, their free will, or their individuality in the process. They had become estranged, presenting themselves in odd postures ranging from stiff to animated, ecstatic to withdrawn. There was something eerie about them, but it was nothing you could put your finger on.

None dared call it crazy, not in any clinical sense. In some ways, cult members functioned even better after their conversions. Most could not be accused of even the most familiar frailties or conceivable vices. They had stopped smoking and drinking; often they had given up drugs and sex as well.

Nevertheless, alarmed by the changes they were witnessing, desperate parents began to take extreme measures to rescue their children. They sought help from "deprogrammers" who would kidnap cult members and attempt to free them from the groups' effects. Then the legal battles began, as young people sought to prosecute those who had tried to prevent them from practicing the professed religion of their choice.

A young married couple whom we will call Lawrence and Cathy Gordon made the front page of their hometown paper when their parents managed to recover them from Sun Myung Moon's Unification Church. The article described the organization's wealth, tax status, and political affiliations and gave a detailed history of Lawrence and Cathy's involvement. But the newspaper account didn't reveal what it was like to go through it all. Despite extensive media coverage of the cults, little attention has been given to the personal impact of the cult experience. Early in our research, it became clear to us that America's growing fraternity of ex-cult members hold the key to the phenomenon of snapping. They alone have gone through the most bizarre forms of sudden personality change and come back to tell the story. With the goal of unraveling this mysterious experience, we traveled to the small midwestern town where Lawrence and Cathy Gordon now live and work.

Like the Displaced Homemaker who ventured into TM, encounter groups, and est, the Gordons are everyday people—good, decent, healthy. They are also typical cult members. They are college-educated and come from upper-middle-class homes. Lawrence is a strapping, fair-haired, all-American type. Cathy is diminutive and vivacious, an outdoorswoman with long strawberry-blond hair and a cheery smile.

Cathy began. She took us back to her first close encounter with the energetic recruiting forces of Moon's church.

"I was standing outside the public library when this guy who was about six feet tall came up to me," she said. "He seemed to be very happy, like he had a lot of answers to things. He said they had a group called the New Age Fellowship, just a group of people who would come together and sit around and talk about different things."

For Cathy, who had earned her degree in sociology, the idea of an evening of intellectual stimulation was appealing. She explained that she and Lawrence had spent some time traveling around the country after his thwarted attempt to get into medical school, and they had only recently returned to town and were just starting to become socially established after their long absence. In this casual and friendly context, the "Moonie's" invitation was attractive. To Cathy, it sounded like a way for Lawrence and her to meet people like themselves.

Something odd about this Moonie struck her immediately, however.

"He seemed to be in a different place than most people," she told us. "There was an aura about him. At the time, he seemed kind of spiritual. He asked me to this dinner they had, and I felt strange. I had to lean against the wall. He seemed to be a very powerful person."

Lawrence, who arrived on the scene later, was unmoved by that initial meeting.

"When I drove up," he said, "this guy was talking to her, and I shouted, 'Come on, Cathy!' Finally she broke away from him, and he came running up to my car in the middle of the street. He said, 'Hey, I just invited your wife to this dinner where we sit around and talk philosophy and sing songs.' I said, 'Sure, sure, thanks a lot.' I just wanted to get home. But a couple of days later, when we were talking about it, we said, 'What the heck, let's go check it out and see what it's all about.'"

First encounters with the cults are rarely anything extraordinary. People may sense something strange about cult members, but the decision to check out the cult is usually a casual one. When Lawrence and Cathy attended their first Unification Church gathering, however, the Moonies' impact on them was much less subtle than before. This time Lawrence felt it more than Cathy. He leaned forward in his chair as he described it.

"We went to the dinner, and there was a funny feeling in the room," he recalled. "I couldn't pinpoint it, but the people seemed to be putting on an act. It wasn't something I wanted to think about. They kept the ball rolling; then this speaker came up. He was a very, very dynamic person; he just radiated when he talked. He started off normal and calm; then he got more into it and his eyes just glowed. It was amazing how much power his eyes had. We sat there glued to him as he communicated this urgent message to us about saving the world. As he talked, he walked around. Every muscle was involved; he was talking to us with his whole body. Because of him we decided to take up the invitation to the weekend workshop in the country, to find out what made him so enthusiastic."

Cathy put in, "My initial reaction to these people was, *I don't know what they have, but I want it.* They all seemed serene, ecstatic, or very, very loving."

"That Friday, all the way up to the workshop we were singing," Lawrence remembered. "Like we were going to summer camp or something. They woke us up at six o'clock the next morning and made us hurry to the lectures. We did exercises—stretching, shouting, singing, running through the trees—then had breakfast and toured the camp. There was a lecturer who introduced himself and then began talking about something called the Principles of Creation. You couldn't deny the first lecture. It was about God's love for man —it was perfectly in line with Catholicism in every way. Lecture Two was the Fall of Man, which was a very heavy lecture. It made you feel guilty for the way you were living and the general attitudes of society. It had a lot to do with sexuality."

After each lecture, the Gordons and about twenty or thirty other new recruits were assigned to small groups where church members answered their questions.

"I kept asking about Masters and Johnson," Lawrence told us, with a boyish grin, "but they said you should totally deny all your sexual feelings and your feelings for other people. I didn't believe it right away, and they said, 'Didn't you feel that way when you were young? Didn't you feel guilty and want to cover yourself up?' I said, 'No, I didn't,' and the Moonies all said, yes, they did."

Cathy had been more affected by the exhortations of the second lecture.

"When they were talking about the Fall of Man," she recalled, "they said that we all had Satan's blood spiritually in us. I felt really dirty, and I had this sense of shame that made me feel even worse."

The final lectures were a mixture of traditional religious references and themes from history, philosophy, and American politics.

"They went through Hellenism and the Reformation," said Lawrence. "Then they arrived at this twenty-one-year period of history—which was supposed to be what Jacob went through—when Communism would be at its peak because Vietnam was a failure and the American people hadn't rallied behind Nixon, which was an indemnity thing because MacArthur didn't save Southeast Asia from the Communists because of President Truman."

Cathy picked up the original thread. "At the end of the weekend workshop," she said, "they left us with the idea that Christ could be coming very soon; in fact, he could already be here. You say to yourself, *Wow, could this be true? Could it be?* But they still hadn't even mentioned Reverend Moon."

Then, according to Lawrence, just before that weekend of much talk and little sleep came to an end, the church leaders made their first direct attempt to bring the two of them into the fold.

"They spent two straight hours trying to talk us into staying," he said. "They told us that when we went back down into the regular world, Satan would invade us. I'd never believed in Satan before, but somehow they got to me. When we left and were driving down, I felt really weird, and it kept up the whole next day while we were getting our business done so we could go back up."

Even though at this early stage the Gordons could feel the "weird" effects of Moon's conversion technique, they were unable to focus their impressions. As Lawrence described it, he and Cathy returned to an everyday world that had grown alien and sinister.

"When we came back down, we thought we were still in control of ourselves," he explained, "but when I look back on it now I can see how heavy their influence was. As soon as we walked into the house, my mom and dad looked at us and said, 'What's wrong with you? What's wrong with your eyes?' But we had been told to anticipate this, that the rest of the world would see us as different because we knew the truth. I just thought, *Aha! Maybe I'm getting spiritual or something!*"

Cathy explained the resolution of that first confrontation with Lawrence's family.

"We had been told that a lot of times people will get sucked back into the real world and Satan through their families, and you had to cut that emotional tie and look at your parents objectively. Lawrence's mother got frantic when she realized we were going back; she ran out to the car crying, but we remained very cool and untouched by her. As we drove away, I said, 'It must be hard for you to see your mother like that.' And Lawrence said, 'That's not my mother. That woman who is crying and carrying on is not my real mother.' And I was proud of him then, for seeing things the way they were."

Lawrence and Cathy drove back to the Moon camp, confident that they were at last seeing the world in its proper perspective. Once formally in the cult and swayed further by repeated fervid lectures, they became totally engulfed.

"I remember looking in the mirror one time," said Cathy. "We were told not to look in the mirror, because it was such a vain thing, but I just glanced at it as I was walking by and I saw my eyes and I thought, *Oh, boy, my eyes are on fire. I'm really high, spiritually high!*"

Then they described the same kind of high that led to Jean Turner's emotional breakdown in est, which grew for them into a sustained alteration of awareness.

"By the end of the next week, I remember feeling objective about the world, really detached from it," said Lawrence. "The first day of that seven-day workshop, the lecturer had said to us, 'By the end of the week, you're all going to be just like me. You're all going to be walking around smiling.' And we were."

Along with the other new converts, the Gordons experienced not just one but frequent peak moments when they felt as if they were receiving a revelation.

"Two other people and I were asked to pray for all the new members," Cathy recalled, "so we prayed out loud for three hours. At the end of the prayer, the leader came in and said, 'You've been praying long enough. Why don't you break it up in a few minutes.' I realized that I had one more minute to make this prayer really count, so I prayed even harder and just then I felt like everything I was saying was being sucked into a vacuum. When I stood up, I felt like thin air; I had to brace myself. I felt this energy, it was kind of an ecstasy. It just flowed through me like a sensation of tingling. It sent shocks through me, and I equated it with divine love."

Here again was the moment of snapping in its most intense physical form. Lawrence reported having a similar experience, "when I felt my spirit opening up."

"One day I started to have doubts, so I said to myself, *I have to go out and pray about this,* because that's what you're supposed to do when you're weak. So I went out and prayed just like Cathy did, and after—I don't know how long, I have no recollection of time—I started to get strong again. I felt a tingling in my back like raindrops, and I thought, *Wow, this is a sign!* It felt cool; it lasted about ten seconds, like God was about twenty feet above me with a little sprinkler."

Soon after they moved into the church, Lawrence and Cathy were separated. Cathy's participation remained largely subservient, the woman's fate in many cults, while Lawrence was sent halfway across the country to begin fund-raising activities. Securely anchored in his altered state of awareness, he returned to the everyday world, dressing up in the Moonie's familiar dark suit and tie to begin solicitations that would often keep up twenty hours a day. Now, on the streets, the same power Cathy had noticed when she met her first Moonie had become an unmistakable feature of her husband's own demeanor.

"I felt a rush when we were out campaigning, a real high," Lawrence told us. "I was bursting with joy. People would open the door in a humdrum mood, and as I talked they would get high with me."

According to Cathy, the effect was contagious.

"When we came back from a weekend workshop," she said, "Lawrence talked to his sister for a couple of hours. She was affected for days. People where she worked noticed it all week."

The high that communicated itself so effectively, however, was frequently marred by the Gordons' discomfort and personal misgivings.

"Every day of fund raising people would make comments to me," Lawrence told us. "I was getting all the negativity that the church predicted, but it was supposed to be Satan attacking me. We were told to be humble toward people and say, 'I'm sorry you feel that way.' But many times doubts came up in my mind when I was fund raising. I'd think, *Do I really want to go into this plush restaurant and bother these people who are having a nice dinner with their family? Do I want to do that and make a fool of myself?* But the church said, *Try always,* and I'd find myself at banquets, going from table to table asking people for money." (He accomplished his goal. The first year he was in the Unification Church, he raised $50,000.)

Exhaustion was a far more pervasive problem in the Gordons' life in the Unification Church. According to church doctrines, it is considered a sin to be sleepy.

Another former Moonie we interviewed later told us more about this problem.

"I'd be out fund raising in a parking lot somewhere, feeling very heavy, having trouble keeping my eyes open, and I'd go back somewhere and lie down," he said. "One time some people called the police. They thought I was dead. I saw other members fall asleep while they were talking, just leaning in a car window, right in the middle of a sentence.

"Anyone who can't stay awake is said to have *sleep-spirit* problems," he went on. "Sleep spirits were supposed to be the spirits of people who had died. They were very low—they came from Satan's world—and if church leaders found someone with sleep-spirit problems, they would treat him very badly. One time at their training center in Barrytown, New York, a Japanese member slugged me very hard. When we would get tired, they'd tell us to go take a cold shower. Sometimes they would use squirt guns to keep people awake."

The Unification Church holds a special place among the cults. With a membership that has been estimated as high as 60,000 to 80,000, it is one of the largest and richest actively recruiting cults in America today. Despite numerous questions raised by private citizens and government investigators regarding its business practices and tax-exempt status, the church has survived virtually unscathed every claim made against it. Despite many legal battles over the kidnapping and deprogramming of its members, it continues to operate without restraint in nearly every major city and on most college campuses in America.

The Reverend Sun Myung Moon, the founder of the Holy Spirit Association for the Unification of World Christianity, is a wealthy Korean industrialist turned evangelist. While church members state publicly that Reverend Moon makes no claim to be the Messiah, former Moonies we interviewed told us that within the church he is openly referred to as the Messiah and that he himself claims to be a divine being sent to earth to finish the work of Jesus Christ, which he sees as the breeding of the "ideal race."

Since it was founded in Korea in 1954, the Unification Church has grown to enormous proportions and has accumulated immense wealth. In addition to his munitions interests in Korea, Moon owns factories that produce ginseng tea, titanium products, pharmaceuticals, and air rifles. Members of his church can be seen selling flowers on street corners throughout the United States. In recent years, the church's profits have been used to make sizable investments in American real estate, including a huge retreat in Barrytown, New York— Moon's primary American residence—and the old New Yorker Hotel in midtown Manhattan, purchased for a reported $5 million in 1976 and now serving as the church's national headquarters.

In the last few years, the Unification Church has done much of its recruiting under the name of CARP, the Collegiate Association for the Research of Principle. The church has denied reports that it operates through a number of organizations, among them the International Federation for Victory Over Communism, the Professors Academy for World Peace, and the Little Angels of Korea. Several years ago, until they were identified, Moon had church members doing volunteer work for many members of the U.S. Congress. A church front organization was reportedly contracted to clean the rugs in the FBI headquarters in San Francisco in 1976. In 1977, the church began publishing a daily newspaper in New York City, the *News World*. The Washington *Post* has twice reported alleged links between the Unification Church and clandestine

American activities of the South Korean Central Intelligence Agency.

In our opinion, the Unification Church is the most sophisticated of the cults in its activities as well as its conversion process. In order to further Moon's cause, fund-raising activities are kept up almost around the clock. A number of members report that they are not given adequate time to rest or to even begin to think about anything other than the urgent mission of the church. For many weary cult members laid low by exhaustion, doubt, and fear of the outside world, relief comes only in the form of intense snapping moments.

Before our meeting with the Gordons came to an end, we heard yet another account of this extraordinary phenomenon. We were struck by its frightening resemblance to the many vivid, first-hand descriptions of death and dying that have been published in recent years. For us, it indicated an equally significant form of personal dissolution.

"Once we were in the vans and our fuel pump broke and I curled up on the back seat to go to sleep," Lawrence told us, still obviously baffled by the experience. "Then I felt my body was going numb, going away, and I had many sensations all at once, like I was physically dying but spiritually being pulled out of my body. At the same instant, this thing was opening up before me. I could see a light and feel something coming toward me to get me or help me. Then I heard this heavenly singing, all different kinds of ranges and pitches, like *Ahhhhh!* But because I felt my body physically dying, I became petrified and pulled myself back together and sat up."

To us, Lawrence and Cathy's year and a half in the Unification Church sounded like a waking nightmare, a winding descent into a world devoid of free will, where personal survival loses all meaning, feelings for others disappear, and the outside world takes on dark, supernatural dimensions. We found very few people who got out of the Unification Church or any other cult on their own. In some cults, we were told members are warned to fear invasion by Satan. In others, they are told that leaving the group will result in reincarnation as an insect or in death to a family member. Apparently, many cult members experience these threats as totally believable, and they are helpless to act against them.

Can this state of mind possibly be conveyed by the term "religion" as we know it? Were the ongoing highs experienced by Jean Turner and the Gordons the result of true enlightenment or revelation? Before we can draw any conclusions about the phenomenon we call snapping, we must first examine these intense experiences within their original context of religion and then investigate the common ground that underlies both these psychological and spiritual transformations.

4 The Roots of Snapping

Religion claims to be in possession of an absolute truth; but its history is a history of errors and heresies. It gives us the promise and prospect of a transcendent world—far beyond the limits of our human experience —and it remains human, all too human.

—Ernst Cassirer,
An Essay on Man

THE MIRACULOUS HEALING of Jean Turner's legs in est and the moments of ecstasy and revelation experienced by Lawrence and Cathy Gordon in the Unification Church have their counterparts, throughout history, in every culture and civilization. In ancient Greece, audiences experienced catharsis, a moment of purgation and purification, at the height of Greek dramas and religious rituals. To this day, in Nepal, Sufi dervishes whirl around until they are overcome with religious fervor, and voodoo tribes in Africa and Latin America pursue the same moment in fiery, drum-beating, earth-pounding black masses. In each instance, the activity gives way to a moment of overwhelming physical sensation.

But physical sensations alone do not account for the violent upheaval that Jean Turner experienced in the aftermath of her est training or the abrupt change that overtook the Gordons in the course of their initial three-day Unification Church retreat. Our culture has never witnessed transformations of precisely this kind before, although there have been many similar examples throughout the history of religion. In the infinite richness and variety of religious experience, individuals have perceived an extraordinary refocusing of awareness as a great spiritual breakthrough in one form or another—spiritual, for although it is felt "in the flesh," it cannot be directly linked to any immediate physical cause. Lacking understanding, and with no reliable method for investigating the phenomenon, people through the ages have grappled imaginatively with their experiences, looking to some higher order and ascribing these changes in awareness to a source outside the body. They have been explained as messages from beyond or gifts of revelation and enlightenment, personal communication that could only be delivered by a universal being of infinite dimensions, a cosmic force that comprehends all space, time, and earthly matter.

In the course of human development, every culture has recognized this spectacular phenomenon. The Greeks called it the *kairos* or divine moment, for since ancient times it has been characterized by awesome sensations and celestial visions. Every major religion, including Islam, Hinduism, Buddhism, and Zoroastrianism, stems from the similar experience of its founding figure. Among Western religions, Judaism is replete with the moment in the divinations of its prophets and seers, and the story of Christianity overflows with incidents of "revealed truth." The pages of history tell very little about the actual circumstances surrounding these incidents, but they provide undeniable proof of the universality of the experience.

While not a commonplace occurrence, the experience of enlightenment may be seen as a completely natural one. Stripped of its supernatural components, it is simply a moment of fundamental human growth, of overwhelming feeling and understanding when an individual pushes through to those higher levels of consciousness that distinguish us as human beings. For the prophet, the genius, and the average citizen alike, life moves forward in such sudden leaps, peak moments, and turning points.

In the course of our own travels and interviews, we spoke with many individuals who told us they had experienced the "divine moment" of enlightenment. Collecting their stories, we were amazed to find the variety of contexts in which these experiences occurred—from huge public gatherings to lonely roads, in childhood and old age alike. The kinds of changes in awareness and personality ranged from the dark transformations we are concerned with in this book to glorious breakthroughs that seemed to us undoubtedly worthy of genuine religious recognition.

The most beautiful and moving example of this latter form of experience was told to us by a woman we will call Helen Spates. A devout Christian in her late forties, she is a gentle person with rich black hair and wide, youthful eyes. We came upon her in the South, and we sat in her kitchen and drank tea as she recalled the circumstances that led to her first spiritual awakening, which took place at a very early age.

"I had my own personal experience as a child," she told us. "I really came into the awareness that there is something higher that is wonderful and beautiful. My mother died and I was very despondent. I just wanted to die along with her because she was a part of me; she was the one I loved. Here I was in the first grade and the children in school would throw rocks at me and just add to my loneliness. Then one day I was underneath a tree, a big cottonwood tree on our farm, and I was spread out just lying there in an old wagon, looking at the sky and the white clouds. Their beauty overwhelmed me, and from the cottonwood tree I saw these beautiful, shiny leaves, and I thought, *New life, new life, how can there be such beautiful creativeness? There must be someone that brought all this about. There must be."*

She looked at us, searching our faces. She explained that she was embarrassed to have such an intimate part of her life tape-recorded, but then, eager to share with us, she went on.

"I was just overwhelmed with everything," she said, "and I started singing my problem to God. I just blurted out to him exactly how I felt. I told him that my father was a drunkard and my mother was dead, and I was an orphan child and I just didn't know where to lay my head. Then I stopped singing and just lay there, and I felt something real warm overwhelming me. It was in just a moment, yet it was like an eternity. No sooner did I become aware of this warm peace overwhelming my little body when a joy, such a joy hit me with such tremendous force that I jumped out of that wagon and ran. I ran past an orchard, I ran on a ditch bank, I ran and ran. Then finally I stopped. I looked at my dad's acreage of alfalfa in full bloom and the butterflies dancing overhead, and I raised my arms and sang, *My heart is taking over. It's learning how to love!"*

Helen Spates's profound personal experience had apparently released her from the enormous emotional stress she had been forced to contend with as a young girl—the loss of her mother, the insults of her schoolmates, the constant torment of an alcoholic father—and had signaled the resolution of those conflicts. Of all the stories we heard, hers stands as the most unchallengeable instance of enlightenment in the best sense of the word. It was a moment in which she broke through to a new level of awareness; it took her beyond her painful emotions to an understanding that left her with new feelings of joy and love.

We spoke with other people who had experienced this natural moment during the course of their adult lives. For each of them, as well, the experience marked the end of a period of personal torment from which they had found no release. Another woman, a recent convert to Christianity, told us about a crisis that was resolved in an instant and led directly to her conversion.

"When I finally accepted Christ I was in a desperate situation," she confessed. "I had fallen and gashed open my head, and I thought, *Nothing is accidental.* I thought that I had done this to myself. I was going crazy thinking that I had these self-destructive impulses. My mind was going on and on like that and I was really scared. I was afraid I was going to throw myself off a cliff and not be able to stop it. I thought, *How can I stop this craziness?*

and said, *God, if you can make this go away I'll serve you.* And instantly I felt calm. I felt really crazy, then I felt really calm."

As this woman described her experience, it seemed obvious to us that a sudden physical shock had set off a reaction which nearly snowballed into tragedy. Yet, in contrast to Helen Spates, in the calm that followed, this woman had the sensation not simply of newfound feeling and awareness but of having entered a whole new state of being, a transformation of personality on its most intimate level.

Among Christians in America, this powerful experience is called being Born Again, and it is a surprisingly widespread occurrence in the United States. A recent Gallup poll reported that half of all adult Protestants, or nearly one third of all Americans, say they have been Born Again. This means that at least 50 million individuals in this single faith alone have experienced sudden spiritual renewal. Among this number are many prominent figures in business, the arts, and politics.

Some have even made their private experiences public. One of the more astonishing Born Again Christians in recent years is former White House counsel and Nixon aide Charles Colson. Colson vividly described his experience in his best-selling autobiography, *Born Again.*

"Something began to flow into me—a kind of energy," Colson wrote, recounting an event that came on him suddenly while he was sitting in his car. "With my face cupped in my hands, my head leaning forward against the wheel, I forgot about machismo, about pretense, about fear of being weak. Then came the strange sensation that water was not only running down my cheeks, but surging through my whole body as well, cleansing and cooling as it went. They weren't tears of sadness nor of joy, but tears of release. I repeated over and over the words, *Take me.* . . . Something inside me was urging me to surrender."

And Colson did surrender, cooperating fully with federal prosecutors in one of the most baffling personal turnabouts of America's Watergate era. As in the two previous accounts, Colson's spiritual metamorphosis can be linked to tangible circumstances. His rebirth came at the height of his legal peril for his role in the Watergate crimes. The intense physical sensations he experienced seem often to accompany the Born Again moment, and they were confirmed for us by many other Born Again Christians we interviewed. A tingling of energy appears to be common, along with alternating feelings of heat and cold. Frequently, the individual will have the impression of a cleansing flow of water, which is usually accompanied by an uncontrollable surge of tears.

Possibly an even more unlikely figure than Colson, former Black Panther leader Eldridge Cleaver says he, too, was Born Again while hiding overseas from prosecution in the United States on charges of assault and intent to murder. In an interview in *Newsweek,* Cleaver described another mystifying feature of the Born Again experience: the divine vision, which may be a powerful spur to life-changing action.

"I was looking up at the moon," said Cleaver, "and I saw the man in the moon and it was my face. Then I saw the face was not mine but some of my old heroes. There was Fidel Castro, then there was Mao Tse-tung. . . . While I watched, the face turned to Jesus Christ, and I was very much surprised. . . . I don't know when I had last cried, but I began to cry and I didn't stop. I was still crying and I got on my knees and said the Lord's Prayer. I remembered that, and then I said the Twenty-third Psalm because my mother had taught me that, too. It was like I could not stop crying unless I said the prayer and the Psalm and surrendered something. . . . All I had to do was surrender and go to jail."

In the aftermath of his divine vision, Cleaver gave himself up to foreign police and was returned voluntarily to federal custody in the United States.

Many skeptics have questioned the sincerity of dramatic religious conversions such as those of Colson and Cleaver, but there can be no doubt about the existence and extensiveness of the Born Again moment in the United States. In the stressful situations just described, being Born Again was an intensely private, personal experience. Yet for many other Americans, their rebirth took place in a group religious gathering held by one of America's numerous branches of Evangelical Christianity.

This public spiritual experience dates back as far as man and society, and it has been a vital feature of religion in America as well. The first Great Awakening of Colonial America in the 1740s was led by the Puritan minister Jonathan Edwards, whose fire-and-brimstone sermons reached peaks of emotion that sparked a New Light among whole assemblies of colonists. In the 1800s, Baptists, Mormons, and other nationwide religious groups joined in frenzied services of devotion that rivaled the ecstatic rituals of the more esoteric Quaker and Shaker sects. It was not until this century, with the emergence of American Evangelicalism and its extravagant Holy Rollers, that the experience of divine enlightenment reached out to touch great masses of people in the United States. Long before the human potential movement began hailing encounter highs and peak experiences, America's Pentecostal and Charismatic Christians set off a grass-roots revolution of their own. Since the days of the Reverend Billy Sunday and Aimee Semple McPherson, Evangelical Christianity has grown into an international movement spanning a broad spectrum of faiths that includes such worldwide religious crusades as those of Billy Graham and Oral Roberts.

The explosion is generally acknowledged to have begun on the first day of the year 1901, when the long-established tradition of Christian evangelism, the ardent preaching of the gospel, was itself reborn in a new and potent form. In a Bible school in Topeka, Kansas, directed by the Methodist minister Charles Parham, people "laid hands" on one another and prayed that the Holy Spirit might be given to them with the sign of "speaking in tongues."

Even to most Born Again Christians, the experience of speaking in tongues remains something of a mystery. Historically, it has its origin in the New Testament, in the Acts of the Apostles. According to that passage, at Ephesus, in what is now Turkey, the early Christian Paul came upon some Christian disciples who had not received the Holy Spirit according to Christ —they had only received the baptism according to his cousin John. In that first recorded instance of the Born Again Charismatic experience, Paul told them about the baptism according to Jesus; "On hearing this, they were baptized in the name of the Lord Jesus. And when Paul had laid his hands upon them, the Holy Spirit came on them; and they spoke with tongues and prophesied."

In that ancient moment, according to the Bible, those who felt the spirit spoke in a language unknown to man; as a result of that experience, their lives were instantly transformed. Their awareness underwent a sudden change, which they attributed to the spirit of Jesus Christ, and they became devout followers of Christianity, their faith confirmed by intense physical sensation.

In that same Evangelical tradition, the Holy Spirit did in fact appear to Parham's congregation in Topeka, first overwhelming a young woman student and then visiting others in that assembly. From Topeka, the Christian Charismatic movement has spread around the world to an estimated fifteen million communities. Unlike other modes of religion, which require great leaps of faith on the part of their followers, the Charismatic movement, as one tract describes, sees itself as "a powerful new sign of the spirit adapting to the needs of our modern era." In keeping with the time-honored tradition of Evangelicalism, which promises personal renewal through the "living experience" of Christianity, the Charismatic movement strives to bring its adherents to frequent personal encounters with the Holy Spirit. Strengthened by that experience, the individual is then sent forth into the world with a newfound joy, inner peace, and—as one minister described it—"a love for God and neighbor." From then on, among many Charismatic sects, a major focus of the new convert's devotion becomes the activity of "witnessing," or giving personal testimony of his experience in the hope of winning new converts to the movement.

As with Helen Spates's natural moment of enlightenment, we found many instances where the group "personal encounter" proved to be a source of genuine personal growth. The potential benefits of this form of worship were poignantly demonstrated to us during a conversation we had with a gentleman we will refer to as Martin Young, a thoughtful husband and loving father of two small children who, for many years, has been a successful businessman in the Midwest. A Roman Catholic all his life, in the late sixties he joined the growing Charismatic movement within the Catholic Church, which has become a point of controversy in recent years between traditional and more liberal Catholics. In contrast to the popular image of Charismatics as Bible-thumping religious extremists, we found Martin Young to be a polite, easygoing individual, a short, handsome man who was happy to share with us his first experience of "baptism in the Holy Spirit." He ushered us into his living room one afternoon, built a roaring fire in the fireplace, and poured three glasses of white wine.

"There were about seven of us and we went into a prayer meeting," he began solemnly. "After the regular meeting they asked if some of us would like to come upstairs and pray together. We went into the upper room. There were other people laying hands on, and I was kneeling in the circle. I just knelt —I wasn't asking for it—and all of a sudden I came into a chant in tongues. Now I'm not much of a singer, but it came out a very beautiful chant. My wife was standing beside me observing, and she received tongues without even knowing it."

As Martin Young described it, he and his wife had a personal experience of the presence of the Holy Spirit in their small Christian Charismatic prayer group. Along with other members of the group, they uttered sounds which have no meaning in any modern or ancient language, but which they interpreted in terms of the traditional Christian scriptures. The tongues chant, Young told us, has often been likened to ancient Middle Eastern and Asian dialects, but extensive scholarly research has failed to establish its derivation or even a definite vocabulary or grammar. Regardless of its origin, speaking in tongues appeared to be a profoundly compelling group experience which, Young said, may visibly affect both participants and observers. He tried to convey to us the essence of the Charismatic ritual that had become so familiar to him.

"When you come into a prayerful atmosphere," he said, "anyone can sense a different feeling. If you walked in here when we were having a prayer meeting with a smaller group, you could feel the intensity of the fervor with your whole being—your heart, your mind, everything. You can see the reverence of the people. You can tell which people have been in the prayer group before; you can feel that they are immersed in the spirit of God."

Following his first Charismatic encounter, as others had professed in the Born Again moment, Martin Young experienced a sudden refocusing of awareness which he anchored to the established doctrines of Christianity. From his own account, it became clear to us that strict adherence to this traditional body of moral teachings and guidelines for living enabled him to grow socially as well as personally. He explained how his awareness was altered for the better as a result of his tongues experience.

"After you have received tongues," he said, "you are transformed. You come with new eyes, the eyes of God. You look for new ways of liking people; instead of focusing on their weaknesses, you find something good about them. You turn to the positive, to the beautiful—this is living Christianity. I'm not saying that we are not still weak and creatures of habit, but walking with the Lord is a process. It's a journey. It's a mode of change."

From our point of view, Martin Young's understanding of his transformation seemed remarkably perceptive, although, as he described it, the entire experience was contained within the framework of his firm religious belief. Traditionally, religion in America has facilitated and encouraged this kind of personal growth through spiritual belief. It took the Evangelical movement, however, to fuse religious faith and intense physical experience into what amounts to an organized program of personal renewal, curing bad habits, vices, and addictions and offering a set path of daily life and worship for those in search of one.

For the most part, the expressed doctrines and values of Evangelicalism are in keeping with the most basic ideals of American life. They do not depart greatly from other traditional religions in the United States that have played autonomous but integral roles in this nation's social and political development. Yet, unlike America's other religious traditions, the Evangelical movement shares many characteristics with religious cults and mass therapies. Its ecstatic moments are sought after and intense; conversion is sudden and profound. The movement boasts miraculous cures for lifelong ailments and engages in the zealous recruitment of new members. Moreover, like many cults and mass therapies, in recent years the Evangelical movement has multiplied its enormous wealth and following through the use of sophisticated mass-marketing techniques, bringing its heavily advertised crusades to prime-time television and even linking television, radio, and publishing interests around the country into Evangelical networks to promote fund raising and solicitation.

This use of sophisticated technology and mass-marketing strategies is a relatively new trend in Evangelicalism, but in a few short years it has become the movement's primary mode of recruitment. It is in this leap of that "old-time religion" into the arena of big business that Evangelicalism intersects the phenomenon of snapping in America, raising some of the most difficult—and sensitive—questions of our investigation.

Perhaps the most visible form of this new attitude can be seen on highways across America, where huge blue and white billboards and innumerable bright yellow and black bumper stickers proclaim the simple phrase "I

Found It." This vague message is now almost universally recognized as the catchphrase of America's burgeoning Evangelical movement, yet few Americans are aware of the massive scope of the heavily financed and well-coordinated public relations campaign behind it. The creation of a Harvard Business School graduate and former adman for Coca-Cola, I Found It places the number of recruits it has won for Jesus at 600,000 in some two hundred cities, by its own estimate. In 1976, donations alone added up to $29 million, and sales of literature—hardcover books, paperbacks, and pamphlets—totaled an additional $3 million.

The parent organization of I Found It is the Campus Crusade for Christ International, Inc. One of its board members posted the bail money for Eldridge Cleaver, who, while awaiting trial, made public appearances on behalf of the group. In one of Campus Crusade's numerous copyrighted pamphlets, *Jesus and the Intellectual,* the group's president and spiritual leader, Bill Bright, draws quotes from the Bible to bolster his argument for the "surrender of the will," the same surrender that both Colson and Cleaver testified to in their Born Again stories. According to Bright, the key to becoming a Christian is "the surrender of the intellect, the emotions, and the will—the total person." Only then, as it is stated in Corinthians, does an individual become a "new creature" in Christ, as "old things are passed away" and "all things are become new." In its similarity to the appeals of so many cult recruiters and lecturers, this traditional Christian doctrine—and the suggestion contained in it—takes on new and ominous overtones.

Is the I Found It crusade a cult? When we began this investigation, we were asked that question by many traditionally religious people, including a number of ardent Born Again Christians. At the time, we dismissed it as an impossible charge, for our initial acquaintance with the crusade revealed none of the prominent features we had come to identify with a cult. Members did not cut family ties or leave school to live in communal homes. They did not work around the clock in cult fund-raising efforts or donate their possessions and life savings to the organization, nor did they engage in arcane rituals and erratic behavior or demonstrate an inability to communicate with the world at large. In our early interviews with dozens of Born Again Christians around the country, we found many of them as amiable as Helen Spates and Martin Young: aware, concerned, delightful individuals who were actively engaged in furthering their communities both socially and politically.

Others, however, shocked us considerably. There were individuals who, at the end of what we thought was an open and genuine discussion, declared flatly that we would be condemned to Hell for the opinions we expressed and the beliefs we held. One young woman implied that our project was foolhardy because it was contrary to "God's plan"—a keynote of the I Found It philosophy. "It's the intelligent people, like yourselves," she informed us, "who have such difficulty coming to Christ." Another crusader handed us a little booklet written, she said, "just for our Jewish friends." Copyrighted by the American Messianic Fellowship, it excerpted Hebrew scriptures from the Old Testament to verify that the "Messiah Jesus" would cleanse the reader "from all your filthiness." In our travels, we were also astonished to see how many Born Again Christians, most of them I Found It people, had in fact become completely absorbed in their newfound faith, devoting the bulk of their lives, their time, and their money to organizations whose most visible activities appeared to be soliciting donations and recruiting new members.

What is the line between a cult and a legitimate religion? In America today that line cannot be categorically drawn. In the course of our investigation, however, it became clear to us that many Born Again Christians had been severed from their families, their pasts, and society as a whole as a result of a profound personal transformation. It is not in keeping with the purpose of this investigation to comment on the far-flung Evangelical movement in its entirety, but our research raised serious questions concerning the techniques used to bring about conversion in many Evangelical sects. In order to further our understanding of those techniques, we paid a visit to America's foremost Charismatic leader, Holy Roller, and faith healer—retired.

Marjoe Gortner was the first Evangelical preacher to blow the whistle on his profession. In his documentary film *Marjoe*, made in the late sixties, he revealed age-old tricks of the trade and exposed some of the entertainment aspects of the popular movement that have made it big business.

If he lives forever, Hugh Marjoe Ross Gortner will most likely always be "The World's Youngest Ordained Minister." Born January 14, 1944, Marjoe was almost strangled during delivery by his own umbilical cord. The obstetrician told his mother that it was a miracle the child survived, and thus "Marjoe"—for Mary and Joseph—the Miracle Child took his place at the end of a long line of Evangelical ministers.

From the beginning, his preaching skills were meticulously cultivated. Before he learned to say "Mamma" or "Poppa," he was taught to sing "Halleluiah!" When he was nine months old his mother taught him the right way to shout "Glory!" into a microphone. At three, he could preach the gospel from memory, and he received drama coaching and instruction in every performing art from saxophone playing to baton twirling. On Halloween, 1948, at the age of four, Marjoe was officially ordained and thrust into a wildly successful career as the Shirley Temple of America's Bible Belt, the sprawling nongeographic community of strict adherents to the Christian scriptures. In the following decade he preached to packed tents and houses coast to coast, as enthusiastic audiences flocked to see the Miracle Child who allegedly received sermons from the Lord in his sleep. Owing to his mother's careful training, harsh discipline, and indomitable ambition, Marjoe's sermons were flawlessly memorized, right down to each perfectly timed pause and gesture. Frequent Halleluiahs and Amens punctuated his performances, which were cleverly promoted with titles such as "From Wheelchair to Pulpit" and "Heading for the Last Roundup," which Marjoe preached wearing a cowboy suit.

Marjoe's captivating sermons rarely failed to fill the church collection plate to the brim, and his renowned faith healings were miraculous even to him. In his teens, however, Marjoe grew disenchanted with the continued deception of his divine powers. He left the Evangelical movement in search of more legitimate means of employment. He spent some time in a rock band, trying to move with the changing times; then he returned to the Evangelical circuit to make his revealing motion picture. *Marjoe* is one of those frank films that delves deeply into sensitive areas of American morality that slip over the line into profiteering.

We found Marjoe in Hollywood last year, where he now resides on a secluded hilltop estate in Laurel Canyon. After we drove up the winding dirt road that leads to his lofty home, Marjoe greeted us cordially and ushered us into his sunken living room, where he pointed out some familiar features of the sprawling southern California landscape visible through his wall-sized picture window. We told him that we had come to hear about his miraculous powers of "saving" and "healing," trade secrets that neither his film nor his subsequent biography unraveled satisfactorily. Tall, handsome, with lion-colored curls and a penetrating stare, even in T-shirt and faded jeans Marjoe had an air of power about him. From the outset of our talk, however, he squashed all notions we might have had that his talents were in any way extraordinary.

"I don't have any power," he started off, just to set the record straight. "And neither do any of these other guys. Hundreds of people were healed at my crusades, but I know damn well it was nothing I was doing."

Yet, Marjoe admitted, he remained somewhat baffled by the thousands of souls he helped to "save" and the numerous illnesses he seemed to have cured. His own insight into his preaching skills was on a decidedly earthly level. Based on his years of training and experience, he located the source of his divine power squarely out among the flocks who assembled to receive his gifts.

"You start with a guy who obviously has a problem," he explained. "You've got to begin on that premise. Things haven't worked out for him, or he's looking for something, or whatever. So he goes to one of these revivals. He hears very regimented things. He sees a lot of people glowing around him

—people who seem very, very happy—and they're all inviting him to come in and join the clique and it looks great. They say, 'Hey, my life was changed!' or 'Hey, I found a new job!' That's when he's ready to get saved, or Born Again; and once he's saved, they all pat him on the back. It's like he's been admitted to this very special elite little club."

Marjoe downplayed his own role in the proceedings. As he saw it, the real show was in the audience; he served primarily as a conductor.

"As the preacher," he said, "I'm working with the crowd, watching the crowd, trying to bring them to that high point at a certain time in the evening. I let everything build up to that moment when they're all in ecstasy. The crowd builds up and you have to watch it that you don't stop it. You start off saying you've heard that tonight's going to be a great night; then you begin the whole pitch and keep it rolling."

For Marjoe, who has seen it a million times, the divine moment of religious ecstasy has no mystical quality at all. It is a simple matter of group frenzy that has its counterpart in every crowd.

"It's the same as a rock-and-roll concert," he asserted. "You have an opening number with a strong entrance; then you go through a lot of the old standards, building up to your hit song at the end."

The hit song, however, is spiritual rebirth, the product of a time-tested recipe for religion to which the preacher and every member of the audience contribute some small but active ingredient. Then, according to Marjoe, the only fitting encore to the overwhelming moment of becoming saved is a personal demonstration of the power of that newfound faith. This is the motivating factor that prompts speaking in tongues, also known as the "receiving of the glossolalia." As Marjoe explained it, this well-known Evangelical tradition requires even greater audience participation on the part of the tongues recipient and the entire audience.

"After you've been saved," Marjoe continued, "the next step is what they call 'the infilling of the Holy Spirit.' They say to the new convert, 'Well, now you're saved, but you've got to get the Holy Ghost.' So you come back to get the tongues experience. Some people will get it the same night; others will go for weeks or years before they can speak in tongues. You hear it, you hear everyone at night talking in it in the church, and they're all saying, 'We love you and we hope you're going to get it by tonight.' Then one night you go down there and they all try to get you to get it, and you go into very much of a trance—not quite a frenzy, but it is an incredible experience.

"During that moment the person forgets all about his problems. He is surrounded by people whom he trusts and they're all saying, 'We love you. It's okay. You're accepted in Christ. We're with you, let it go, relax.' And sooner or later, he starts to speak it out and go *dut-dut-dut.* Then everyone goes,

'That's it! You've got it!' and the button is pushed and he will in fact start to speak in tongues and just take off: *dehandayelomosatayleesaso* . . . and on and on."

Marjoe paused. Flo was dumbfounded by his demonstration, although he hadn't gone into the jerking, trancelike ecstasy that is commonly associated with the tongues moment. I'd seen the classic version in his movie, yet even in this restrained demonstration, Marjoe appeared to be triggering some internal releasing or babbling mechanism. I asked him how he brought it about.

"You'll never get it with that attitude," he joked. Then he went on to explain the true nature of the experience. His perspective showed it to be a process that requires a great deal of effort to master.

"Tongues is something you learn," he emphasized. "It is a releasing that you teach yourself. You are told by your peers, the church, and the Bible— if you accept it literally—that the Holy Ghost spake in another tongue; and you become convinced that it is the ultimate expression of the spirit flowing through you. The first time maybe you'll just go *dut-dut-dut-dut,* and that's about all that will get out. Then you'll hear other people and the next night you may go *dut-dut-dut-UM-dut-DEET-dut-dut,* and it gets a little better. The next thing you know, it's *elahandosatelayeekcondelemosandreyaseya* . . . and it's a new language you've got down."

Except that, according to Marjoe, it's not a real language at all. Contrary to most religious understanding, speaking in tongues is by no means passive spiritual possession. It must be actively acquired and practiced. Although the "gift" of tongues is a product of human and not supernatural origin, Marjoe displayed tremendous respect for the experience as an expression of spirituality and fellowship.

"I really don't put it down," he said. "I never have. It's just that I analyze it and look at it from a very rational point of view. I don't see it as coming from God and say that at a certain point the Holy Spirit zaps you with a super whammy on the head and you've 'gone for tongues' and there it is. Tongues is a process that people build up to. Then, as you start to do something, just as when you practice the scales on the piano, you get better at it."

Already, we could see the difference between Marjoe and some of his modern-day fellow preachers and pretenders. Unlike many cult, group, and Evangelical leaders, Marjoe has always held his congregations in high regard. During his years on the Bible Belt circuit, he came to see the Evangelical experience as a form of popular entertainment, a kind of participatory divine theater that provides its audiences with profound emotional rewards. Marjoe realized that his perspective would not be shared by most Born Again Christians.

"The people who are out there don't see it as entertainment," he confessed, "although that is in fact the way it is. Those people don't go to movies; they don't go to bars and drink; they don't go to rock-and-roll concerts—but everyone has to have an emotional release. So they go to revivals and they dance around and talk in tongues. It's socially approved and that is their escape."

Within that context of social entertainment, Marjoe took pride in his starring role as a traveling evangelist.

"It was my duty to give them the best show possible," he said. "Say you've got a timid little preacher in North Carolina or somewhere. He'll bring in visiting evangelists to keep his church going. We'd come in and hit the crowd up and we were superstars. It's the charisma of the evangelist that the audience believes in and comes to see."

What got to Marjoe, he explained, and eventually drove him out of the business were many of the same disturbing aspects of the Evangelical movement we had noticed in our own travels and interviews.

"When I was traveling," he said, looking back on the old days, "I'd see someone who wanted to get saved in one of my meetings, and he was so open and bubbly in his desire to get the Holy Ghost. It was wonderful and very fresh, but four years later I'd return and that person might be a hard-nosed intolerant Christian because he was better than anyone who drinks and better than the world because he had Christ. That's when the danger comes in. People want an experience. They want to feel good, and their lives can be helped by it. But then as you start moving into the operation of the thing, you get into controlling people and power and money."

Marjoe shook his head sadly. Indeed, he didn't strike us as the type of person who would be comfortable in that role. In the sixties, while he was exploring new outlets for his talents, he watched his former profession grow to vast international dimensions. Since then, he has followed the curious rise of America's religious cults, among them Reverend Moon's Unification Church.

"Moon is doing the same thing I do," said Marjoe, "only he's taken it one step further. He's suggesting to people that he *is* the Messiah. In my religion, the old-time religion, it's total blasphemy to suggest that. Moon has gone too far, but that's a very heavy number on people, because everyone wants to meet a Messiah."

Marjoe was quick to point out that Moon's preaching powers, like his own, are by no means divine or even innate. Marjoe acknowledges that his power over an audience derives primarily from the skills he perfected as a child, techniques of rhetoric and public speaking that have been passed down to us from the Greeks. These tools have long been in the public domain, and they make up the stock-in-trade of everyone whose work involves personal contact with other individuals and groups.

"It's the same whether you're a preacher, a lawyer, or a salesman," he told us. "You start off with a person's thought processes and then gradually sway him around to another way of thinking in a very short time.

Although Marjoe no longer consciences the use of his preaching talents for evangelical purposes, he still uses his skills in areas that have nothing to do with religion.

"I was campaigning for Jerry Brown when he was running for governor," he said. "I gave speeches when he couldn't show up. This was a whole different kind of speech for me, because I didn't know the people and the whole thing was political. One time I was supposed to go to a rally for a thousand AFL-CIO workers in San Francisco, and I thought, *Oh, no, how am I going to talk to these guys?* I needed a hook to get the audience, because I knew a person's mind is usually made up within the first minute or so. If they like you and you say the right things at first, then you can take them on to other things they might not ordinarily agree with. But all I had to go on was that, and structures of speech I knew from preaching."

He paused again, allowing us a moment to consider his predicament.

"When I got there they were a little hostile," he continued, "and I was very nervous about it. There was a podium with two flags on it, an American flag and a California state flag. I walked up—it was very quiet—and as I was walking up there it just came to me, I don't know from where. I grabbed the American flag and I crinkled it in my hand. I looked at it and sort of gave it a little toss back against the wall and said, 'I remember when Betsy Ross made that flag. Today it's made in Japan.' Well, a roar went up as that struck a chord in those workers, and I was God from that moment on."

Today Marjoe restricts the use of his talents to his acting career and to social causes he deeply believes in. Foremost among those causes is informing the public about some of the rhetorical techniques that are being used to manipulate their thoughts and emotions. Most techniques Marjoe is in command of are simple and age-old, but so effective that they can be equally powerful even when an audience has been explicitly forewarned of their use. Toward the end of our conversation, Marjoe told us a story that revealed the fineness of his rhetorical skills. In contrast to the massive physical experiences such as intense group rituals and intimate personal crises that have been recognized as major contributors to the snapping moment, Marjoe demonstrated how words alone, artfully manipulated, may be used to influence groups and individuals, even to the point of evoking the overwhelming emotional response of being "saved."

"I lecture in about twenty colleges a year," he began, "and I do a faith-healing demonstration—but I always make them ask for it. I tell them that I don't believe in it, that I use a lot of tricks; and the title of the lecture is 'Rhetoric and Charisma,' so I've already told them how large masses are manipulated by a charismatic figure. I've given them the whole rap explaining how it's done, but they still want to see it. So I throw it all right back at them. I say, 'No, you don't really want to see it.' And they say, 'Oh, yes. We do. We do!' And I say, 'But you don't believe in it anyway, so I can't do it.' And they say, 'We believe. We believe!' So after about twenty minutes of this I ask for a volunteer, and I have a girl come up and I say, 'So you want to feel better?' And I say, 'You're lying to me! You're just up here for a good time and you want to impress all these people and you want to make an ass out of me and an ass out of this whole thing, so why don't you go back and sit down?' I really get hard on her, and she says, 'No, no, I believe!' And I keep going back and forth until she's almost in tears. And then, even though this is in a college crowd and I'm only doing it as a joke, I just say my same old line, *In the name of Jesus!* and touch them on the head, and wham, they fall down flat every time."

5 Snapping as Something New

everybody happy?
WE-WE-WE
& to hell with the chappy
who doesn't agree

      —e. e. cummings

OUR CONVERSATION with Marjoe gave us a rare view of the many ways in which rudimentary rhetorical skills can be used to manipulate the emotions of individuals and whole audiences. But it did not explain what happened to Jean Turner in est or to Lawrence and Cathy Gordon in the Unification Church. To understand those experiences we need to take a closer look at America in the sixties, an era that began in a clutter of powerful new therapeutic techniques and religious practices and ended in a runaway, mind-altering technology of experience.

The wheels of this new technology began to turn in the fifties, when America was still on its snowballing course of postwar affluence and conspicuous consumption. By the end of that decade, the simple high of material splendor had already begun to flatten out. Around the country, people awoke from the American Dream in a cold sweat of existential despair, as the triumphs of business and applied science which had showered America with "things" was overpowered by a crying hunger for new and meaningful *experience*.

The first steps in that direction were taken by the poets and writers of the Beat Generation, who set off to mine the rich spiritual lodes of the East. Zen Buddhist practices first cropped up in the poetry and literature of Allen Ginsberg and Jack Kerouac. The benefits of meditation were expressly laid out in the popular writings of Alan Watts, most notably in his book *The Way of Zen,* which opened the East to a stream of traffic that has been bumper to bumper ever since. And perhaps the most influential figure of all was British author Aldous Huxley, whose short, brilliant essay *The Doors of Perception*, as far back as 1954, linked emerging trends in Eastern thought to psychedelic drugs and blasted a gaping portal in our Western notion of reality.

These sparks touched off the consciousness explosion, a cultural revolution that brought Timothy Leary, Richard Alpert (Baba Ram Dass), and LSD out of Harvard and led an entire generation to "turn on" to new modes of thought and experience. Before long, in California's fertile climate of open enjoyment and experimentation, these rituals and practices blossomed into a full-fledged movement for the exploration of man's untapped human potential.

It was Abraham Maslow, father figure of the new movement as well as of its related discipline, humanistic psychology, who set the upper limit of that potential when he marked off the realm of peak experience. He identified it as the "core-religious" or "transcendent" experience, the nucleus of every known high or "revealed" religion; the mystical, revelatory, ecstatic moment that was universally endowed with supernatural significance. Maslow's intention, however, was to view this peak objectively. He proposed that this new category of human experience be examined on its own merits, free of religion. He cited the promise of psychedelic drugs as just one manner in which all human beings could investigate moments of peak experience for themselves.

Maslow's endorsement of peak experience sounded the keynote of the sixties. It became the pot of gold at the end of the search, the breakthrough for which all that vague despair of the fifties had been longing. At the Esalen Institute in Big Sur, California, the cradle of the newborn movement, innovative techniques for creating intense sensory and intellectual experience were experimented with in a receptive atmosphere. There our knowledge of how individual personality may be affected by intense experience was undoubtedly pushed forward many decades in the period of only a few years. Along the way, Esalen's spiritual and psychic voyagers spent fleeting moments in realms of consciousness the human mind had only dreamed of until then, or mentioned cryptically or cloaked in metaphor.

In no time, Eastern practices and psychedelics became high fashion among both scientists and casual experimenters. The fledgling movement spurred an outpouring of new therapeutic techniques from what had been largely private, professional settings into loudly public, experiential arenas. The encounter group or T-group, as it was originally called, one of the first to appear, had as its birthplace the National Training Laboratories of Bethel, Maine. Before long, a glut of radical therapeutic techniques—some old, some new—came out of the woodwork. Among them were psychodrama, a role-playing therapy developed in the twenties by a Viennese physician named Jacob Moreno; psychosynthesis, a combination of group and individual therapeutic techniques developed by an Italian psychoanalyst; guided fantasy, a systematic daydreaming technique outlined in the forties by a French psychotherapist; bioenergetics, a body therapy from the fifties developed by American psychiatrist Alexander Lowen, a former student of Wilhelm Reich; and Rolfing, a form of deep-muscle manipulation pioneered in California by Dr. Ida Rolf, a biologist turned therapist.

Each technique was capable of producing emotional highs, peak experiences, and other dramatic personal breakthroughs. Throughout the sixties, they were intermixed ad-lib, along with drugs and Eastern practices of zen, yoga, and other forms of meditation, to bring about profound adventures in human awareness. In this popular free-for-all of experimentation, these powerful techniques lacked even the most general guidelines for such extensive and nonprofessional use. In the aftermath of all their peaking, bursting, and mind-blowing ecstasy, individuals broke through boundaries of human awareness into unforeseen—and unruly—reaches of consciousness and personality. One man's outburst of screaming and violence became another's "release of blockages" and still another's "cosmic vision," for at the time no one could say with certainty who was doing what to whom. And with what. And how.

The only indisputable interpretations were in fact spiritual ones, for the new field of humanistic psychology, still in the process of defining itself, was unable to supply sufficient alternative explanations to meet the demand. So in the late sixties the movement began to strip to its essentially theological underpinnings. The notion of transcendence became entangled in its fundamentally Eastern, Hindu roots, and the theory and practice of encounter edged closer to its revivalist forerunners. By the end of the decade, the human potential movement had become a roving, raving potpourri of therapy and religion, science and mysticism, the avant-garde and the occult.

Suddenly, the golden age of Esalen and the human potential movement began to tarnish. The drugs got out of hand, the techniques went awry, and the vision of mankind emerging to meet its destiny grew nearsighted. In the early seventies, along with the souring of so many counterculture themes, the voyage to self-awareness made a series of wrong turns and lost its way. The Aquarian dream hit the skids during the final agony of Vietnam and bottomed out concurrent with the nightmare of Watergate. In that time of social and political pandemonium, the energy and excitement of the sixties were consumed, and the vibrant culture of that decade fell into a state of aimlessness and torpor. It took just one more hammerblow to drive the final nail into the coffin.

That blow landed hard in the consummate American element of mass marketing, as the methods of big business were brought into the movement, took it over, and changed its character altogether. Mass-marketed therapies led the way, pooling bits and pieces of psychoanalysis, psychodrama, and other old techniques with the new group techniques of encounter and guided fantasy, and with Eastern practices of meditation. The first original conglomerations of these techniques were neatly packaged and distributed coast to coast under names like Mind Dynamics, Arica, and Silva Mind Control. Transcendental Meditation was already being peddled like speed reading; Scientology's Dianetics had been mass-marketing its own popular therapy since the fifties. At the same time, America's religious cults got into the swing, fanning out quietly across the country in massive fund-raising and recruitment drives. Cults such as the Hare Krishna, the Divine Light Mission, and the Unification Church cleaned up their images and outfits, honing their sales techniques to razor sharpness and making use of expert business and legal counsel.

In many instances, these new programs were being engineered by top experts from Madison Avenue. The Hare Krishna hired its own admen; like I Found It, est gave a top position to a former Coca-Cola executive. And it worked! The right buttons were pushed and Americans let their appetites for experience run hog-wild. Suddenly, without apology, as if another world war had just ended, the early seventies saw Americans take to meeting their own needs for experience and little else. It was the coming of what social analyst Peter Marin termed the New Narcissism, an era that pop-critic Tom Wolfe dubbed the "Me" Decade. In their eyes, the noble desire for self-realization had turned into a simple obsession with self-indulgence and immediate physical sensation.

What no one noticed, however, was the important change that was taking place at a much more fundamental level. As a direct result of techniques and practices that have profound effects on the workings of the mind, people were not merely shifting their attention and changing their beliefs in the seventies; they were snapping.

The cults provide some of the most vivid examples of the way in which America's technology of experience has been used to bring about fundamental alterations of personality. For many cult members, the phenomenon of snapping is the product of a comprehensive attack on human awareness. During the first moments of contact, potential converts may be manipulated with precision by the rhetorical ploys that Marjoe so deftly demonstrated: personal confrontation, conversation, group lectures, and other modes of persuasion. Once they have been drawn into the cult, they may be bombarded with intellectual concepts and religious doctrines that they cannot fit together and led through religious rituals that induce intense emotional highs and overwhelming peak experiences.

Converts may then be subjected to additional personal encounters in which their new experiences are given prescribed cult interpretations. Very often during this period, physiological stresses such as poor diet and exhaustion further weaken their resistance to suggestion and command. In some situations throughout recruitment, conversion, and initiation, each individual is given specific orders to refrain from doubt and told not to question the wisdom of cult doctrine.

Inevitably, under the cumulative pressures of this sweeping physical, emotional, and intellectual blitz, self-control and personal beliefs give way. Isolated from the world and surrounded by exotic trappings, the converts absorb the cult's altered ways of thought and daily life. In a very short time, before they realize what is happening, while their attention is diverted to contrived spiritual conflicts and further weakened by lack of food and sleep, the new cult members slide into a state of mind in which they are no longer capable of thinking for themselves.

It is our contention that this comprehensive attack strikes at the heart of consciousness, undermining fundamental processes of thought and feeling that make up individual awareness, volition, and personality. Yet to zealous cult members this new state of mind often has another name: happiness. Their characteristic public pronouncement is that they have found true happiness, fulfillment on both personal and spiritual planes in the simple life and labor of the cult. Their ongoing state is a constant high, an emotional peak that maintains itself. When it falters for whatever reason, cult members may resort to any of a number of techniques of meditation, chanting, or fervent prayer in which they have been carefully instructed, all guaranteed to return them to the state of bliss that is their reward for unqualified devotion.

Except for the religious component, virtually all the mass therapies use the same basic techniques. They recruit their participants through similar informal channels—posters, telephone and mail solicitations, and word of mouth. Here the individual is drawn into an intense group setting or therapeutic session in the hope of having some life-changing breakthrough. Then, as in est, these profound experiences may be created by various individual and group processes and "training" techniques. Group leaders may instruct participants in meditation or guide them through vivid fantasies. They may give interminable lectures, filled with psychological and scientific jargon, or sow intense conflicts in these individuals over the entire range of their life experiences, from infancy through childhood and adolescence to their current work and family relationships.

Caught in this crossfire of verbiage and long-buried emotion in the context of a physically grueling group ordeal, the individual may reach a state of explosive overstimulation or emotional collapse. In the aftermath of this overwhelming new experience, he or she may enter a state of mind that is perceived as a kind of renewal or rebirth and which may be, in fact, a protracted physical and emotional high. Successful mass-therapy graduates may achieve a state of euphoria, their problems solved because they have, in effect, stopped worrying about the things that were bothering them.

At the present time, our language has no appropriate term for this new way of coping with the problems of life. We can describe the process as one of shutting off the mind, of not-thinking. In our view this is the underlying appeal of nearly every religious cult and mass therapy in America today, as well as the unstated attraction of many branches of the Evangelical movement.

What kind of cultural environment breeds this widespread need to shut off the mind? It could be argued convincingly that the need is universal, that everyone—from Athenians to Sufis to voodoo tribesmen to modern Americans—must have some periodic release from the ordeal of being human. In that sense, the rituals and techniques which throughout history have been used to create peak experiences and moments of enlightenment may be looked on as vital sources of rest and relaxation for the mind, momentary breathing spells that hold great powers of insight, healing, and renewal.

But what value can there be in engineering these experiences to shut down the workings of the mind altogether, to stunt the process of thought and leave people numb to their own feelings and the world around them? Throughout history, this kind of attack on human awareness has proved an efficient method of controlling members of tribes, societies, and whole nations in which little value is placed upon individuality. The state of mind it produces has a tradition that dates back to the dawn of civilization.

In the remote bush country of Australia, aboriginal tribes still engage in rituals perfected more than 16,000 years ago to induce a state of mind in their adolescents that is surprisingly similar to the plight of thousands of America's brightest youth today. Joseph Chilton Pearce described the technique in his book *The Crack in the Cosmic Egg.* Around puberty, the young male of the Ananda tribe of central Australia is taken from his mother, isolated in the wilderness, and deprived of food for a prolonged period of time. He is kept awake at night in a state of constant fear by the eerie, whirling sound of the bullroarer, a native hunting device, until the combined physical and emotional stresses reach their maximum effect. At that moment, the elders of the tribe converge on the terrified youth wearing grotesque masks and covered with vivid body paints and proceed to subject him to a painful ritual of initiation into manhood. If he survives the ordeal, the young man emerges from the ritual in a drastically reduced state of mind, his awareness continuing at a level only sufficient to allow absolute adherence to the strict laws and taboos of the tribe. The adult

Ananda tribesman may spend his entire life in this altered state the natives call Dream Time. He will stand on one leg for hours, completely motionless, in a waking trance so deep that, as Pearce says, flies may crawl across his eyeballs without causing him to blink.

In recent years, the aboriginal Dream Time has been hailed as a state of profound sophistication in human awareness. Anthropologists point to the aborigine's physical endurance, spiritual satisfaction, and telepathic powers as marks of advanced evolution in a tribe that may represent the longest unbroken line of cultural development. However, they make the error of implying that this efficient and admittedly remarkable form of social control and spiritual fulfillment in a primitive, unchanging environment holds some promise for the future of our complex, rapidly changing, advanced technological society. Yet, following a decade like the sixties, it is ironic to find Americans who seek greater awareness and self-determination accepting instead a contemporary counterpart of Dream Time. What turn of events could have struck such an ancient chord in our modern time?

In the sixties, people rebelled against another modern version of Dream Time: the corporate mentality of the fifties which turned so many active, imaginative individuals into soulless organization men. But the consciousness explosion that tore through our society unleashed more awareness than many people were prepared to deal with: awareness of the empty rewards of most jobs and careers, the confining traditions of marriage and family relationships, worn-out social stereotypes and sex roles, the dangers of nuclear war, the threats of environmental pollution and dwindling energy resources, and the moral bankruptcy of our political institutions.

For a decade, Americans took action on every front and won many stunning victories, politically, culturally, and environmentally. But there were problems that would not yield to mere awareness, the best intentions, or even affirmative, aggressive action. In the seventies, people found themselves confronted with a world of overwhelming trade-offs: environmental quality versus technological progress, international diplomacy versus basic principles of morality, the freedom and independence of the single life versus the sharing and loving of intimate relationships. These uncompromising dilemmas—and others—gave rise to a new form of expanded awareness, one born of a maturing realism rather than the youthful idealism of the sixties.

In the wake of the fifties, America's postwar era of omnipotence and immortality, and of the sixties, a colorful, space-age decade in which people lived their dreams and accomplished the impossible without blinking, the new realism of the early and middle seventies was tainted with the specter of lowered sights. For many, it teetered midway between resolve and resignation. Cheap energy was running out, and no alternative sources appeared imminent;

diplomatic breakthroughs were accomplished, but many sincere negotiations ended in stalemate or betrayal; our old social traditions and institutions had been shattered, but no new ones were evolving. Everywhere, our individual lives seemed to be less important than the demands of our mass society. The problems, pressures, and pace of modern life were irreversibly snowballing, threatening to trap each individual in a tangle of pollution, inflation, exhaustion, loneliness, boredom, and frustration.

For many Americans, the only way out of this nightmare was to stop worrying altogether, to dive into work or play with the hope of finding something that would bring results. So in the seventies, as others have observed, our entire culture took off on its last desperate, narcissistic pursuit of happiness. Panicky college seniors forged rationalized "practical" career goals that exempted them from the commitments of the sixties. Young couples settled for new "realistic" relationships that freed them from their earlier desires and standards. Runaway husbands and wives spun intricate webs of faulty logic to excuse themselves from prior responsibilities. Late-blooming hippies and disillusioned political activists set off on gung-ho back-to-nature expeditions, while businessmen in mid-life crisis and mothers with "empty-nest syndrome" sought ever greater material diversions to disguise their own lack of meaning and direction.

This shift in our basic attitudes, opinions, lifestyles, and relationships has fed into a social and cultural environment that in its own tacit way offers heady rewards for not thinking. How easy it is to be carried aloft and swept along by God's "revealed plan" or to buy some technique that causes problems to "cure up in the process of life itself." Shutting off the mind in this way provides instant relief from anxiety and frustration. It evokes pleasure by default, salvation through surrender, and, even better, its simple happiness is self-perpetuating.

Indeed, the moment when we stop thinking may be one of overwhelming joy, the moment when the search at last comes to an end. Journalist Sally Kempton, writing in *New York* magazine, described a series of personal and professional crises that brought her to a large-group audience with the Swami Muktananda, one of the less mercantile of the growing number of Eastern guru entrepreneurs. Sitting quietly before Muktananda along with a hundred other devotees, Kempton sought enlightenment from the Swami. She found it in a single, casual remark.

"And finally," she wrote, "out of the welter of questions about lights and visions and experiences of transcendental love, came the one question that seemed to apply to my situation: 'What do you do about negative emotions?' a woman asked, and Muktananda said, 'Let them go. . . .'"

That simple instruction may not have been as profound as it was propitious, yet it set off a chain reaction of thought and feeling that is one of the most vivid accounts of snapping to reach the media:

Perhaps it wasn't what he said that struck me, but how he said it. Or maybe it was both. One of my deepest assumptions was that the thing to do about negative emotions was figure out where they came from, talk them over with your friends, work them out, *deal* with them. The last thing I had ever thought to do about negative emotions was to let them go. But Muktananda's words did something to me. It was as if they entered my mind, sinking through my assumptions like a kind of depth charge. It sounds strange, but for a moment I felt as if his words had actually knocked the voices of irritation out of my mind. I hadn't even realized they were there, those voices, until I noticed how good I felt without them. And for the rest of that intense and dream-like afternoon I sat feeling empty and absorbent, until at last Muktananda picked up a large tambourine and banged on it, and I sat up with a start. A chant was beginning, sweet and melodic, and also rhythmic; and five minutes into the chant I noticed a warm ache in my throat and liquid in my eyes, and wondered why I was crying. I didn't feel at all sad.

Driving home on the freeway afterward, I noticed that I had a lot of energy. In fact, I had so much energy that I didn't quite know what to do with it, and so I went home and ate a huge meal and talked loudly for two hours with my friend Jane, and then went into my room and lay down on my bed and closed my eyes and the whole thing started.

What it made me think of was Alice falling down the rabbit hole. I felt as if a huge pool had opened in my heart *(Oh, God, I thought, it's all true what those creeps were saying),* and the pool was full of soft air, and I was floating on it. It was the most intensely sensual feeling I had ever had. It felt so good that my first reaction was a sharp pang of guilt, a feeling that I had stumbled into some forbidden region, perhaps tapped a pleasure center in my brain, which would keep me hooked on bodyless sensuality, string me out on bliss until I turned into a vegetable . . . then I forgot about thinking, and just let myself drift on it.

6 Black Lightning

I do not doubt that in the course of time this new science will be improved by further observations, and still more by true and conclusive proofs. But this need not diminish the glory of the first observer.

> —Galileo
> (writing in praise of William Gilbert,
> pioneer in the study of magnetism)

IN ALL THE WORLD, there is nothing quite so impenetrable as a human mind snapped shut with bliss. No call to reason, no emotional appeal can get through its armor of self-proclaimed joy.

We talked with dozens of individuals in this state of mind: cult members, recent est graduates, Born Again Christians, and even some Transcendental Meditators. After a while, it seemed very much like dancing to a broken record. We would ask a question, and the individual would spin round and round in a circle of dogma. If we tried to interrupt, he or she would simply pick right up again or go back to the beginning and start over.

Soon we began to realize that what we were watching went much deeper. These people were not simply incapable of carrying on a genuine conversation, they were completely mired in their unthinking, unfeeling, uncomprehending states. Whether cloistered in cults or passing blindly through the world, they were impervious to the pain of parents, spouses, friends, and lovers. How do you reach such people? Can they be made to think and feel again? Is there any way to reunite them with their former personalities and the world around them?

A man named Ted Patrick has developed the only remedy currently available. A controversial figure called by the cult world Black Lightning, Patrick was the first person to point out publicly what the cults are doing to America's youth. He investigated the ploys by which many converts are ensnared and delved into the methods most cults use to manipulate the mind.

He was also the first to take action. In the early seventies, Patrick began a one-man campaign against the cults. His fight started in southern California, on the Pacific beaches where, in the beginning, organizations such as the Hare Krishna and the Children of God recruited among the vacationing students and carefree dropouts who covered the sands in summer and roamed the bustling beach communities year round. The Children of God approached Ted Patrick's son there one day and nearly made off with him. Patrick investigated, was horrified at what he found, and immediately set out on a personal course of direct action. His personal experiences with cult techniques and their effects led him to develop an antidote he named "deprogramming," a remarkably simple and—when properly used—nearly foolproof process for helping cult members regain their freedom of thought.

Before long, Ted Patrick was in action all over the country on behalf of desperate parents. He made front page headlines in the East for his daring daylight kidnappings of Ivy League cult members, he made network news in the Northwest for his interstate car chases to elude both cult leaders and state troopers, and eventually he made American legal history. In his ultimate defense of the U.S. Constitution, Patrick challenged the confusion of First Amendment rights surrounding the cult controversy and drew an important distinction between our guaranteed national freedoms of speech and religion and our more fundamental human right to freedom of thought. In precedent-setting cases, American courts have begun to confirm Patrick's argument that, by "artful and deceiving" means, the cults are in fact robbing people of their natural capacity to think and choose. Until recently, it was never considered possible that a human being could be stripped of this basic endowment. Patrick's efforts have been aimed at calling attention to the significance of this new threat and to the urgent need to deal with it in new professional and personal ways.

In many courtroons, however, Ted Patrick has lost his case for freedom of thought, gathering a mounting stack of convictions for unlawful detention. In unsuccessful attempts to free cult members from their invisible prisons, Patrick has been repeatedly thrown into real ones, in New York, California, and Colorado. In July, 1976, Patrick was sentenced to his longest term in prison, one year, for a cult kidnapping he did not in fact perform.

In February, 1977, we visited Ted Patrick in the Theo Lacy Facility of the Orange County Jail to learn about deprogramming from the man who coined the term. It was dark when we arrived, and we had to squeeze past the evening's incoming offenders at the main desk and make our case for visiting a prisoner after hours. Theo Lacy, we were told, is not half as bad a place as some of the others Patrick had seen. Yet upon showing our credentials, we were ushered into a glaring, airless cubicle under fluorescent light and constant surveillance. Minutes later, Patrick joined us.

A short, sturdy, round-faced man with dark skin and close-cropped hair, his physical appearance conveyed little of his notorious reputation. He wore large dark-rimmed glasses, a plain white prison shirt, and baggy trousers. Even in this depersonalizing environment, he projected an unmistakable presence. There was a sense of command about him, and even a measure of charm in his guarded smile.

When we told him something of the nature of our investigation, Patrick seemed to warm to our visit. In a sentence, he ticked off the physical and emotional stresses that make up the basic cult technique as he sees it. "They use fear, guilt, hate, poor diet, and fatigue," he said. We had heard that from many people, we told him. What we had come for was his unique perspective on the way those techniques may affect the mind. Suddenly, our interview came alive.

"The cults completely destroy the mind," he said without qualification. "They destroy your ability to question things, and in destroying your ability to think, they also destroy your ability to feel. You have no desires, no emotion; you feel no pain, no joy, no nothing."

Patrick confirmed our own perspective when he described the method of control used by many cults, beginning with the moment the recruiter "hooks" his listener.

"They have the ability to come up to you and talk about anything they feel you're interested in, anything," he said. "Their technique is to get your attention, then your trust. The minute they get your trust, just like that they can put you in the cult."

It was the classic sales pitch, carried off so smoothly that it amounted to what Patrick called "on-the-spot hypnosis." Then, he said, once the potential member is hooked, the cult keeps up a steady barrage of indoctrination until conversion is complete.

"When they program a person," said Patrick intently, "they use repetition. They give him the same thing over and over again, day in and day out. They sit up there twenty-four hours a day saying everything outside that door is Satan, that the world is going to end within seven years, and that if you're not in their family you're going to burn in Hell. When a person goes under, he feels guilty if he goes outside in that bad, evil world. He is terrified of what will happen to him out there." ·

Patrick stopped. His version was almost identical to the experiences Lawrence and Cathy Gordon had reported (although they had not been deprogrammed by Patrick but by one of his former clients). He leaned forward, resting his powerful arms on the table between us as he continued.

"There's just so much the human mind can take," he said. "You can stay up just so long without sleep. You can hear the same thing over and over and then it breaks you down. I went into one of the cults with the intention of staying a week. I stayed four days and three nights, and if I'd stayed six more hours I would have been hooked. I'd have never left."

It was in 1971 that Patrick infiltrated the Children of God, the cult that had tried to recruit his son, Michael, one Fourth of July on Mission Beach in San Diego. Patrick's initial concern over the cults was personal, but it also had a public side. A number of worried parents had already appealed to him for help in his official capacity as head of community relations for California's San Diego and Imperial counties. Patrick had moved to San Diego some years earlier and had become active in local politics, acquiring a reputation for his work against discrimination in employment. During the Watts riots of 1965, he helped calm unrest in the Logan Heights section of San Diego, an act of public service that won him recognition in a *Reader's Digest* article. The article caught the attention of California's Governor Ronald Reagan, who appointed Patrick—an active Democrat—to the community relations post.

In his brief experience with the Children of God, though he was alert to the cult's tactics, Patrick found that he was not immune to their effects.

"You can feel it coming on," he explained. "You start doubting yourself. You start to question everything you believe in. Then you find yourself saying and doing the same things they are. You feel like you're sinking in sand, drowning—sometimes you get dizzy."

Here, according to Patrick, was that moment when the individual first goes under, when he may experience the overwhelming emotional release characteristic of snapping. From then on, the new member is taught daily rituals of chanting and meditation which effectively prevent him from regaining control of his mind, or wanting to.

"Thinking to a cult member is just like being stabbed in the heart with a dagger," said Patrick. "It's very painful, because they've been told that the mind is Satan and thinking is the machinery of the devil."

Having gained personal insight into the manner in which that machinery may be brought to a halt, Patrick developed his controversial deprogramming procedure, the essence of which, he explained, is simply to get the individual thinking again.

"When you deprogram people," he emphasized, "you force them to think. The only thing I do is shoot them challenging questions. I hit them with things that they haven't been programmed to respond to. I know what the cults do and how they do it, so I shoot them the right questions; and they get frustrated when they can't answer. They think they have the answer, they've been given answers to everything. But I keep them off balance and this forces them to begin questioning, to open their minds. When the mind gets to a certain point, they can see through all the lies that they've been programmed to believe, and they realize that they've been duped and they come out of it. Their minds start working again."

That, according to Patrick, is all there is to deprogramming. Yet since Patrick first began deprogramming cult members, both the man and his procedure have taken on monstrous proportions in the public eye. The first and most obvious reason for this is that, by nearly all current standards, deprogramming should be wholly illegal in the United States. It would seem to be a flagrant violation of individual freedom to hold a person captive in what, on the surface, can only be construed as an attempt to change his religious beliefs.

There is also the volatile question of physical force. Patrick's legendary kidnappings (a tactic he employs only as a last resort) often bring him into physical confrontation with cult members who have been warned that Black Lightning is an agent of Satan who will subject them to unimaginable tortures to get them to renounce their expressed beliefs. An individual in a cult state of mind may object violently and vehemently to having even a simple conversation with a deprogrammer, and in the course of his efforts, Patrick said, he has been slugged, kicked, spat at, and threatened with kitchen knives. Primarily out of self-defense but also to establish his authority, Patrick generally meets force, when he encounters it, with force. On occasion, Patrick told us, he may thrust a battling cult member into a chair or against a wall, not to harm the individual, he insisted, but simply to demonstrate his capacity to match his opponent's strength and determination. During deprogramming, however, Patrick has no qualms about employing a variety of shock tactics designed to jar his subjects out of their otherwise impenetrable bliss. In order to evoke an emotional response from a cult member who is attempting to "tune him out," Patrick may tear up photographs of the individual's cult leader before his eyes. And with the permission of the subject's parents (who in almost every case are present at the deprogramming), Patrick may remove a cult member's ritual beads or even, in the case of some male members of the Hare Krishna cult, cut off the ponytails many preserve on their otherwise clean-shaven heads. In some cases, the boldness of Patrick's moves alone may be enough to shake a cult member out of his unthinking state. In others, however, it only serves to further outrage him.

In the eyes of the law, of course, such strong-arm tactics can only be interpreted as assault. In fact, several cult members who managed to escape their parents and Patrick before being deprogrammed have run to the media with horror stories about the procedure. One young woman charged on national television that Patrick had ripped her clothes off and chased her nude body across the neighbors' lawns. Other active cult members claim to have been brutally beaten by Patrick. Yet no parent, ex-cult member, or other reliable witness we talked to ever substantiated any of those charges.

In truth, Patrick told us (and others later confirmed), many of the exaggerations and distortions that have been disseminated about deprogramming are part of a heavily financed and well-coordinated campaign by several cults to discredit his methods. Yet in the end, he declared, the propaganda only works to his advantage.

"The cults tell them that I rape the women and beat them. They say I lock them in closets and stuff bones down their throats." Patrick laughed. "What they don't know is that they're making my job easier. They come in here frightened to death of me, and then, because of all the stuff they've been told, I can just sit there and look at them and I'll deprogram them just like that. They'll be thinking, *What the hell is he going to do now?* They're waiting for me to slap them or beat them, and already their minds are working. The more they say about me in the cults, the quicker I can deprogram them."

The heart of Patrick's deprogramming technique, however, has nothing to do with fear, coercion, or intimidation, nor does it consist of simply pleading with the individual—as a parent might—to give up his odd or irrational beliefs. If deprogramming were that simple, anyone could do it; yet in many cases Patrick alone has succeeded where parents, long-time family friends, clergymen, and even psychiatrists have failed. What makes Patrick so special? In our opinion, it is the wealth of personal experience he has acquired and the extraordinary understanding and sensitivity he brings to his task. In the beginning, Patrick admitted to us, he had to develop his method by trial and error, attempting to reason with cult members and learning each particular cult's rituals and beliefs until he cracked the code. In the process, he read everything that has been written on brainwashing and related subjects. Then he proceeded from those textbook cases to the new forms of conversion he had encountered. Refining his procedures with each new case, Patrick came to understand exactly what was needed to pierce the individual's unique mental shield. Almost like a diamond cutter, he had to probe with his questions the rough surface of speech and behavior until he found the exact spot, the key point of contention, at the center of each member's beliefs. Once he found that point, Patrick hit it head on, until the cult member's entire programmed state of mind gave way, revealing the personality that had become trapped inside.

As Patrick began to loosen up, his spirit and confidence came through more freely. We asked him, first, if he would explain his manner of beginning the deprogramming process and, second, how he knew when a person had been deprogrammed; that is, when he could say for sure that he had done his job.

"The first time I lay eyes on a person," he said, staring at us intently, "I can tell if his mind is working or not. Then, as I begin to question him, I can determine exactly how he has been programmed. From then on, it's all a matter of language. It's talking and knowing what to talk about. I start challenging every statement the person makes. I start moving his mind, slowly, pushing it with questions, and I watch every move that mind makes. I know everything it is going to do, and when I hit on that one certain point that strikes home, I push it. I stay with that question—whether it's about God, the devil, or that person's having rejected his parents. I keep pushing and pushing. I don't let him get around it with the lies he's been told. Then there'll be a minute, a second, when the mind *snaps*, when the person realizes he's been lied to by the cult and he just snaps out of it. It's like turning on the light in a dark room. They're in an almost unconscious state of mind, and then I switch the mind from unconsciousness to consciousness and it *snaps*, just like that."

It was Patrick's term this time—we hadn't said the word—for what happens in deprogramming. And in almost every case, according to Patrick, it comes about just that suddenly. When deprogramming has been accomplished, the cult member's appearance undergoes a sharp, drastic change. He comes out of his trancelike state, and his ability to think for himself is restored.

"It's like seeing a person change from a werewolf into a man," said Patrick. "It's a beautiful thing; the whole personality changes, the eyes, the voice. Where they had hate and a blank expression, you can see feeling again."

Snapping, a word Ted Patrick uses often, is a phenomenon that appears to have extreme moments at both ends. A moment of sudden, intense change may occur when a person enters a cult, during lectures, rituals, and physical ordeals. Another change may take place with equal—or even greater—abruptness when the subject is deprogrammed and made to think again. Once this breakthrough is achieved, however, the person is not just "snapped out" and home free. Patrick's method always requires a period of rehabilitation to counteract an interim condition he calls "floating." To ensure that the cult member does not return to his cult state of mind, Patrick told us, he recommends that his subjects spend some time living in the home of a fully rehabilitated deprogrammee. He feels that the best way to keep a person from "backsliding," as he calls it, is to return him to everyday life and normal social relationships as quickly as possible. In that environment, the individual must then actively work to rebuild the fundamental capacities of thought and feeling that have been systematically destroyed.

"Deprogramming is like taking a car out of the garage that hasn't been driven for a year," he said. "The battery has gone down, and in order to start it up you've got to put jumper cables on it. It will start up then, but if you turn the key off right away, it will go dead again. So you keep the motor running until it builds up its own power. This is what rehabilitation is. Once we get the mind working, we keep it working long enough so that the person gets in the habit of thinking and making decisions again."

Patrick's deprogramming procedure adds a whole new dimension to the already complex mystery of snapping. In one sense, deprogramming confirms that some drastic change takes place in the workings of the cult member's mind in the course of his cult experience, for only through deprogramming does it become apparent to everyone, including the cult member, that his actions, and even his expression, speech, and appearance, have not been under his own control. In another sense, deprogramming is itself a form of sudden personality change. Because it appears to be a genuinely broadening, expanding personal change, it would seem to bear closer resemblance to a true moment of enlightenment and understanding, to the natural process of growth and newfound awareness, than to the narrowing, traumatic changes brought about by cult rituals or artificially induced group ordeals.

What is it like to experience the sudden snap of a deprogramming? As a result of Ted Patrick's untiring efforts, there are now thousands of answers to the question. Patrick himself claims to have deprogrammed fifteen hundred cult members, and there are numerous others who have been deprogrammed by his former clients. In the course of our travels, we spoke with dozens of ex-cult members around the country, many of whom had been personally deprogrammed by Ted Patrick. In every instance they praised the process and its inventor. As far as we could see, Patrick's clients showed no scars, either physical or mental, from their deprogramming experience. Almost without exception, they seemed to be healthy, happy, fully rehabilitated, and completely free of the effects of cult life.

In contrast to the many tales of cult conversion that we heard, which after a while began to sound virtually identical, each story of deprogramming was its own spellbinding adventure, rich with intrigue and carefully planned to the last detail. The first step in the process is almost always to remove the cult member from the cult, which may be accomplished by abduction, legal custodianship, or, as Patrick seems to prefer, simply a clever subterfuge. One of the more suspenseful examples of this tactic was told to us by a young woman we will call Lynn Marshall, a former member of the Love Family, also known as Love Israel and the Church of Armageddon, a small, arcane Christian cult in the Pacific Northwest. She described her shanghaiing by Patrick and her family.

"I was kidnapped at the prompting of my parents," she told us. "My mother invited me to have lunch with her, but you weren't supposed to go anyplace by yourself in Love Israel—especially not with somebody from the outside world—so a guy went with me, the one we all called Logic, who in real life is the son of Steve Allen from television. We went out with my mother and had lunch. She was with a man she said was a friend of the family. They had a rented car and were going to drive us back, and when we got in the car they had me sit in the back seat with my mother while Logic sat in the front seat with her friend. We headed off in the wrong direction, and Logic said, 'We're going in the wrong direction,' and my mother's friend said, 'Well, I have a friend to visit.' He started to get on the freeway, and he stopped to pick up this guy who was hitchhiking. I thought to myself, *He's going to pick up a hitchhiker with my mother in the car?* They made Logic get out because they said they wanted the hitchhiker to sit in the middle. Then when Logic got out they closed the door and left him standing there on the on-ramp. I thought my mother had gone crazy, but we sped off and my mother said, 'We're taking you home.' The hitchhiker was Ted Patrick."

Not all of Patrick's legendary kidnappings go off like clockwork, however. Another ex-cult member we spoke with, Tom Koppelman (not his real name), a former "devotee" of the Hare Krishna, recalled the advance warning he had received about deprogramming. He told us about his abduction; then he went on to describe the deprogramming process itself.

"They didn't talk about the deprogrammers much in Krishna," Koppelman said, "but I remember this one devotee was about to leave once with his parents, and this guy mentioned that you had to be careful because there are people parents hire called deprogrammers and they beat you up and make you eat meat and parade prostitutes in front of you and put ice on the back of your neck to keep you awake."

With those fears instilled along with other fears of the outside world, Koppelman did not go gently into his own intricately planned kidnapping several months later.

"I guess my father had the idea to tell the Krishnas that they were going to take me to the dentist to get my teeth checked," he recalled. "So my mother picked me up and I went alone because my cult leader said I could. He said we had to keep my teeth in shape for Krishna. So we were driving the right way to the dentist, and suddenly my mother pulled behind this car and I asked, 'Why are you stopping?' and I looked up and these big guys got out of this Pontiac. They scared the hell out of me because I knew what was going on. They lifted me right out of the front seat into the back seat. I was scared to death. I was sure I was going to get taken to a motel and beaten up. So I started kicking and shouting and chanting *Hare Krishna* in the back seat."

When a cult member first realizes that he has been abducted, some kind of extreme reaction usually follows. He may chant or pray or struggle until he sees the futility of his efforts. Then he may reverse his approach, but even cooperation does not mean that the cult member has come out of his cult state of mind. Koppelman's response was typical of many others we heard.

"I stopped shouting when they said they weren't going to do anything to me," he remembered. "They said they were only going to talk to me and that was all. Then I relaxed completely. I said to myself, *Boy, here's my chance. I'm going to convert all these people.* I also remember thinking, *This is sure going to make a great story when I get back to the temple.*"

From the moment of abduction, the deprogramming process is under way. At the outset, the cult member may faithfully defend his cult, but just by listening to the deprogrammer and observing other people and the world outside, he may start to sense the strangeness and alienation of his cult state of mind. For Koppelman, this was the first inkling of doubt after months as an unwavering devotee.

"First I felt very strong," he explained. "Then they got me to the house and I started to feel very small, very unimportant, sort of like a withdrawing feeling. I felt like I was starting to blend in with the wallpaper. I thought about trying to escape. I remember looking at the window and somebody mentioned, 'No, it's nailed shut.'"

Surprisingly, to deprogram this ascetic follower of Krishna, a Hindu God, Patrick used the same tool he might use on a Moonie or a Jesus Freak: the Bible.

"Patrick knew a great deal about religion and I respected that," said Koppelman. "He started pulling out verse after verse from the Bible that really cut down the Krishna movement. I think the last one was 1 Timothy 4, which said, essentially, *There will be those who depart from the faith and with consciences as if seared by a hot iron will command not to marry and forbid the eating of meats, which God hath put us on this earth to be taken with Thanksgiving*—something like that. That really got to me; it blew the groundwork out of the whole vegetarian business."

Here, as Patrick himself had described to us earlier, he determined from his initial questions that the core of Koppelman's bond to Krishna was the cult's argument against killing and eating animals, a belief that was intricately tied to the Hindu cult's doctrine of reincarnation. Patrick pressed this sensitive issue until he broke through Koppelman's main line of defense.

"Then something happened in my mind," Koppelman said. "I was sitting there and it was like there was this tremendous chasm that went way down; it looked like it was endless. Here I was on one side, and I knew this side wasn't right. Things were just going around in my brain. I was still on the Krishna side at this point, but I could feel myself rushing toward this edge which I was crossing over. I was scared. I really wanted to say, Well, who do I follow now? But suddenly, bang, I was on the other side. In my mind, I could actually see myself leaping over this chasm. It was very vivid. There was a dark mist and this deep chasm. I moved toward it and hesitated at the edge; then I sort of went over. It's like in a dream when you jump and everything is in slow motion and then suddenly you wake up. I just snapped out of it completely and immediately got my sense of being human back. Instantly. Bingo!"

For Patrick, it was a familiar moment of confirmation. He noticed the change immediately, as did Koppelman's parents, who were present throughout the deprogramming. For everyone assembled, final proof came seconds later.

"The first thing I said was, 'Where are the prostitutes? I'm disappointed.' That was the first time I'd cracked a joke in six months."

As we listened to Koppelman's story, it became clear to us that he certainly had not been asleep all those months, nor had he been unconscious. Yet his state of mind was a deep "chasm" apart from our usual notion of human awareness. He was conscious the whole time, but not thinking; as Patrick says, he had been robbed of his *freedom* of thought. Immersed in a fantasy world, Koppelman was cut off from that vital quality we in the West used to refer to as free will. Without it, he was a different person altogether, blank and humorless, until Patrick's deprogramming procedure broke through the shell of his less than fully human existence.

Sometime after we spoke with Koppelman, we interviewed an ex-member of another Hindu cult, the Divine Light Mission, which is led by a rotund teen-age guru named Maharaj Ji. Bill Garber, as we will call him here, painted a slightly different picture of the deprogramming process.

"Ted took me to the limits with a series of questions," he told us, "and I found myself wondering what was going on, since I supposedly had a monopoly on truth and love and he didn't, and I was not supposed to be able to be talked out of my faith. Ted's questions had to do with people in other groups. He asked me what made me think that I had the only true way when they all felt that they had the only true way. I knew I couldn't handle that one, so I just started meditating and waiting for the guru to send me the answer. Then Ted said, 'Meditation is okay, but not when someone is using it to control your mind. You have been brainwashed without your knowledge or consent.' I stopped meditating and a few ideas popped into my head. I began thinking about the interrelatedness of selling techniques and brainwashing. Ted didn't know it, but I had been an encyclopedia salesman some years before."

As Garber described it, the moment when he snapped out was more abstract than wildly dreamlike. Yet for him, as for Tom Koppelman, its abruptness was unforgettable.

"The effect was something like whipping through a deck of IBM cards," he remembered. "A couple of ideas fell together with a kind of a *zap*. It was the first imaginative thinking I'd done in a considerable period of time. Everything came together with such a suddenness that Ted didn't even know what he had done."

And for Garber, the moment when his mind switched back on was accompanied by extraordinary physical sensations.

"I sat there with this dazed look on my face," he said. "I was jolted, as if by a shock, and there was a momentary visual distortion which was part of the overwhelmingness of it, like having a zoom lens built into your eyes. All of a sudden, Ted's face went *zip-zip*. I never experienced that before, and I haven't experienced it since."

One puzzle of snapping that the deprogramming process illuminates is the enormous amount of mental activity that takes place in the cult member's unthinking, unfeeling state. Ironically, most of the individuals we spoke with fought desperately to preserve their blissed-out states, although they were saturated with fear, guilt, hatred, and exhaustion. In the beginning this seemed to present us with a disturbing contradiction: How could an individual whose mind has apparently been shut off, who has been robbed of his freedom of thought, display such cunning and initiative? What the deprogramming process demonstrates is that the cult member does not simply snap from a normal conscious state into one of complete unconsciousness (and vice versa during deprogramming). Rather, he goes from one frame of waking awareness to another in which he may be equally active and perceptive. We talked with an ex-member of the Church of Scientology, one of the oldest and cagiest of America's cults, who was capable of taking even greater steps to preserve his cult frame of mind.

"I tried doing insulting things," he told us. "There were four people in the room, and I took my clothes off and got into bed right in front of them. But Ted kept talking and occasionally he would move my bed a little so that I couldn't go to sleep. I sat up on my elbow and I said, 'How would you like it if I kicked your ass?' And he came and stood over me and said, 'Yeah? You just try it!' That kind of scared me, even though I'm much bigger than he is."

In this case, however, as in most of Patrick's deprogrammings, neither party resorted to violence. Instead, Patrick's adept conversational skills held the cult member's attention until he snapped out.

"I tried to pretend that I was listening," this former Scientologist told us, "but I also tried to stay spaced out and not really pay attention. Occasionally, something would go *pop*, and I would suddenly be listening to him. The feeling was mainly caused by his continuous talking and changing the speeds of how he was talking. He made his own rhythm and his own changes of high-pitched and low-pitched tones that was really refreshing. From his continuously talking like that, he just snapped me out of the spaced-out state I was in. All of a sudden I felt a little flushed. I could feel the blood rushing through my face."

Then there are those deprogrammings in which the cult member remains relatively docile from the outset, sometimes openly admitting to be in a state of doubt and confusion. We spoke with a young ex-cult member whom we will call Teri O'Connor who went through a particularly difficult deprogramming with Patrick. Now fully rehabilitated, she told us her story, providing a glimpse of just one of many profound human moments that seem to epitomize the spirit of Patrick and his work.

"He kept saying this stuff and I was trying to rationalize it," she remembered, "but it was impossible to rationalize. I began to get very uncomfortable, and I said to him, 'I feel like I've been crazy these last few months.' I was so scared, I could see myself being in the nuthouse for the rest of my life. I was a little jellyfish, and if someone other than Ted Patrick had gotten ahold of me, they could have done anything they wanted. Then it was like a light going on. I definitely felt it and my mom said she saw it in my eyes.

"In the beginning, I didn't want to say too much about the deprogramming. I was still afraid, but if it hadn't been for Ted Patrick, I would just be crazy today. I owe him my life, actually, I really do."

To further our understanding of deprogramming and its controversial inventor, we looked into Patrick's background and, during our interview, asked him questions about his childhood, discovering a depth of personal experience that gave clues to his pioneering insights into the tactics used by the cults. Born and raised in Chattanooga, Tennessee, young Theodore Roosevelt Patrick had even more social handicaps to overcome than just being poor and black. The man who today works wonders with words was born with a speech impediment. This brought him into contact, at an early age, with many dubious forms of religion.

"My mother carried me to every fortune-teller, faith healer, Holy Roller, false god, prophet, voodoo, and hoodoo—every one that came into town; but you could hardly understand a word I was saying," Patrick told us. "My sister had to interpret for me. Then suddenly it came to me. I thought, *Are you asking God to do something that you are not willing to do for yourself? Have you tried? And I knew I hadn't.*"

So Patrick cured himself.

"I'd always been afraid of words," he admitted to us. "I was unable to say a lot of words because I was afraid they'd come out wrong. So I started correcting myself over and over again, out loud. Even when I was in church, my mind would be correcting itself over and over again. That's how I got to the point where I can talk now."

After overcoming his initial disadvantages, Patrick progressed through ten years of public school, leaving high school to embark on his varied career of social activism in defense of minority rights. Later, when he began his battle against the cults, it must have seemed ironic to many who knew him that he had become passionately engaged in what superficially appeared to be a fight against the rights of individuals and minorities. When he first began deprogramming, Patrick was well aware that he was technically violating the First Amendment freedoms of the cult members he abducted. In view of the circumstances, however, and the observable changes that had come over the cult members, Patrick was led to draw his fine and now hotly debated distinction between constitutional and human freedoms.

"When you're born into this world, you're born into the laws of nature," Patrick asserted, "and only then are you introduced to the laws of the land. Anytime someone destroys your free will, when they take away your mind and your natural ability to think, then they've destroyed the *person*. As long as you remain in that condition, you have no more constitutional rights to violate."

From the beginning, Patrick spoke out boldly in defense of freedom of thought, knowing that his new procedure would cost him his job and his own freedom as well. Although he has been deprogramming cult members full time for several years now, Patrick remains a deeply moral and religious man. Nevertheless, in his deprogrammings, he takes great care never to impose his own religious beliefs, or anyone else's, on the young people he rescues.

"When I deprogram people," he stressed, "I don't make any mention of a church or whether or not I even believe in God. That's beside the point. My intention is to get their minds working again and to get them back out in the world. I've been through the Bible, I know it backwards, but I didn't begin to understand the Bible until I got out of school, when I hit the streets and started studying people. That's the only way to use the Bible; you must relate it to everyday life. When the twenty-fourth chapter of Matthew says, *There will be many coming in my name, saying, I am Christ; and they will deceive the very elect,* then people should relate it to all these false gods today."

There are some signs that people are beginning to understand. Within the last few years, a number of other deprogrammers have started working around the country. All former clients, students, or self-confessed imitators of Patrick's style, they have benefited greatly from the trailblazing efforts of Patrick and his energetic colleague, Sondra Sacks. While Patrick was in jail, his followers and imitators began making headlines of their own, and many also began charging parents astronomical fees for their services. Some of these new deprogrammers, however, lacking adequate training and understanding, chalked up failures in surprising numbers, as their clients slipped back into the cults or suffered emotional breakdowns as a result of inept deprogrammings or ineffective rehabilitation periods. In the course of talking to Patrick and many of his former clients and then to other deprogrammers and their subjects, we quickly learned that, despite all the attention this controversial technique has received, few of Patrick's high-priced imitators share his expertise. Many know the legal ropes of gaining temporary custody of cult members, most have done their homework on the essentials of brainwashing; but only a few seem to have mastered the vital human elements of trustworthiness and sincerity that can reach even the most distant, detached cult member. For the deprogrammer guided by those qualities, breaking through the cult's wall of mindless happiness may be accomplished with deceptive simplicity.

"A lot of times deprogramming is just a matter of telling a person what life is all about," Patrick told us. "It's a simple thing to tell somebody to take life for what it is, not what it should be and not what you'd like it to be. But sometimes that's all it takes."

That evening, as we prepared to leave the cramped cubicle within sight of the front door of the Orange County Jail, Patrick told us of his immediate plans to write a manual of deprogramming, one that would clear up some of the public and professional confusion surrounding his technique and place it in a broader framework that, in the future might prove to be of value in treating other forms of mental and emotional disorders. Patrick grew philosophical as we touched upon the implications of his work.

"A lot of people who are in mental hospitals have nothing wrong with them," he said. "They just don't know how to accept life for what it is, and not what they want it to be. Like in here, for instance, I adjust myself to this jail. I enjoy myself in prison because I'm stuck here." As he continued, his powerful dark eyes began to twinkle. "I got them organizing here," he confided. "It's been booming the past week. One hundred and five inmates signed a petition requesting a grand jury investigation of my case."

After eight months in prison, apparently, Black Lightning was back in action.

Three days after we left him, he was released from jail.

Few people have spoken up in defense of Ted Patrick and what he is trying to do. No professional organization or established institution has taken a stand on behalf of his commitment to freedom of thought. Part of the problem may be attributable to Patrick's own manner of action. In his single-minded focus on rescuing cult members, he minces no words and wastes little time on social niceties. As a result, he often irks and alienates those parents, law enforcement officials, and mental health professionals who might otherwise be his natural allies.

Yet, regardless of his style, the grave questions Patrick has so flamboyantly brought to public attention are not ones we can choose to like or dislike —nor will they simply go away if we ignore them. Is an individual free to give up his freedom of thought? May a religion, a mass therapy, or any other institution systematically attack human thought and feeling in the name of "happiness" and "fulfillment"? These are questions that we in America are not prepared to deal with, because they challenge long-standing assumptions about our minds, our personalities, and our human freedom.

In the weeks and months following our trip to the Orange County Jail we spoke with many people about Ted Patrick: parents, ex-cult members, other deprogrammers, and a number of people who were only dimly aware that there was such a thing as a controversy over some alleged forms of religion in America. We heard some denounce Patrick as a villain and a fascist, while others hailed him as a folk hero and a dark prophet of what lies ahead for America. Yet Patrick himself shows little concern for titles or media images. All he seems to ask is that people take him seriously.

We saw him a second time, during the summer of 1977, in Colorado, where he had gone voluntarily to serve out the last few weeks of an earlier kidnapping conviction in that state. There, in a private visiting room at the Denver Jail, he greeted us warmly, his hands and shirt covered with bright-colored paint from some work he had been doing in the prison workshop. He spoke highly of the treatment he was receiving from guards and prison officials, who had invited him to address them on the subject of deprogramming. Our talk turned to recent developments in the cult controversy and his own worsening legal and financial situation because of a flood of lawsuits filed against him by several large, wealthy cults. Patrick once again became somber, concerned over what he saw as the public's growing apathy in the face of the cult world's increasing wealth, power, and social legitimacy.

"The cult movement is the greatest threat and danger to this country that we have ever had," he said gravely, "but the people won't wake up, the government, Congress, the Justice Department won't wake up until something bad happens."

With regard to his own work, Patrick felt a greater urgency than ever, he said, and he was already marshalling his forces to go back into battle immediately upon his release. He said he would try to stay within the law wherever possible in future, but if it became a question of crossing over the line in order to save a cult member's captive mind, he had no doubt about what his top priority would be. At the same time, Patrick assured us, he would continue to appeal to the government and representatives of America's mental health establishment for their help, although he saw little hope of receiving support for his efforts.

"Sooner or later, they're going to have to recognize deprogramming as a profession," he said. "They're going to be forced to. But right now they don't believe that this is something that can happen to anybody. Everybody's vulnerable. I want to make people aware of that."

7 Wanted: Professional Help

'Life is a very wonderful thing,' said Dr. Branom. . . . 'The processes of life, the make-up of the human organism, who can fully understand these miracles? . . . What is happening to you now is what should happen to any normal healthy human organism. . . . You are being made sane, you are being made healthy.'

'That I will not have,' I said, 'nor can understand at all. What you've been doing is to make me feel very very ill.'

—Anthony Burgess,
A Clockwork Orange

IN HIS EFFORT to gain support for his battle against the cults, Ted Patrick has made repeated personal appeals to America's mental health community. The professionals, however, have almost totally ignored his insight into cult techniques and their effects, and they have flatly refused to become involved in the public controversy over his deprogramming procedure. But Ted Patrick is not the only person who has been brushed aside. A much less controversial figure, William Rambur of Chula Vista, California, has been similarly disregarded in his efforts to bring the cults' destructive new threat to personality to the attention of mental health specialists.

William Rambur is another who has gone to bat for the perplexed, embarrassed, angry, heartbroken parents of America's cult members who have been legally handcuffed in their efforts to rescue their sons and daughters. Since 1971, Rambur has been an outspoken activist in the battle against the cults. In 1973, he helped organize the Citizen's Freedom Foundation and became its first president. With over 4,000 members, the CFF is the largest parents' organization among many combatting the cults. Since the organization was founded, Rambur and his colleagues have formed a nationwide network to help locate cult members who have disappeared from their schools and homes. They have circulated newsletters and given lectures throughout the country in their program of public education, and they have appeared in Washington asking for government investigation of the cults.

In our swing through southern California, we stopped at the CFF office in Chula Vista, near San Diego, where we spent an emotional afternoon that stretched into evening with William and Betty Rambur. There we heard perhaps the most appalling story of our investigation.

Like Ted Patrick and so many other Americans who have taken up the fight against the cults, the Ramburs' outrage stems from personal, painful experience. In July, 1971, the Ramburs' daughter, Kay, vanished abruptly from her job as a registered nurse. A few days after her disappearance, William and Betty Rambur received a letter from their daughter informing them that she had joined a cult called the Children of God and that she had decided to devote her life to the service of Jesus Christ. Kay had always been a religious girl, but, given no further explanation, the Ramburs were baffled by her decision. After repeated attempts to find her, they finally located Kay on a Children of God farm in Texas, where they were horrified to see for themselves all the signs of the cult state. As we sat surrounded by great bins of mail in the cluttered CFF office, William Rambur, firm but mild-mannered after his many years as a high school teacher, told us what it felt like to see his daughter in that condition.

"You know how when you look at people," said Rambur, "you look them in the eye and it seems like they're looking back at you? In the case of the cult members, you look in their eyes and they're not looking back. It's a strange thing, especially when it's your own daughter, and you look in her eyes and you remember how she looked the last time you saw her, and now there's nothing, no emotion or anything left. It's just like a void, and you look in the other people's eyes who are in these cults and you see the same sort of thing. It's kind of scary."

On the COG farm, Rambur told us, he walked with his daughter in a field and convinced her to return home to Chula Vista. As they were driving away, several COG members sped up in another car and blocked them from leaving. Without a word, Kay unlocked the car door and went back with the other members. Several months later, Rambur finally managed to talk Kay into returning home for a weekend visit. Once she was free of the closed cult environment, Rambur said, he and his wife succeeded in questioning Kay and reasoning with her until they effected a crude deprogramming of sorts.

"Finally she came out of it," Rambur recalled. "She seemed like her old self again. She was happy. She said, as far as the Children of God were concerned, they could go to hell, she was out of it."

When Kay snapped out of her cult state, she gave her father some very specific instructions.

"She said, 'Dad, all of those people in there need help,' " Rambur told us. " 'But we've got to help them from the outside, because nobody can help themselves from inside.' She said, 'Dad, don't ever give up fighting, because if you ever give up fighting, they'll never get out by themselves.' "

But Kay Rambur's amateur deprogramming was far from complete. For the next few days she lingered in the precarious floating state described by Ted Patrick, a twilight zone of uncertainty and vulnerability to suggestion. During that time, Kay and her father attempted to free Robert, another cult member who had been married to Kay by the cult leaders in what Rambur interpreted as an attempt to further remove her from her father's pursuit and legal jurisdiction. Rambur and his daughter telephoned Robert to invite him to spend a few days at their home. Rambur told Robert that he was welcome, and he heard his daughter say, "Robert, it's beautiful, you've got to come." Then he and his wife left the room to let Kay talk to Robert alone.

"That was our mistake," Rambur told us sadly, "but that was before anyone really knew."

While Robert and Kay were talking, Betty Rambur picked up the phone to extend her welcome to Robert. She heard him tell Kay, "If you leave the Children of God, you'll be responsible for the deaths that follow. The blood will be on your hands." Astounded by what she was hearing, Betty Rambur told Robert that he was welcome in their home, but that she wouldn't tolerate that kind of talk. Then she put down the receiver, and a few minutes later Kay emerged markedly transformed.

"When Kay came out of that back room she was just a different person," said Rambur. "She was only on the phone a couple of minutes, but when she came out she was like a zombie again."

The nightmare that followed was as incomprehensible as it was horrifying. Rambur told us that just after Kay talked to Robert, two neighbors received anonymous telephone calls warning them that if they didn't stop associating with the Ramburs they would be killed and "there wouldn't be enough bones left to bury." Children of God members lined the Ramburs' street in trucks and vans, and Kay rushed out screaming that the Devil was in the house. As Rambur and his son brought Kay back inside and tried to calm her, Kay wrestled her brother to the ground and started to choke him. Then she hit one of the Ramburs' neighbors across the neck and kicked another in the groin. Finally, the Ramburs called the police, who responded promptly, restored peace, and recommended that Kay be hospitalized. At this point, Rambur had his first confrontation with the mental health profession.

"When we got out to the hospital there was a woman doctor who we later discovered had been contacted by the Children of God," said Rambur. "They called the hospital when they found out we were coming and told her that an upset father was trying to bring his daughter in to have her committed. When we walked in there, the first thing she said to Kay was, 'You're not crazy, are you?' She refused to admit her to the hospital. She said, 'There's nothing wrong with her. I think it's the father who is upset. He's the one who needs help.' "

At the time, Rambur couldn't believe his ears. He said, "Look, if you think that's how it is, put me in, too! Put us both in here." But the admitting doctor steadfastly refused. A nurse who had been watching said, "This is the craziest thing I've ever seen. That girl needs help, and it looks like everyone on this staff is preventing you from helping your daughter."

"We just didn't know what to do," Rambur admitted, reliving the scene. "This whole episode had gone on for close to a week, and most of us had had no sleep during that time and we were getting pretty distraught. There was no place else we could turn. We'd reached the end of the line, so I told my daughter, 'Look, you think I'm persecuting you? I'll not persecute you. I will not try to find you, but I want you to remember this: If you ever need me, I'll come. Now I'm going to leave, I'm going to walk out because I don't know what else to do.' "

They left her there, got into their car, and drove home and went to sleep. After about an hour, however, William and Betty Rambur woke up and said to each other, "Why are we doing this? How could we abandon her?" Desperate, they called the hospital and talked to the chief of staff, who told them a psychiatrist had examined Kay, found nothing wrong, and released her.

"That was six years ago," said William Rambur, looking over to his wife, then back to us, "and no one has seen her since."

In the years that have followed, police in twenty-seven countries have been unable to trace Kay Rambur's whereabouts. William Rambur has remembered his daughter's plea, however, and travels around the United States to help other parents find their children and free them from cult control. Time after time, Rambur has appealed to the mental health community, but the strange new disorder he has brought to their attention poses a peculiar dilemma for their expertise.

"I phoned many psychologists and psychiatrists and asked if they would help; if we could get a youth to come to them, would they give us some insight into the situation?" Rambur remembered. "Several said that they would try. Once, after getting the youth there, the psychiatrist called me and said, 'Look, we're wasting our time. That person has to admit that he has a problem' "— which is something few cult members are prone to do under any circumstances.

Since then, Rambur has taken his plea to other areas of the mental health field, only to meet with a similar lack of comprehension.

"I spoke to a group of sociologists and explained to them what was happening," he told us, exasperated. "They could follow me up to a point; then we got to this threshold that I couldn't make them go beyond. They wouldn't believe this is something new that they should study. They said, 'Why don't you parents go home and relax, and after a certain period your children will come back to you and everything will be fine.' They wouldn't entertain the possibility that what is going on is very different."

Rambur did not dismiss the many traditional responses he has received from psychiatrists and psychologists. As a teacher, he was among the first to admit that parental upbringing and social pressures may be major factors in cult conversion. But too often, he felt, these simplistic explanations beg a larger and more immediate question concerning the cults' conversion techniques.

"Psychologists and psychiatrists who are not aware of what is happening will try to base their opinions on past behavior," said Rambur, "and they lose sight of the fact that there is a new element here that they know nothing about."

Rambur paused; we agreed, and he asked us to convey a message to the mental health profession.

"We've reached the threshold of something new and different," he repeated. "Now we have to add to what we knew before and go beyond that into a new area of study of the mind."

He speaks eloquently but he knows, like Ted Patrick, that without proper credentials no one will listen. After six years, William Rambur's voice of experience has grown hoarse.

"They've studied cases in their textbooks," he said with a measure of resignation, "but I've studied the real thing. You would think that psychiatrists and psychologists would sit down and talk to me."

———

We talked with dozens of parents around the country who, like William Rambur, have sought in vain to find professional help for children who had become unwitting victims of America's cults. They told similar stories of being pacified and sent home by psychiatrists and psychologists who advised them not to worry or become unduly upset, that their children were just "going through a phase" and that they should not "overreact." Many mental health professionals charged that parents' stories were exaggerations. Others refused to believe them altogether. In some cases, they even examined cult members and, as with Kay Rambur, could find nothing wrong. Several other parents who are very active in the anticult fight confirmed William Rambur's impassioned complaints. They described their own attempts to bring the cults to the attention of countless local and national psychological associations. But because they were the parents of the individuals involved and because they lacked professional credentials, their cries fell on deaf ears.

As frustrated as parents are who have been unable to secure help for their children, the situation is immeasurably harder for cult members who have, themselves, desperately sought professional guidance. We spoke with one, a young man we call Paul Davis who is a rare figure among America's growing fraternity of ex-cult members. In 1976, after nearly two years in the Unification Church, Davis left the Moonies on his own, first choosing to visit his family for a weekend, then simply deciding not to return to his life in the church. Davis never underwent deprogramming, however, and he never snapped out of his cult state. For three months after he left the cult, he endured an excruciating emotional ordeal accompanied by severe physical side effects. His encounter with a psychiatrist was typical of the quality of professional help described to us by victims of religious cults.

"I had an uncomfortable feeling in my head," Davis recalled the day we met, his voice still shaky. "I was unable to focus my consciousness or my thoughts. I couldn't differentiate between what was true and what was not. It was a very emotional thing, like what might happen to you in a disaster where your whole family was killed. I was almost in a state of shock. I was unable to relax, always spaced out. My pupils were dilated, I couldn't focus on anything or talk to anybody in a normal way. So I went to a psychiatrist and told him I was in very bad trouble. He couldn't comprehend it. He said someone had planted unconscious things in my mind."

For the next few months, Davis said, he continued to flounder in alternating states of fear, confusion, and despair. He tried to resume a semblance of a normal life, taking up residence on his own and seeking part-time employment to provide an income while he completed his education; but his torturous emotions refused to subside. Another psychologist he went to provided some slight comfort and reassurance, but very little of the understanding he so urgently sought. Finally, he admitted, he tried to cover up his inner torment to the best of his ability. When we spoke, the passage of time alone had served to diminish the effects of his years in the Unification Church. But he couldn't comprehend what had happened to his mind and was still having difficulty making his way in the outside world.

"Unconscious things," Davis was told. We could virtually catalog the number of professional interpretations of "the cult syndrome" that have been passed along to us by parents and ex-cult members. According to various representatives of America's mental health establishment, the sudden personality changes that take place in the cults are caused by "serious failures in family life," "underlying anxieties," and "guilt-ridden insecurities." They are the product of "ego conflicts," "masochistic reactions," and "emotional immaturity." They can be traced to "environmental factors," "antecedent conditions," or "deep-seated subconscious needs."

In recent years, a small number of psychiatrists and psychologists around the country have begun deprogramming efforts of their own, supplementing Ted Patrick's basic deprogramming model with various psychiatric and psychological tools. In some cases this added background has proved helpful, providing professional deprogrammers with additional keys to unlock captive minds. Yet in many instances the professional concepts and jargon have served only to obscure the primary goal of deprogramming, which is to help the cult member regain his natural ability to think for himself. Instead, many professionals pour irrelevant issues and worn-out notions into their subjects' already confused and chaotic minds. The net result is often a deprogramming that is intellectually cluttered and emotionally unclear.

On our way back east, we spoke with one young woman who, months later, was still struggling to understand the changes of mind she had experienced. Unlike Paul Davis, Mary Troy (not her real name) didn't leave the Unification Church on her own. After nearly a year in the service of Reverend Moon, she was kidnapped by her parents and a psychologist from the Midwest newly active in the lucrative business of professional deprogramming. In the style of Ted Patrick, she was abducted and taken to a motel. In contrast to Patrick's seasoned method, however, the psychologist's deprogramming technique was one of inept confrontation, mere badgering, and transparent psychological ploys.

"At first they tried to get me to feel anger," Mary Troy recalled, "but they didn't succeed. So they started digging into my childhood—which wasn't exactly ideal. They brought up something very personal from my past, and I said, 'I can see what you're trying to do, but I don't want to go along with your games.'"

Eventually, after several days in the motel room, her parents and the deprogrammer hit upon a past trauma that managed to loosen her captive thought processes. Unlike the characteristic distinct moment of deprogramming common to other ex-cult members we spoke with, the psychological approach Mary Troy's deprogramming took, as she described it, resulted in a slow and fuzzy reemergence.

"At the end, it wasn't like fireworks going off," she said. "I just realized, *Well, everyone seems to think I'm normal again. I guess this is that moment.*"

In the months that followed, Mary Troy returned to the psychologist for regular sessions of long-term therapy. There she was given reasons for why she had joined the cult and a basic understanding of the techniques of "mind control." But the psychologist did not succeed in helping her understand the feeling that she had entered a new state of being since her deprogramming, a sense of self quite different from the one she knew before she joined the cult.

"The first few weeks out of the cult I had no idea who I was," she said. "Yet I wasn't uneasy about it, I looked on it as kind of exciting. But whoever I was before the cult, I'm not anymore. I'm a different person now; a lot of things have happened to my mind."

In marked contrast to some of Patrick's former clients, Mary Troy did not appear to us to have been reunited with her former self. The difficulty seemed to stem from the purely intellectual content of her psychological treatment. What was missing in this professional approach with its efficient explanations was some sign of the feeling and mutual respect between deprogrammer and subject which Patrick's clients conveyed to us. Without these vital components, her professional deprogramming had merely replaced Mary Troy's religious answers with a new set of psychological ones. It never managed to rekindle the spark of her own individuality.

We interviewed the psychologist who deprogrammed Mary Troy. He told us what the recognized authorities on brainwashing, mind control, and "coercive persuasion" had to say, but he refused to take a professional stand on behalf of Patrick's deprogramming technique, which, he implied, was not a properly scientific procedure. His own method of deprogramming called for detailed probing into the individual's childhood and upbringing and usually required several months of expensive follow-up therapy. Yet to our amazement, despite the numerous cult victims he had treated, he equivocated on the cult controversy.

"Some people are better off in cults," he informed us, adding, "As a psychologist, I'd rather not comment until some sort of statistics are derived on what kind of people become cult members."

William Rambur's frustration and anger at the response of the mental health community is understandable. Among the professionals we contacted from New England to California, we encountered many of the same attitudes Rambur found in relation to the cults. Like so many parents, we sat quietly while professional people told us that "there wouldn't be any kids in cults if we had better reading programs in our schools" and that "involvement in clans and secret societies is a normal part of growing up." The majority of professionals, however, refused even to discuss the problem, fearing involvement in religious controversy or some threat to their stature among their colleagues. One world-renowned expert on the mind told us flatly, "I'll have nothing to say about the cults." Another gave us some leads to pursue, saying, "Don't forget, you never heard of me."

In the face of mounting public concern over the visible dilemma of the cults, and with an increasing number of Americans falling victim to mass-marketed therapies, America's mental health establishment has had almost nothing to contribute to our national understanding of the problem. Their old theories fail to match up with the new facts; their analyses are based on concepts left over from eras that bear little resemblance to America in the seventies. While parents and cult members alike cry out for help, few professionals are looking at the cult experience itself, at the specific techniques used by the cults, and at the effects of those techniques on the mind.

Above all, America's mental health community has shown no sign of assuming the leadership role that would seem to be its responsibility. To better understand why, we felt it necessary to extend our investigation into that field's problems and dilemmas. In our research it became evident to us that —like so many other people and institutions in the United States today—the mental health community is showing symptoms of a sudden, drastic alteration of its own identity, a refocusing of awareness in the wake of the consciousness explosion. This sweeping transformation, we discovered, has brought it to the point of crisis in its dealings with the public—and within its own ranks as well.

8 The Crisis in Mental Health

The present crisis of psychology (which, however, has already lasted for some 30 years) can be summarized as the slow erosion of the robot model of man.

—*Ludwig von Bertalanffy,*
General Systems Theory (*1968*)

THE ENTIRE RANGE of phenomena that fall under our general heading of snapping comprise a domain of personality disorders that the mental health community has been unable to explain or treat. America's epidemic of sudden personality change, however, is itself a symptom of a far-reaching crisis in the mental health of the nation as a whole. This crisis can be traced to the consciousness explosion of the sixties, which had a profound impact on mental health practice throughout the country and on the personal lives of many mental health professionals as well.

Until the early sixties, Western psychological thought cleaved neatly along two theoretical lines: the Freudian, or psychoanalytical, and the behavioristic, often called experimental, Skinnerian, or positivistic. The psychoanalytical branch separated human personality into a set of mental subdivisions called ego, id, and superego, which were governed largely by the subconscious. The behavioristic school, on the other hand, dealt solely with observable behavior, insisting that mental activity and "internal states" were of little significance in human affairs because they could not be observed or reproduced experimentally.

The psychoanalytical and the behavioristic schools of psychology are generally considered to be diametrically opposed to one another in both theory and therapy. The first looks inside the "psyche" to the subconscious; the other stands back to validate only the observable product of behavior. Yet both psychological models share a common assumption about human beings: that an individual's conscious experience of the world around him is, at best, of secondary importance in the development of his personality and the determination of his behavior. In the Freudian tradition, the unknowable and unreachable subconscious governs personality. In behavioristic theory, a mind-boggling number of environmental forces automatically condition an individual's responses. This common assumption unites the traditional forces of psychology in our culture; both relegate an individual's awareness of his thoughts, feelings, and actions to some form of external or hidden internal control. Taken together, they comprise the "robot model" of man, the theoretical base of psychology upon which our modern technological society has evolved.

In this century, application of the robot model has become a major preoccupation of our free enterprise system in particular and of our society in general. American business has developed perhaps the most sophisticated fusion of the two schools. Its marketing and advertising strategies prey upon basic human needs and fundamental insecurities in order to create and fulfill consumer demands with scientific predictability. Throughout our society, the unconscious control of human beings has become the focus of some of our most powerful institutions. It is taken for granted in education, where the principles of behavior modification govern teaching, not only in school but also in the home. It is the subject of continuing experimentation in factories and other work environments. It has burgeoned in the seventies in a spate of best sellers advising readers how to exploit tactics of "power," "assertiveness," and "winning through intimidation" to turn the unawareness of others to their own personal advantage.

Predominant as the robot model of man has been—and continues to be—in American business and social life, there has always been an alternative force in psychology. It, too, has gained strength and popularity in recent years. In the late fifties, a number of splinter groups from the main currents of Freudian and behavioristic theory began to coalesce into a new and comprehensive school of thought on human nature. This so-called Third Force in psychology was made up of many of Freud's early disciples and later rivals, among them Alfred Adler, Otto Rank, and Freud's protégé, Carl Jung. These towering figures were joined by emerging existential or humanistic psychologists such as Gordon Allport, Gardner Murphy, Carl Rogers, and Abraham Maslow and by dynamic social psychologists such as Kurt Lewin and Jacob Moreno. By the early sixties, after many of its founders had died, this Third Force came to be known as humanistic psychology, the new discipline that would lead the way in the exploration of man's uniquely human capacities. In recognizing this unlimited potential, the Third Force rejected the robot model of man and gave primacy instead to the shaping power of human awareness.

The new techniques and therapies of humanistic psychology offered impressive demonstrations of that power. It used intense, immediate experience to alter not simply patterns of behavior but the individual's state of awareness, even his whole personality. During this time, "experience" came forward as if it were a new discovery of human nature, and "consciousness" burst upon the American scene as an exciting new arena of adventure.

Almost overnight, humanistic psychology and its offspring, the human potential movement, transformed our popular attitudes toward mental health beyond recognition, first on the West Coast, then spreading quickly eastward. Suddenly, people drastically reduced their participation in psychoanalysis, psychotherapy, and traditional group therapy—small weekly or twice-weekly groups led by a psychiatrist or psychologist, devoted primarily to open discussion along traditional lines. Instead, they entered into weekend encounter groups and radical therapies, therapies that used physical and emotional experiences such as arm wrestling, body massage, intense verbal attacks, and prolonged confinement to produce those now familiar peak experiences and breakthrough moments.

In the beginning, the new methods of humanistic psychology received a cool reception from tradition-bound mental health professionals. Most psychoanalysts, psychiatrists, and clinical psychologists were content to work with the tools they had available; the field already seemed more than adequately fragmented with its long-standing theoretical dichotomies and splinter factions. But more importantly, the basic principles of encounter and other experimental therapies contradicted almost every rule of traditional mental health practice. By urging physical contact and personal confrontation, these new approaches trampled the sacred accord of the doctor–patient relationship, overturning inviolable canons of formal conduct and professional detachment.

The first results achieved by the new techniques were difficult for the mental health establishment to ignore. Very often, people would return to their traditional therapy sessions raving about the fun and excitement they had had in an encounter group and declaring that they had accomplished more in one weekend than they had in years of private analysis or group therapy. As the consciousness explosion took off, and despite their skepticism, many of the professionals were forced to pay attention to this personal testimony. Before long, however, the brush-fire spread of these new concepts and therapies circled back and threatened to consume the profession of psychiatry itself.

The dark side of this new world of human potential was evident from the beginning. In a climate of heedless experimentation, many searchers strayed into no-man's-lands of human awareness. As new attitudes burst forth to fuel the sixties' environment of revolution and alternative lifestyles, a growing number of individuals began to find themselves adrift or run aground—and they began to react accordingly. Around the country, people began to "flip out" and go visibly crazy, engaging in violent and self-destructive behavior. Others, in contrast, "flipped in" and snapped, dropping into states of fantasy, terror, and disorientation that were, in those early days, wholly unforeseen and inexplicable.

Predictably, the burden of treating the new casualties of the conscious-ness explosion fell squarely on the shoulders of the psychiatric profession, on the medical doctors who manned the nation's emergency rooms, crisis units, and psychiatric wards. They were the first to see those people in most urgent need of professional help. However, psychiatry was not prepared to deal with this new monster of "experience," nor was it capable of treating the unusual disorders of personality that resulted. Psychiatrists are doctors, trained in physiological diagnosis and grounded in the traditional models of psychology. When in the sixties they began to identify a brand-new category of mental and emotional disturbance, one that was caused neither by chemical, motor, or neurological dysfunction nor by childhood or environmental factors, they found they could not diagnose it as either medically based mental illness or traditional psychological malaise. It came to be called a "critical situational response," a crisis brought on by some new and intense experience, such as psychedelic drugs, encounter groups, Eastern mystical practices—or by every-day social problems of undefinable origin.

For treatment, the traditional tools of psychiatry proved ineffective. There was no longer time or reason for the leisurely analysis of a person's entire emotional past; the principles of behaviorism likewise were inadequate for understanding and treating these new afflictions of human awareness. Psy-choactive drugs were helpful in dealing with severe emotional traumas and nervous breakdowns, but the vast majority of patients never deteriorated to these extreme conditions. Instead, they succumbed to fantasies and delusions, withdrew into themselves, or simply behaved in odd and eccentric ways.

Slowly, as the old approaches proved increasingly useless, the recognized limits of psychiatric treatment began to give way to whole new systems of interpretation. For the first time, psychiatrists began to look beyond the clinic, the couch, and the laboratory in an effort to incorporate the insights of humanistic psychology into their own models and practices. By the late sixties, comprehensive new approaches to mental health, such as family therapy and community counseling, were being developed to deal with the new problems affecting individuals in all kinds of groups and everyday life. In addition to psychiatrists, other mental health professionals—clinical psychologists, social workers, and rehabilitation counselors—began to create expanded follow-up functions and move into new supporting roles in order to cope with the greatly increased number of adults and adolescents who had begun using counseling services, drug rehabilitation facilities, and crisis centers from coast to coast.

Not all the changes taking place in psychiatry and the mental health field were confined to questions of patient treatment, however. By the end of the sixties, professionals at the forefront of American psychiatry and psychology were immersed in firsthand experimentation. In their quest for insight many of them ran into a peculiar double-edged dilemma. On the one hand, they were looking into these new techniques in search of new modes of treatment and understanding; yet, like others around the country, they themselves were not immune to the effects of the techniques. Faced with the added problem of distinguishing their research and experimentation from its inevitable personal impact, many professionals found themselves unable to integrate their dual paths of experience. In many instances, their traditional backgrounds in physiological disease and psychopathology left them ill-equipped to deal with the emerging humanistic notions of creativity, play, and spontaneity and unprepared for the moving peak experiences and alterations of awareness they encountered. Like a growing number of their patients, many psychiatrists became victims of the search.

By the early seventies, surviving traditionalists within the ranks of psychiatry continued to mind their own business while the rest of the profession was growing overloaded and exhausted. As many of its younger and more vocal members fled the field for other careers, psychiatry no longer had the internal strength or organization to exert the leadership that was in order. The profession ignored its social responsibility to issue warnings, establish guidelines, or set any other criteria that might aid the millions of Americans searching indiscriminately for some ill-defined personal breakthrough. By mid-decade, the mental health establishment had pulled back even farther from the wave of experimentation still coursing through the country. In an effort to reestablish itself as a valid field of scientific inquiry and medical practice, the psychiatric profession took a protective step in the direction of its traditional medical foundations. With no clearer alternatives, psychiatrists turned increasingly toward pharmacological methods of treating emotional disorders. In many areas, they simply abandoned their earlier clinical commitments and public service activities. Left without leadership, the rest of the mental health community remained silent while powerful new group techniques, radical therapies, and other tools for the alteration of awareness and personality slipped into the hands of cult leaders and mass-market entrepreneurs.

At the end of the seventies, America's varied mental health professions remain visibly divided. Psychiatry is once again anchored to the biological foundations of traditional medicine, and pharmacology has emerged as the focus of most new research in the profession. In major psychiatric institutions around the country, however, other vital clinical, counseling, and rehabilitation functions of the field are being dramatically reduced in size or cut back financially, prompting the public to seek out religious and commercial versions of these much-needed services.

In our conversations with representatives of the mental health profession we found confirmation, not surprisingly, that psychiatrists and psychologists are as susceptible to snapping as anyone else. We even heard of some professionals who had become entrapped in religious cults. Furthermore, we discovered, quite apart from any experimentation with specific cult or group techniques, that the profession seems to breed its own strain of snapping. We gained perhaps the most insightful view of this peculiar problem from an articulate young doctor named Gilla Prizant, whom we met one smogless afternoon in Los Angeles.

Dr. Gilla Prizant is a representative of the new generation of young psychiatrists coming out of the nation's medical schools to take on the challenges of turbulence and retreat within their profession. Graduating from Northwestern Medical School, she began her psychiatric training at the end of the mental health field's period of great upheaval. Ever since, she has been earnestly engaged in finding a responsible direction for herself as a professional. When we spoke with her in her office at UCLA's Neuropsychiatric Institute, she shared her private thoughts concerning a side of America's mental health crisis that the general public rarely sees.

"I went to med school wanting to be a doctor," she began, a little wistfully, "but I had tremendous problems on rounds, especially with surgeons, who are notorious for looking at a piece of anatomy rather than a human being. Since then, my orientation has changed considerably."

Her introduction to psychiatry, Prizant told us, got off to a particularly unpleasant start. She interned at one of the nation's largest psychiatric training institutions, a county hospital located in southern California. There she was appalled at the hospital conditions and the quality of psychiatric care available to the poor and underprivileged.

"I was simply overwhelmed," she said, looking back. "It was probably the most chaotic patient experience of my life. We were overworked and understaffed; there was pandemonium. In the admitting area, we were encouraged to 'expedite.' There was no time to evaluate incoming patients. The ward situation was completely drug-oriented. In the adolescent ward, they checked to see how many staff members were going away for the weekend, and if there were marginal numbers of staff they would just go through the charts and raise everybody's medication."

For the young intern, this rigorous on-the-job training proved to be a long nightmare of physical and emotional strain.

"I remember one day the temperature inside the hospital was a hundred and five degrees," she recalled. "Each intern had at least twelve patients. We were walking around with huge plastic containers filled with ice chips. We were becoming dehydrated, popping salt tablets. And that was *us!* We were the *healthy* people! I had one drug-overdose patient hooked on intravenous, so she was confined to her bed. As I was leaning over listening to her chest, a huge cockroach ran across her bed."

Experiences such as these made a deep impression on Prizant as she continued her psychiatric training, and she grew disillusioned with the impending future she foresaw as a psychiatrist.

"I had a helpless feeling of not being able to do anything," she remembered. "I got tired of having no time to enjoy life. I got tired of being tired. I became very aware that the kind of care that is taught as standard psychiatry in medical school is not available to most people in this country. They just don't have the time or money. I began to feel that it was a social injustice to train psychiatrists who would simply go out and open offices in the suburbs and see people who are nice, healthy, ambulatory neurotics."

It is that class of ambulatory neurotics, according to Prizant, which is now being attracted to mass-marketed therapies. Those therapies, in her opinion, offer no solutions to America's mental health problems.

"I have serious questions about the validity of a lot of the things people are calling 'therapies,' to begin with," she said. "On the whole, I think they're irresponsible. They are tampering with dangerous areas of the mind. On the other hand, if positive changes do occur, you really don't know what to attribute them to."

In the course of her training, Prizant had seen numerous victims of mass-group therapies. She described their reactions in such traditional terms as schizophrenic, paranoid, psychotic, and delusional. She recalled one case in particular.

"There was one woman from est," she said, "who came into the day hospital for six months after she took the training. She was paranoid and delusional. She believed that est had somehow infiltrated her body and everyone else's body. She was projecting all kinds of things."

When we asked her about the cults, however, Prizant confessed that she hardly ever came upon cult members in her psychiatric work. As we had been told, few of them ever manage to break free of their cults and seek help on their own. Prizant recalled treating cult members frequently back in medical school, however, not in regard to their mental health but for physical conditions.

"I remember one Krishna woman I had on my rotation on OB-GYN [Obstetics and Gynecology]. She was about eight months pregnant and eating no protein. She was, essentially, living on orange juice," Prizant said. "I remember my incredible sense of rage—not because of what she was doing to her own body, but at what she was doing to that unborn child. I felt a sense of injustice."

As we talked about various cult and mass-therapy techniques, Prizant told us that many of the rudiments of those group techniques are now part of every young psychiatrist's basic training, a remnant of the wave of experimentation that nearly overwhelmed her profession a few years back. Today, however, they are taught as necessary tools.

"There were several group experiences for first-year residents," she said. "We had one group experiment in regression designed to teach the participants about authority, leadership, and responsibility by blurring the boundaries between individuals in an intense group setting. It was supposed to teach us about defensive projection—putting your feelings onto someone else, not knowing where that person begins or where you begin—but if you ask me it was actually an experiment in group psychosis."

In this particular group situation, she said, many of the young psychiatrists found themselves unable to maintain their professional detachment. Despite their training, some proved to be no more immune to the impact of group techniques than many cult members or mass-therapy participants.

"One member of our group became quite regressed," said Prizant. "He was incessantly giggling, and the group consultants made a fairly dramatic intervention at that point to reintegrate him. In another group, some people did become psychotic and began acting out fantasies outside the group, driving the wrong way in traffic and things like that."

Prizant reported these reactions without comment. When we turned to her own response, however, she admitted that she too found the ordeal trying.

"I wasn't quite sure how I was supposed to extrapolate that experience to what happens when you're leading a group and one of your patients starts projecting things onto you. It was an interesting experiment, but one I wouldn't repeat. The next day I had to fly back to Chicago to see my fiancé, and I found it very difficult."

As we talked about the various forms of sudden personality change we had encountered among cult members and group participants, Prizant brought a new one to our attention, one that she found particularly alarming: the change she witnessed in her colleagues over the course of their three-year training.

"You really can't see the forest through the trees until your third year of psychiatry," she said. "Then it's very interesting to watch the third-year residents interact as a group and with other people. Everything is analyzed to the nth degree; everything gets discussed in terms of the jargon. Very subtly, they learn the rules of the game—how you are supposed to act when you're a psychiatrist."

For several years, Prizant has watched the young professionals in the classes ahead of her march down similar paths to secure and lucrative private practices.

"There is a definite trend among third-year residents to go scurrying around finding all the neatest offices in the wealthy suburbs and trying to take their hospital patients out with them," she said. "There seems to be an inverse correlation that develops between a psychiatrist's amount of training and his social responsibility."

Prizant admitted that she found the trend to be particularly dismaying, but she sympathized with those who got caught up in it.

"I'm not sure why it happens, except that, quite frankly, you get very tired of putting off everything—financially, emotionally, experientially—in order to become a doctor. So when you finally make it, everything else kind of goes by the wayside. A lot of us went into medicine for noble reasons, we wanted to help people, but it's very difficult to hang onto your humanistic ideals."

Prizant shook her head. It sounded to us as if she were doing a fairly successful job of steering her own course through her training, but she claimed that she, too, was struggling to contain that type of personal detachment she views as a specific hazard of her trade.

"Psychiatry definitely changes you as a person," she said, with more than a hint of sadness. "You become desensitized to people. I learned very early in medicine that if I identified with my patients to the extent of thinking, *My God, this could be me or my mother or my grandmother!* I would soon go bananas. You can't function with that kind of mental set. And when you go into psychiatry it becomes even scarier, because what you're dealing with is not objective. When you're treating neurotic patients—the obsessive compulsives, the hysterical personalities, the people who feel super-depressed and want to kill themselves—you're dealing with a patient population you could very easily become part of. Psychiatrists are all pretty much neurotic; to go through medical school these days you have to be sort of neurotic. There are reasons why our divorce and suicide rates are so high, but you just have to turn yourself off to it."

To counteract the effects of psychiatry on her own development, Prizant told us she was taking positive steps to make sure she stayed personally and socially responsible. She was assuming an active role in the Southern California Psychiatric Society and working toward a master's degree in public health. Her current goal, she said, was to forge a career for herself in health-care planning, avoiding the pitfalls of private practice altogether.

"We're not all money-mongers," she said confidently, "and we're not all aloof. I'm trying to safeguard myself from becoming that way by seeing things from their broader perspectives."

At the end of our conversation, Gilla Prizant smiled warmly and told us to be sure to call her if she could be of further help. Touched by her views, we left with a new sense of respect for psychiatrists like Prizant who have managed to remain committed before the onslaught of their profession, and we felt compassion for those whose own prestigious careers contain elements of the kind of emotional detachment we had come to recognize as a symptom of snapping.

We talked with a number of psychiatrists around the country who shared Gilla Prizant's commitment as well as her concerns. They painted a picture of a profession that is, today, as one told us, "a mixed bag of disciplines and trainings." In order to be truly responsible, another said, a psychiatrist must be familiar with the wide range of new drugs, techniques, and therapies and become a "sort of quick-change artist," yet also learn how to "leave it alone when you go home at night."

Another psychiatrist was quick to point out that no serious practitioner in his profession can compete with a cult leader or mass-marketer who offers "instant cures and easy answers." With the proliferation of nonprofessional therapies and the increased demands of government agencies, insurance companies, and other "third-party payers" for tangible results, psychiatry has been forced to resort to such concrete methods as drugs, he said. Yet, like the nation as a whole, the psychiatric profession seems to be emerging from a period of adolescent boldness into one of more restrained realism, and today's young psychiatrists are among the first to call for caution.

"A psychiatrist has no easy answers," one new practitioner told us. "I can't make any guarantees. I'm a doctor, not a messiah, and all we can do is our best."

9 Beyond Brainwashing

"At Panmunjon the American imperialists and their running dogs and lackeys, the British capitalist ruling clique, are holding up the peace talks. In the imperialists' prison camps they are torturing, starving and killing the Korean and Chinese prisoners, but we will remain calm and will never torture or kill you. You are safe with us. We shall always self-consciously carry out the Lenient Policy and thus shall continue to give you the chance to study and learn the truth, and see how your leaders are catching the people in a web of lies and preparing to extend the Korean conflict, and unleash a third world war."

> —*Commandant, POW camp in Korea, 1954*
> *(quoted in a British chaplain's account*
> *of his imprisonment)*

WHILE the mental health community was grappling with the consciousness explosion, the "critical situational response," and the changing picture of mental health in the nation as a whole, the appearance of the cult syndrome with its total transformation of personality posed an added and unwanted challenge. Sudden personality changes had been taking place in American religious circles for decades, but they had been practically ignored by the mental health field, first because they posed few legal or social problems but also because religion and psychiatry, like church and state, had traditionally refrained from crossing into one another's territory. With the rise of the cults, however, and the growing legal concern for the constitutional rights of cult members, the mental health community, with considerable caution and reservation, slowly began to examine this bizarre form of personality change.

For the past few years, a group of about a dozen professionals around the country—psychiatrists, psychologists, and social workers—has begun to acknowledge that what is happening to America's cult members is something new. Their tiny, loose-knit, fledgling organization, Return to Personal Choice, represents the first professional attempt to understand the cult experience and aid cult members in need of treatment, and what these professionals are being forced to admit is that their tools of analysis and treatment are inadequate to the task.

In 1976, Dr. John G. Clark, Jr., a professor of psychiatry at Harvard Medical School and Massachusetts General Hospital and a member of Return to Personal Choice, testified before a special committee of the Vermont State Senate investigating "the effects of some religious cults on the health and welfare of their converts." In his statement, Clark cited the known health hazards, both physical and psychological, and noted that point beyond which his profession has been unable to go. Said Clark:

> The fact of a personality shift in my opinion is established. The fact that this is a phenomenon basically unfamiliar to the mental health profession I am certain of. The fact that our ordinary methods of treatment don't work is also clear, as are the frightening hazards to the process of personal growth and mental health.

In their efforts to account for this new kind of "personality shift," Clark and a number of other professionals have turned to the only body of research that relates to the phenomenon: the various inquiries conducted by their colleagues into the way the human mind responds in situations of extreme duress. Several decades ago, this topic took on national urgency with the discovery of extreme examples of sudden shifts in belief, behavior, and personality which came quickly to be identified with a process known as brainwashing. Since the celebrated trial of Patricia Hearst in 1976 and the widely publicized court verdict in early 1977 in which five members of the Unification Church in San Francisco were released in their parents' custody to be professionally deprogrammed, the media, the courts, and the general public have seized upon this term. Few people, however, realize its limited applicability to the wide range of sudden changes in personality taking place in America today.

The word "brainwashing" was first introduced into the popular vocabulary in the early 1950s. Then it served as a vivid explanation for the technique that had been employed by the North Koreans to extract allegedly voluntary confessions of war crimes from U.S. airmen downed in the Korean war. When it was first brought to light, this new, uncanny, and sinister method of inducing personal change seemed to have sprung out of nowhere, having no comparable tradition in the West and no apparent foundation among the ancient rituals of the East. Threatened and intrigued, the U.S. government supported a number of research projects aimed at unraveling the mystery.

Of many early studies of brainwashing, the most widely recognized is that of Yale psychiatrist Robert Jay Lifton, who was among the first American doctors to examine victims of the process, both soldiers and civilians. In his book *Thought Reform and the Psychology of Totalism,* published in 1961 (a comprehensive report on studies published earlier in professional journals), Lifton analyzed the method of brainwashing as it was developed by the Communist Chinese during their political takeover of the mainland in the late forties. From his essentially psychoanalytic orientation, Lifton described the various physical and emotional stresses used by the Chinese to induce feelings of "guilt anxiety" and create a condition of "ego-destruction" in their subjects, after which they proceeded to "re-educate" them in accordance with the principles of Chinese Communism. In his book, Lifton described the process as one of "depersonalization" accomplished by repeated attacks on the individual's sense of self, overt death threats, and complete control of the surrounding environment, followed by sudden reprieve—lenient treatment in return for full cooperation. He wrote about the traumas individuals suffered in the symbolic terms of "death and rebirth" associated with the confession of past wrongdoing and reindoctrination and even noted the familiar "thousand-mile stare" that often characterizes brainwashing victims.

Lifton's work is significant and important, yet it demonstrates the limitations of his Freudian underpinnings and lexicon. His phrase "ego-destruction" connotes the sweeping impact of the brainwashing process on personality, but his analysis offers little insight into the mechanics of the process by which the Chinese affected the minds of his research subjects. Instead, his theory proposes a complicated explanation based on deep-rooted unconscious factors, where simpler and more accessible answers would suffice.

A more concrete approach, in keeping with recent trends in psychiatry, has been to seek medical answers to questions of brainwashing and "personality shift"; for although psychiatry can say very little with certainty about how brainwashing affects the mind, it has discovered a great deal about how it affects the body. The physiology of both brainwashing and religious conversion is now a well-established and extensively documented subject of medical inquiry. The acknowledged expert in this field is British psychiatrist William Sargant. In his seminal work, *Battle for the Mind,* published in 1957, he explored in detail the role of intense physical experience in bringing about sudden changes in religious and political belief. In support of his argument, Sargant cited his own work with battle-weary soldiers during World War II, research in psychotherapy using drugs, electroshock, and neurosurgical methods, and experiments on laboratory animals, to draw an elaborate picture of what happens to the central nervous system during rituals of brainwashing and religious conversion.

Sargant addresses questions of more immediate relevance to our investigation. His book sheds light on two distinct sets of physiological factors that may be involved in the creation of spiritual or revelatory experiences. The most common techniques produce states of overexcitement in the nervous system, which, according to Sargant, can be accomplished by means of drumming, dancing, singing, praying, or "by the imposing of emotionally charged mental conflicts needing urgent resolution." Sargant identified these techniques in the black masses of voodoo tribes and the dances of Sufi whirling dervishes, as well as in American religious practices such as those of the Shaker dancers of Connecticut, the snake-handling Christian sects of Tennessee, and the fiery preachers of Evangelicalism. His second analysis is nearly opposite in every way, declaring that the sensation of enlightenment or newfound awareness may also be produced by practices that, in effect, reduce or inhibit the activity of the nervous system, such as fasting, meditation, and other forms of sensory deprivation. Sargant noted the common use of these techniques among practitioners of Eastern religions.

In each case, Sargant holds, the dramatic conversions that follow these experiences are the product of a physiological dysfunction of the brain which renders it receptive to new ideas and physically incapable of judging or evaluating the wisdom or correctness of those ideas. Sargant's argument is impressive but, as he acknowledges, by no means original. The first data on the subject was compiled early in this century by the Russian neurophysiologist I. P. Pavlov. Pavlov's studies of the effects of stress on the higher nervous systems of dogs provided Western science with an entire terminology of psychological malaise. He accurately mapped the successive stages of "protective inhibition" of brain function as a response to overwhelming stimulation, and he described the physiological and behavioral effects that resulted from it.

Following in the medical tradition of Sargant and Pavlov, those members of America's mental health profession who have begun to investigate the cult experience have confirmed the physiological effects of stresses such as reduced sleep and caloric intake on the nervous systems of cult members. Verifiable links have been discovered between the cult state of limited awareness and a decrease in peripheral vision. Connections have also been established between physical stress, poor diet, and fatigue and the disruptions of the endocrine system found among cult members that may cause women to stop menstruating and men to lose such secondary sex characteristics as facial hair and a deep voice. These insights have been helpful in treating the physical damage caused by extended periods of cult life, but they lead away from—not toward—a fuller understanding of the effects of cult techniques on the mind.

This medical approach also ignores situations in which intense spiritual experiences and sudden conversions are brought about in individual and group settings that present no physical stress or deprivation whatsoever. Our own research revealed numerous instances: Jean Turner's first encounter high, for example, and, most spectacularly, Sally Kempton's audience with the Swami. In these contexts, the only elements that can be identified as triggering the overwhelming individual reactions are a few well-placed words or, at most, some intangible quality in a rather exotic and alien environment.

The two most popular theories of brainwashing, Lifton's and Sargant's, offer no explanation for these experiences. In the literature of brainwashing, the only related insight can be found in a lesser-known study by a social psychologist named Edgar Schein. Schein, like Lifton, participated in the first army studies of brainwashing. In contrast to his medical colleagues, Schein's primary focus was on the psychological force inherent in the group processes used by the Chinese to change beliefs, attitudes, and opinions. He based his theory of "Coercive Persuasion" on models of small-group interaction developed by M.I.T. social psychologist Kurt Lewin (today referred to in human potential circles as "the father of the encounter group"). Schein's contribution, however, gets lost in the plethora of opposing references he brought together, and his overriding emphasis on the element of coercion renders his work particularly inapplicable to our investigation.

Studies of brainwashing, while historically significant, fall far short of explaining the phenomenon we call snapping. The Chinese program of Thought Reform was designed simply to change political belief and induce full cooperation among Chinese citizens and captive Westerners. What is happening in America today is very different. Instead of physical coercion and threats of death, the minds of American citizens are being swayed and altered by the promise of exciting new adventures in human awareness. While some of these dramatic experiences may be created by certain kinds of physiological stress and group pressure, no one has been able to explain the profound effects and personality shifts often produced by cults and mass therapies: the disorientation and delusion found among many est graduates we spoke to, the sensation of experiencing higher realms of consciousness widespread among Transcendental Meditators, the ongoing ecstasies common to other mass-therapy participants and many Born Again Christians, and the bizarre trancelike states that characterize many cult members.

The only other tool available to explain these individual responses in terms familiar to professionals and the general public is hypnosis, a widely used but little-understood technique for influencing the mind. Introducing the concept of hypnosis, however, only serves to compound the problem at hand, for the age-old art remains the black sheep of Western science. Although the techniques and effects of hypnosis have been widely demonstrated and reproduced, science has yet to explain the prodigious power of suggestion that enables a skilled hypnotist to put people in trance states where they may perform feats of superhuman strength, demonstrations of complete imperviousness to pain, and acts of memory and imagination that defy all waking capability.

Many have tried and failed to explain hypnosis in scientific terms. As early as 1755, the notorious F. A. Mesmer, the Viennese physician who pioneered the development of modern hypnosis, offered a theory of "animal magnetism" to explain the phenomenon, for which he was condemned as a fraud by the most revered minds of his day (among them, the American statesman and scientist Benjamin Franklin). In fact, the effects of hypnosis have nothing to do with man's animal or biological nature. It has been shown repeatedly that animal response to the techniques of hypnosis is almost exactly opposite to that of human beings in every instance. While fear and physical stress may produce a temporary state of catatonic immobility in dogs, sheep, and other animals, this effect has nothing to do with the modern practice of hypnosis, although many scientists, including Pavlov, have made the mistake of explaining hypnosis in terms of animal response.

In recent years, science has come to understand hypnosis a little better, and most of our previous beliefs about it have been directly overturned. The myth of the trance state has been shattered; the previously held notion that an individual must be put to sleep in order to be hypnotized has been categorically disproved. The old dangling watch fobs and swirling spirals of the mesmerist served merely to distract the subject's attention, rendering him more susceptible to suggestion and command. Gone, too, are the naïve convictions that hypnosis cannot be put to harmful use and that an individual will not perform an act under hypnosis that is contrary to his conscious nature. Traditionally, practitioners of hypnosis have exercised extreme caution and responsibility in the use of their mysterious skill, but many admit that, through lies and carefully contrived suggestions, a hypnotist could prompt his subject to commit any action, even a crime, in the firm belief that he was performing the act to accomplish some greater good.

In these latest findings about hypnosis and the power of suggestion there are important clues to the destructive effects of many cult and group techniques, but—like "brainwashing," "ego-destruction," and "coercive persuasion"—the term "hypnosis" tells nothing about the dramatic alterations of awareness and personality and the lasting disruptions of thought and feeling we learned about from participants in cults and mass therapies. The techniques employed by cult and group leaders bear no resemblance to the classical induction of hypnosis, nor are the effects confined to simple trance states or feats of memory and imagination. Their attack is comprehensive and profound, not simply altering belief and behavior, as in brainwashing, but producing lasting changes in the fundamental workings of the mind. And their tools are those of everyday communication, ordinary skills, and natural abilities that have been honed to the sharpness of precision instruments.

Invariably, in America, an individual's involvement in a cult or mass therapy begins with voluntary participation. He or she reads a handbill, engages in a conversation, attends an introductory gathering or lecture, accepts an invitation to a group dinner or cult feast. Then comes the decision to take up further offers to attend a weekend seminar, workshop, or spiritual retreat. At any time during these early stages of recruitment—and throughout participation in the cult or group—the individual's actions and responses may be artfully controlled without the use of physiological stress or any physical means whatsoever. In lieu of coercion or hypnosis, cult and group leaders use an altogether different class of strategies: they may misrepresent their identities and intentions; they may lie about their own relationships to their organizations; they may display false affection for the potential member; they may radiate spiritual fulfillment and happiness to the point where it has a profound impact on the individual they are confronting; or they may provoke discussion and debate, creating what Sargant calls "emotionally charged mental conflicts needing urgent resolution."

However, none of these ploys depends upon any form of physiological dysfunction in the nervous system or the brain to be completely effective and produce their most dramatic effects. On the contrary, whatever the ploys, their effectiveness depends on the normal functioning of the human brain in its capacity for communication—without that, they would not work at all. At every stage of involvement, from initial contact through conversion to the most profound states of humiliation and submission, every consequence of cult and group participation that has been explained as a product of physiological stress may also be produced with equal intensity and reliability by means of simple techniques of communication: age-old tools of rhetoric and persuasion, refined methods of propaganda and mass marketing, and as yet little-understood elements of group dynamics and nonverbal communication.

There is nothing casual or informal about the manner in which these sophisticated techniques are employed, nor is there anything mysterious about the way they achieve their predictable and profound effects. Like the distracting watch fob of the mesmerist, the well-known physical stresses used by cult and group leaders serve only to weaken an individual to suggestion and command. Subsequent thoughts, actions, expression, and even level of awareness, however, are controlled by identifiable products of human communication. They are controlled by the specific beliefs, opinions, suggestions, orders, and feelings the individual receives from cult recruiters, lecturers, and others in personal conversations and group rituals and amidst the atmosphere of warmth, love, and total acceptance that is common to each of these diverse groups.

This process of communication reaches far beyond the mere exchange of spoken and written messages between individuals; this complex and sophisticated process controls both our bodies and our minds. Communication, in fact, governs everything we experience as human beings. It is the basic organic process that regulates the functions of our nervous system. The principles of communication that underlie Marjoe's rhetoric, Moon's persuasion and propaganda, and est's group dynamics are one with the natural laws that direct and control the flow of sensation throughout the body and the brain. Through this common process, acts of speech, from sermons to hypnosis to casual conversation, and every other form of communication may affect biological functions at their most rudimentary levels, as well as human awareness in its highest states of consciousness and spirituality.

With the widespread exploitation in our society of sophisticated communication techniques in religious rituals, group practices, and mass-marketing strategies, a new perspective is clearly in order, one rooted in the process of communication which has come to play such a tangible role in our daily lives. Since Pavlov's time, research in animal behavior has made significant contributions to our understanding of elementary human processes and responses, but today this body of knowledge alone no longer provides the necessary base for broader legal, psychological, or social interpretation. Inevitably, theories based on the study of lower organisms are doomed to fail as explanations for events and activities that are uniquely human. Very often they obscure our understanding of individual and social phenomena that have no counterparts in other species. Snapping is such a phenomenon, and in order to understand it, we must first recognize that human beings do not grow and develop in an unvarying world of animal behavior; they do so in a dynamic world of experience that shapes their awareness, their personalities, and their lives.

To reach the core of America's current epidemic of sudden personality change, we must go beyond brainwashing, beyond physiology and psychology, to the process of communication by which human beings exchange thought, feeling, and experience itself with one another. Communication processes account for Jean Turner's first "encounter high" as well as the roller-coaster ride of ecstasy, fantasy, and horrifying delusion she experienced after est. They offer a way to examine the entire course of Lawrence and Cathy Gordon's participation in the Unification Church, from Cathy's feelings of strangeness when she met her first Moonie to Lawrence's vision of death while out fund raising. Moreover, communication provides a way to understand Marjoe's seasoned ability to sway an audience to the point of emotional collapse, as well as an explanation for why Sally Kempton snapped in response to a few empty words from Muktananda. It also confirms why hundreds of cult members have regained their ability to think for themselves after answering Ted Patrick's pointed questions.

In recent years the term "communication" has been used to signify an expanding universe of activities, encompassing such varied disciplines as broadcast journalism and library science. Our aim, however, is not to explore communication in this catch-all sense. Throughout this book we use the term to refer to an identifiable set of human processes which may be clearly understood in the light of recent breakthroughs in physics, mathematics, and biology. With the aid of these basic sciences, we can now forge a new perspective on the phenomenon of snapping. We can build a bridge from our culture's unconscious robot models of personality and behavior to a new view of human beings based on human awareness and experience. The foundation of this bridge is located in the technical sciences of communication—cybernetics and information theory—and the first step in building it requires that we update our understanding of how communication processes affect the human brain and nervous system, the basic biological machinery from which our individual personalities emerge.

PART TWO

A New Perspective

10 Information

Information is information, not matter or energy.

—*Norbert Wiener,*
Cybernetics

IRONICALLY, cybernetics and information theory, the new communication sciences which have given rise to America's space-age hardware and modern technology, offer us a natural point of departure from the robot model of psychology. It is this world of sophisticated machines, not the world of animals, that has been constructed in the image of man. From its raw materials, its basic principles and processes, we can begin to refine our understanding of snapping.

In every form of the phenomenon we can identify a common element, whether it be the most intense physical experience or the most evanescent spiritual moment, the most profound thought, the deepest emotion, or the most mundane phrase or fleeting image that sets off some massive, life-changing individual response. It is something called *information*. Information is what human beings are made of, not simply information in the everyday sense of the word—news, facts, data, telephone numbers—but information in its scientific sense, the substance that flows through the human brain and nervous system. Information, not matter or energy, is the stuff of human consciousness. It is the soul of communication and the key to the phenomenon of snapping. Before we can fit together the different pieces of the puzzle, it is necessary to explore the manner in which the brain receives and processes information. Only within the last few years have scientists even begun to comprehend this amazing process, and, as it turns out, it is not at all as they once suspected.

The concept of information grew out of the science of cybernetics, one of the new aids to understanding which have been developed in recent years.

Cybernetics does not simply represent an advancement in older sciences. It is a whole new field of inquiry, born in America during World War II when teams of leading scientists from a wide range of disciplines were brought together in all-out efforts to solve the concrete problems of modern warfare. Out of such practical engineering tasks as computing intricate enemy flight trajectories and designing tracking mechanisms for antiaircraft artillery emerged the first principles for the scientific study of communication.

Cybernetics, succinctly defined as the study of "communication and control in the animal and the machine," developed quickly into a broad science of automatic control systems: mechanical, electronic, and biological structures that regulate their own internal processes and correct their own errors in operation. The word cybernetics—coined by Norbert Wiener, the brilliant mathematician from M.I.T. and the acknowledged father of the science—comes from the Greek word for steersman and commemorates the earliest known cybernetic device: the automatic steering mechanisms used on ships which monitored the disturbances of wind and waves and adjusted the rudder accordingly to keep the ship on a steady course. In Wiener's terms, the vital element of "feedback" which guided the ship's tiller, like the beam of radar which fed instructions to the automatic antiaircraft guns he helped develop, supplied a "measure of organization" to the system that he identified as "information." Following the war, Americans began to receive the first fruits of these once top-secret labors, as a new generation of automatic, self-regulating hardware and appliances came to the marketplace to ease all sorts of daily chores. Early arrivals included fully automatic washing machines, self-triggering toasters, and electronic supermarket doors, each employing simple feedback devices that responded to some tiny measure of information.

Despite these practical beginnings, the notion of information remained one of the slipperiest concepts to hit modern science since the theory of relativity. Engineers in America tended to view information in terms of organization, order, and "organized complexity," while their British counterparts preferred to view it in terms of selectivity and "variety." The first formal theory of information was proposed in 1949 when Dr. Claude E. Shannon, a research mathematician at the Bell Telephone Laboratories, published a paper in collaboration with Dr. Warren Weaver, then of the Rockefeller Foundation, entitled "The Mathematical Theory of Communication," in which they set out the physical requirements and limits to the communication and transmission of messages. In this initial scientific attempt to give form and substance to that indefinable electronic flux coursing through Ma Bell's telephone lines, Shannon and Weaver introduced the concept of the "bit" (short for *binary digit*) of information, the simple on-off, heads-or-tails choice which they defined to be the smallest amount of information any message may contain. Then, armed with the bit and simple mathematical logarithms, they went on to derive a way of measuring the amount of information contained in *any* message. This scientific reckoning with the intangible provided no insight whatsoever into the value in human terms of any particular communication, but by avoiding the ancient, endless debate over the meaning of words and numbers, it offered engineers a new way of speaking simply—and only— about the math and physics of transmitting those messages as quickly and efficiently as possible.

Together, cybernetics and information theory led to major breakthroughs in engineering and technology. Once scientists could accurately measure the amount of information that could be carried through a wire of a given diameter or transmitted over a radio channel of a particular frequency, the door swung open to the mastery of the most immense and complex systems, from vast telephone and television networks to the lightning logic of the computer.

From the beginning, the new sciences helped technicians reduce chaos and complexity to order, but for the laymen these engineering triumphs seemed to increase the complexity and confusion of daily life. In only a few years, improved global communications and high-speed electronic data-processing systems began supplying people with ever-increasing quantities of information at speeds far beyond their human capacity to process and organize: instant news from around the world, intimate glimpses of remote cultures, and close-up images of natural disasters, wars, social problems, and political crises as they happened. Before long, in countless arenas, human performance was being pitted against the extraordinary capacities of the computer and the near-limitless speeds of electronic gadgetry.

No comparable effort was made to understand the personal side effects of these technological thrusts. Wiener himself repeatedly voiced his concern over the impact of this new technology on human beings. Yet little progress was made in relating information, this newly harnessed physical quantity, to the term in its ordinary sense: the massive outpouring of news and the rush of names, dates, details, and experiences which had begun to bombard our brains from all sides and through all our senses every day.

Even as the new sciences were developing, however, researchers began to explore the application of communication principles such as feedback and self-regulation to the study of human beings. The central nervous system was immediately observed to be a marvel of cybernetic engineering, converting every sight, sound, smell, taste, and touch into the common element of information. Every pinprick triggered its own distinct pattern of electrochemical impulses. Every printed word, every musical theme, every human experience sent its own unimaginably complex flow of information from the body's sense organs to the brain.

The human brain, however, presented insurmountable barriers to scientific understanding. Acclaimed as the most sophisticated computer in the world, it was generally assumed to process information in a manner similar to telephone switching systems and electronic data processors, although its exact information pathways were far too complex and minute for experimental observation. Research ethics prohibited tampering with the brains of living human subjects, and those neurophysiologists who, with scalpels and electrodes, explored the brains of monkeys, frogs, and other animals soon discovered networks of such immense biological complexity that they defied both human and computer analysis.

So, alternatively, at other levels of investigation, psychologists and other social scientists attempted to apply concepts of information transmission and automatic control to the activities of the human brain, borrowing notions such as "channel capacity" and "storage and retrieval" for their behavioral studies of the human processes of memory and learning. To their amazement, however, scientists who endeavored to "input" massive quantities of information to the brains of their test subjects—in experiments designed to solve questions such as "How many letters and digits can a human being process at one time?" —were startled to find that, through various techniques for aiding memory and simple methods of grouping or "chunking" long sequences of numbers, human storage and retrieval capacities appeared to be virtually limitless! Evidently, the human brain did not process information in the manner of a man-made computer. Yet, forced to treat the brain as a "black box," an engineering term for a sealed device with internal workings that remain inaccessible and unknown, experimenters were unable to explain the brain's underlying information-processing capacities.

Faced with this indecipherable complexity, psychologists had no alternative but to incorporate their black box approach to the mind into the prevailing traditions of psychology, simply layering their new concepts on top of the old models of behavior and personality. If anything, these technological ideas served only to support and enhance the robot model of man. In place of the behaviorist's notions of "stimulus" and "response," the black box approach substituted communication jargon such as "input" and "output," creating an illusion of new understanding. Yet these terms had little relevance to human beings or their psychological problems, and by the early sixties, cybernetics and information theory were no longer being acclaimed as powerful new conceptual tools for the study of human affairs.

Nevertheless, since the early days of communication science, its technical concepts have filtered down to the popular level, giving rise to a great deal of loose talk along communication lines and a blast of pseudoscientific verbiage about "failures to communicate," "negative feedback," "channel overload," and so on. In addition, the introduction of these terms into the vernacular has been accompanied by a raft of miracle techniques and therapies with names like "psycho-cybernetics," "hypno-cybernetics," "biofeedback," and "mind control." Although some of these applications, most notably biofeedback, have proved of value in enabling people to gain control over aspects of their biological machinery that normally function automatically, such as heart rate and blood pressure, for the most part these simplistic popular comparisons of man's brain to his machines afford little insight. They succeed instead only in reducing the human mind to the level of mere hardware. Human beings, however, as one engineer informed us, are not electrical circuits, and the brain is not simply a big computer. Rather, it is something much more wonderful and complex: a *living* information-processing organ!

Within the last decade or so, with the arrival of a new generation of electronic technology and the development of mathematical and computer models capable of extraordinarily complex modes of analysis, the study of the brain's living information-processing capacities has grown into a specialized science of its own. In a handful of universities around the country, whole centers for the study of "bio-information processing" have begun investigating the unique manner in which human beings order their daily fare of information. In taking its first steps, this infant science has set out to discover how people interpret their sense impressions, selecting vision, which accounts for almost ninety percent of human information processing, as the best sense for scientific inquiry.

In their initial investigations, bio-information scientists have determined that the eye alone has 128 million information receptors. They have traced the bulk of those signals along the optic nerve to deep within the visual centers of the brain. Using advanced methods of computation specially developed for the task, they have begun to understand how the brain converts the bombardment of photons on the retina into shapes that change in space and brightness over time and then forms those patterns into objects—chairs, people, and so forth—that have some meaning for the individual.

What the new science has yet to learn, however, is how all these signals and patterns come together to create the phenomenon of human awareness, how the individual registers the meaning of what he sees. Bio-information studies have made the first discoveries concerning how our nervous system transforms everything we experience into information, but the field has been unable to connect the hard physical facts of this information in its cybernetic, biological, and, ultimately, electrochemical form with the phenomenon of consciousness, an individual's private experience of the world, which has eluded investigators throughout the spectacular course of Western science.

Early in our collaboration, while developing the framework for our investigation, the two of us found ourselves confronted with this same dilemma. We had been observing and hearing about extraordinary spiritual and emotional experiences which produced profound changes in people's awareness and personalities. Our extensive background research had convinced us that regardless of their personal religious convictions concerning the origin of spiritual revelation, and contrary to popular assumptions which tend to attribute the extraordinary or "supernatural" to the intervention of mystical or cosmic forces, these experiences were natural products of the organic workings of the human brain. For even in its most miraculous feats of consciousness and spirituality, the brain's only known function is one of information processing. Our goal was to account for these extraordinary experiences in concrete, everyday communication terms and to determine whatever impact these experiences might have on the brain's information-processing capacities. Nevertheless, we recognized that even the most careful, thoughtful speculation would draw us to the edge of current scientific understanding, to the frontiers of physics, mathematics, and neurophysiology—and beyond to our own emerging communication perspective on the mind.

In our travels, we contacted a number of prominent scientists around the country, people who have spent their lives studying the human brain, new researchers in the field of bio-information studies, as well as some of the most respected figures working in the "hard" disciplines of math and physics. Nearly all of them encouraged our efforts to make accessible to the general public exciting knowledge that has been confined to scientific arenas for years, in some cases decades. At the same time, nearly all confessed that much of what is known continues to defy interpretation in human terms. We talked with one world-famous engineer who told us that, despite everything he knew about the science of communication, he remained baffled by such accepted practices as speed-reading, which caused him to question how an individual could grasp the meaning of an entire novel in six minutes. "Not as threatening as the cults," he said, "but what does one make of it?" He was deadly serious, however, as were the many other scientists we spoke with who expressed a more far-reaching dismay over what they saw as the enormous gap separating the latest knowledge in math, physics, and biology from an equally substantial understanding of the day-to-day activities of the human mind. The space between, they said almost unanimously, was filled with irreconcilable contradictions, facts of everyday life that collide head on with the laws of nature and modern physics.

Our most fascinating view of these contradictions came out of a conversation we had with Dr. John Lyman, professor of engineering and psychology at the University of California at Los Angeles. Dr. Lyman is a new scientist of the human mind. He began his career in the hard sciences, then went on to apply his knowledge of both engineering and physiology to the practical matter of developing new ways for using technology to extend man's human capacities—a field known today as bioengineering. In his study of the mind, Lyman approaches his all-encompassing subject with the rigor and integrity of a physical scientist, yet throughout he remains a generalist, congenial and refreshingly down to earth.

In the course of two meetings with him—one in his office and one at his cliffside home overlooking the San Fernando Valley—we discussed our investigation of sudden personality change and our communication perspective. He told us that in the early sixties he had the good fortune to meet almost daily for several hours with his long-time friend Norbert Wiener during the last summer of that great scientist and philosopher's life. In many of their conversations, he and Wiener debated the question of what they called "epochal" or life-changing events in human development. As Wiener told Lyman, the subject was of great personal concern; a diabetic, he frequently battled the sudden reversals of emotion and mood characteristic of the disease. Both men recognized, however, that the complexity of the problem extended beyond their learned speculation. Lyman was frank enough to share with us some of the questions that emerged from their discussions, questions which continue to confront scientists working in his field.

"The human being is more than just a sort of super computer," Lyman told us. "The principles from which computers have been developed are certainly very similar to the way in which human beings process information, but human beings do a lot of things that no one has found out about yet."

According to Lyman, human information processing takes place at chemical speeds of roughly 300 feet per second. These neural speeds are far less than the 186,000 miles per second which is the speed of light and the upper limit of any electronic device. Yet human beings regularly perform feats of memory and recall at speeds so extremely fast they cannot be duplicated on a computer. The brain's capacity to search among vast amounts of information and locate specific bits with lightning rapidity is unmatchable by technology.

"We don't know how it's done," said Lyman. "We have some ideas involving hierarchies of information-processing levels, but this is something that's just beginning to be worked on in computer design."

Lyman noted that science has already developed ways of compacting tremendous densities of memory through microfilm techniques and improved technologies of computer memory-bank construction. But he pointed out that computers conduct exhaustive searches through material that must be examined in detail, however swiftly, one item at a time.

This problem of time, Lyman went on to explain, is another dilemma that continues to plague science in both physical and human terms. In human information-processing activities, for example, there are numerous instances where the brain seems to function independently of time altogether.

"When you start measuring dream lengths in relation to their content," he said, "you observe much more dream content than would seem possible in the length of time sleep is going on. The rates of dreaming don't seem to be time-bound—literally, in sequence. The brain appears to restructure things simultaneously. Another example of this phenomenon is when a person sees his whole life flash before him when he's drowning."

To help us understand this peculiar simultaneity of the brain, Lyman offered the analogy of a motion picture reel. Every frame of the picture sequence is already present on the reel, and when the film is run, the images appear to occur in time. The activity of the brain would be equivalent to slicing up the film and spreading out all the pictures side by side. The illusion of motion disappears, and all the information is present simultaneously.

"I don't know if it's true," said Lyman, "but it's possible that when you tell somebody your dream, you may be describing the dream as a sequential thing, whereas when you had the dream, it was like that, like a *snap*"—and he snapped his fingers.

Our word again, but we hadn't even mentioned it to Lyman.

"I can't give you any of the details," he continued, "except that dreams and the time they cover don't match up very well. Most evidence is that dreams apparently covering hours or days of detail take place in a few seconds."

Lyman doesn't see time as much of a factor in the basic functioning of the brain. The time element matters only when the functioning of the brain is translated into action.

"We are time-bound by our ability to express," he said. "Everything we do requires muscular activity, including the movement of our vocal cords. All our outputs to the world are muscular in nature, and the very nature of muscular response is that it has to be temporal, it has to occur in sequence."

Beyond the chemical and cellular levels which underlie its basic information-processing components, the brain has no moving parts, and its activities need not be stretched out over time. As a cybernetic organ, however, the brain has its own set of built-in structural limitations. According to Lyman, rather than being time-bound like the rest of the body, the brain is *space-bound*, or unable to imagine anything outside its three dimensions.

This dependence on space puts us into a perplexing quandary. Exactly where, in any sense, do these complex processes and extraordinary phenomena of mind occur? The majority of information-processing activities are generally conceded to take place in the brain, but beyond that our subjective experiences cannot be located. Certain specific activities such as speech, motor response, and the regulation of biological functions can be traced to particular regions of the brain, even down to small subsections within each region. But neurophysiologists have been unable to establish precise information-processing pathways similar to those that man wires into his computers. They have only been able to trace brain function down to vast "aggregates" of neurons and interwoven "nets" of organization. In fact, scientists have found that the complexity of the brain appears to be irreducible. Minute dissection leads not to clearer understanding of how the brain works but to greater confusion at the most elementary levels of chemistry and physics, and the deeper science delves into the fundamental processes of neural activity, the less it can observe about the brain's most spectacular accomplishments.

Lyman acknowledged the delicacy of the problem.

"There are a lot of subjects that you have to step very carefully on," he said, "because there are many phenomena physics has not put into order yet."

According to Lyman, the final challenge to the study of the mind lies not in biology but in modern physics, which has yet to extricate itself from the paradoxes of relativity. Light, for example, he said, is conveniently conceived of in terms of both particles and waves, despite the fact that the two models contradict each other in fundamental ways. Inside the atom as well, Lyman felt modern physics had reached "the bottom of the barrel," trying to solve the mystery of numerous "elementary particles that can only be given romantic names," he said, such as *quarks*—fractions of mass; *charm*—wisps of electrical charge; and *tachyons*—hypothetical particles that move backward in time at speeds faster than the limit of light.

"The traditional concepts of physics are being profoundly questioned by our own methods," Lyman told us. "Nobody's willing to go mystic and say, 'Okay, we admit that logic doesn't exist.' On the other hand, science is starting to recognize that there's a lot more to relativity than Einstein ever put together."

In Lyman's view, questions of human consciousness will remain unanswerable until the crisis in physics is successfully resolved. As he sees it, the breakthrough that is required here could not be of greater conceptual proportions.

"We had Newton and we had Einstein," said Lyman appreciatively, "but now we need somebody to carry us to the next stage. We need someone to take us beyond $E=mc^2$."

At Stanford University in California, a neurophysiologist by the name of Karl H. Pribram has gone beyond $E=mc^2$. In the course of his lifelong investigation of the inner workings of the brain, this internationally acclaimed scientist has developed a new model of the human brain that is the stuff of which scientific revolutions are made. Sir Isaac Newton looked for answers to puzzles of the universe in the outermost regions of the solar system; Albert Einstein sought ultimate understanding among cosmic forces that doubled back upon themselves at the boundaries of space and time. Unlike them, Karl Pribram has broken through ironclad barriers of physics by seeking answers to questions posed not by the largest or furthermost objects known to man but by what is acknowledged to be the most complex and challenging structure in nature: the human brain.

Pribram's work on the brain spans enormous areas of research. He has made primary investigations into fundamental neural processes to find out how nerve cells communicate with each other, how the brain filters the input it receives from the senses, and what role the brain plays in psychological processes. Pribram's most recent and stunning achievement, however, is his proposed new model of important aspects of brain function, which shatters many of our previously accepted notions concerning such basic activities as perception and memory. His model has evoked widespread discussion and excitement within the scientific establishment, and it is slowly being recognized as a major breakthrough in scientific theory.

Following threads of research loosened by some of the most important figures in brain research, many of whom he has known and worked with personally, Pribram took on the greatest challenge in the field: the mystifying problem of how memory is stored and retrieved in the brain. His approach was brilliantly innovative. Instead of looking for specific bits of information, as most of his predecessors had done, he abandoned this file-drawer model in favor of a new approach to information storage suggested by Dr. Karl Lashley, a pioneer in American brain research. Lashley, who gave up in despair after an unsuccessful thirty-year search for specific memory traces, proposed that memory was not stored in discrete units but rather in intersecting patterns of information flow within the brain. As Pribram was pursuing this avenue of exploration, he came upon a precise mathematical and physical model called the *hologram.* A recent invention of the science of optics, the hologram is by now well-known as a novel way to achieve a photographic "store" from which a three-dimensional image can be reconstructed. What Pribram saw in it, however, was an elegant demonstration of his new theory of memory and perception. The three-dimensional holographic image is the emergent product of the stored "interference pattern" created by two intersecting beams of light —and patterns of light, of course, are simply a visible form of information!

To create a hologram, a beam of coherent light (light waves of a single frequency, in phase, traveling in the same direction) produced by a laser is split through a mirror that is partially silvered and partially transparent. Half the light goes directly to a photographic plate; the other half is reflected off the person, object, or scene being photographed—in this case, *holographed*— and then it too converges onto the photographic plate. The plate records not the actual image, as in conventional photography, but the interference pattern formed by the twin beams of intersecting light. The plate or film, often called the *holograph* as distinct from the image itself, the hologram (although the two terms are also used interchangeably), shows a series of patterns and swirls that mean nothing to the naked eye. To recreate the hologram, the holograph has only to be illuminated by another beam of coherent light, which produces an image with true three-dimensional perspective, an image not on the film but somewhere behind or in front of the film. By looking at the film from a variety of angles, the viewer can see the image from below, above, and either side, perceiving it just as though he were looking at the original object itself from several different positions.

Holography is more than just a photographic gimmick. It is also the most sophisticated method of information storage yet devised. By using different frequencies of light, many interference patterns can be superimposed on a single holographic plate. In recent experiments, 10 billion bits of information have been stored holographically in one cubic centimeter of space! More important than the capacity of the hologram to store enormous quantities of information, however, is the manner in which that information is stored.

In a hologram, the information or light reflected off each point of the object being holographed is spread out and distributed across the entire surface of the film. The holographic film can then be cut into small fragments, and each fragment, when illuminated, will generate the entire image! Damage to any part of the film, even to the majority of it, will not affect the ability of the film to reproduce the whole image.

Karl Pribram seized upon the concept of the hologram as a remarkably appropriate model of how the brain functions in perception. In the process of vision, for example, information that reaches the brain through its vast number of separate channels comes together at several levels to form interference patterns. The result is a "brain representation" (akin to the photographic holograph) that registers beyond the retina (the photographic plate of the eye). The subjective experience is the image created when a visual input reaches this representation deep within the visual arena of the brain. As in holography, this image is projected outward away from the representation and is therefore perceived as an object in the individual's field of vision. The impression of distance, also known as depth of field, is another holographic effect, a phenomenon called *parallax*, caused by the intersection of the twin inputs brought to the brain by the left and right eyes.

Similar processes take place in relation to other sense impressions. Pribram has noted that the principles of holography are not dependent on the physical presence of coherent light waves. Another common form of the holograph is the stereophonic recording. The two channels of sound coming out of the stereo speakers create an interference pattern caused by intersecting waves of vibrating air. The product, a three-dimensional auditory "image," seems to be coming not from one speaker or the other but from somewhere in between—which is, in fact, exactly where the stereophonic image is located. The stereophonic hologram serves as an exact model for the way our two ears function in the process of hearing. Like the eye, the ear sends a vast multiplicity of information through the auditory nerves which conjoins in holographic patterns throughout the network of the brain. Recent research and computer simulations have shown that the same processes are likely to occur with the other senses of taste, touch, and smell. These sensations are not only projections of the enormous quantities of information received by each isolated sense. In many instances, they are products of intersecting patterns from two different sensory systems at once. Our taste impressions, for example, are so heavily dependent on our sense of smell that without the latter many foods would be indistinguishable.

Beyond describing sensation, the holographic model also resolves the conceptual dilemmas of time and space which arise in regard to both memory and dreaming. Its ability to distribute information and retrieve it without searching through endless strings of data bits accounts for many puzzles of the brain's remarkable speed of memory. Presumably, the memory mechanism of the brain is similar to the holographic principle of storing many images within the same space or film by using varying frequencies. One particular wavelength of information will illuminate only one specific image or memory; multiple sources will generate many images simultaneously. This holographic quality would seem to account for the apparent simultaneity of memory in dreaming. In a sense, it enables the brain to relive an entire event from memory or, alternatively, slice apart the separate frames of its time-bound motion picture and, in effect, lay them out side by side, making all the information available at one time. This versatile scheme would also seem to suggest explanations for other remarkable mental processes, from our capacity for free association to those integrative or creative processes that go into imaginative and poetic activity.

A supremely sophisticated and eminently practical form of information storage, processing, and organization, Pribram's holographic model of the brain is highly attractive and entirely plausible. The scientific soundness of the holographic model has been carefully worked out and verified mathematically; the distribution of information has been shown to take place in accordance with precise mathematical "spread functions." In addition, the applicability of the model to the brain has been established experimentally by researchers working independently of Pribram. In 700 operations, Dr. Paul Pietsch of Indiana University has successfully "shuffled" the brains of salamanders—excising, grafting, and literally scrambling their structure and contents—to prove that memory storage does in fact conform to holographic principles. In Pribram's holographic breakthrough, it would seem, science has at last produced a credible theory, mathematical and experimental proof, and, in the three-dimensional holographic image, a working model of consciousness itself.

We drove into Palo Alto one cloudy afternoon in the spring of 1977 to discuss with Karl Pribram the implications of his holographic model. Silver-haired but youthful, even sprightly, Pribram possesses an ageless quality that seems to reflect both greatness and humanity. For several hours, he breathed life into his model of the brain, augmenting his views with photographs, diagrams, and his own colorful manner of expression.

"Holograms do deal with conscious awareness," he said. "When I light up a hologram, the image I see is not on the photographic film. It's somewhere beyond; it's a projection. If the brain is holographically organized, conscious experience will be similarly projected when the right input comes in."

Throughout our talk, Pribram was careful not to state conclusively the implications of his theory, for he was quick to admit that the brain is much more complex and specialized than a simple hologram, combining a variety of modes of information storage, distribution, and organization over the various regions of brain function. Nevertheless, he cited recent research suggesting the broad applicability and flexibility of his basic model. He seemed delighted to surmise about its countless fascinating ramifications, new holographic principles that seemed to resolve long-standing paradoxes of the human mind, and notions which, we suspected, held vital clues to the mysteries of sudden personality change that we were investigating.

Most intriguing to us, and of immediate concern with regard to the descriptions we had heard of abrupt changes in awareness, was the paradox that the brain does not appear to be time-bound in its function, yet meets the sequential demands of every aspect of human activity and bodily function. Pribram accounted for this contradiction with little difficulty, transporting us beyond our traditional notions of space and time into the inner world of the brain.

"Now if the hologram is something that is for real in the brain," he cautioned, "it means that we can store things in our brains in terms of various frequencies of information. Then we can read out the information in either linear or spatial fashion. The linear way is sequential, over time, and the spatial is simultaneous. Space and time are not *in* the brain; they are *read out* of it."

As we contended with this new idea that the brain may be, in fact, the master of its own time and space, Pribram recounted the brief history of the hologram. He pointed out that although his model is a radical one for both biology and psychology, proposing an explanation for intangible qualities of the mind in practical terms, scientists and philosophers have been thinking along similar lines for centuries, developing more and more sophisticated concepts to help them grasp the complexity of the world around them. The first formal principles of holography were introduced in the late forties and fifties by a mathematician named Dennis Gabor, Pribram explained, whose intention was to improve the resolution of electron microscopes, high-powered optical devices that magnify objects to the limits of visible light. Gabor was hoping to find a way to sharpen those ultimate images, as American scientists have since succeeded in "deblurring" images received from satellites in outer space. To do this, Gabor drew upon complex mathematical equations called spread functions, which describe the precise manner in which information is spread out around the entire holographic plate. They also determine how that information is gathered up again to reproduce the original holographic subject.

Pribram cited important historical connections to the mathematics of the hologram.

"The mathematics Gabor used were differential equations, the integral calculus," he said. "And if you go back in your philosophy, you get to Leibniz, who invented calculus. Leibniz first proposed the idea of *monads,* elementary units that contained the entire image of the universe. At the time, everybody thought, *Well, Leibniz is getting old. He's trying to talk about God again, just to make sure he gets into those portal gates of St. Peter.* They thought he was going soft, but it turns out the hologram is nothing but a bunch of monads! In other words, every part of the hologram has the attributes of a monad. It includes everything. All the information is there, from a slightly different window or viewpoint. Nonetheless, each part represents the whole, and that, of course, is Godlike, isn't it?"

Pribram let that idea sink in as well, as our minds raced to make connections. We thought about all the people we had talked to whose experiences with various cults, therapies, and drugs had given them overwhelming sensations of oneness with the universe, or of stepping into other dimensions of reality in which they saw the world "through a different window." We thought about the immensely popular, free-wheeling fiction of Kurt Vonnegut, whose characters frequently came "unstuck" in space and time. And we thought about an astrologer we had interviewed in New York who, in his own nonscientific way, had attempted to convince us that an individual's life is influenced by the entire configuration of the solar system at the instant of his birth. All these ideas, if not holographic truths, were at least holographic possibilities— as was the way our own imaginations triggered one tantalizing association after another. Already we were beginning to grasp the new understanding of human information processing and human experience that could be derived from Pribram's holographic model of the brain. Pribram shared our enthusiasm and helped us ground it in more practical matters as well.

"The holographic notion applies to all of the spiritual ideas we've ever had," he said nonchalantly, "but it also applies to everything we know about social organization."

We had already begun speculating along those lines, for we knew that our emerging communication perspective could not isolate the individual from his larger social nature. The hologram infused new meaning into ideas of interdependence and social relationship to which our society has only recently turned its attention. Each individual can be viewed as a kind of complex hologram of his culture and his time—both the reflection and the focal point of his family, his work, his personal relationships, and his society as a whole. In regard to our own investigation, the social implications of the hologram opened the door to a new understanding of the impact of all group activities, from marathon encounters to religious revivals, lending tangible form to the complexity of interacting sensations, information, and potent communication forces that come together in the individual's sweeping "experience" of the group. On a larger scale, the principles of the hologram mirrored our view of the flow of information in a mass society. Like the rush of sensation to the brain, the flood of mass communication, daily news, ideas, and entertainment is spread out and distributed among every individual, each person receiving his unique mixture and interpreting that information from his own distinctive holographic "window." It seemed to us that, in contrast to the world of matter and energy, the entire universe of information and communication, from the smallest flashes of human awareness to the broadest disseminations of mass culture, may be governed by its own set of coherent laws and properties— which, significantly, appears to conform to the math and physics of the hologram.

Could that same hologram even offer a way to resolve the baffling paradoxes of modern physics? Pribram addressed this larger concern we had heard voiced by so many other scientists.

"We've got to get into a different frame of reference," he declared. "We need a math and physics that will allow us to ask the right questions. We're not asking them now. We're not anywhere near them, and we can't reach them as long as we're stuck within the old Cartesian deterministic coordinates of time and space.

"Look at what is happening in nuclear physics," he said, making reference to the tachyon. "You have a particle leaving here and getting there before it left. Something's wrong! Someone may get a Nobel prize for putting that in diagrams that have time running backwards, but if you ask him what he means by that, he'll say, 'What do you mean, *what do I mean?* I can describe it mathematically, but I haven't the slightest idea what it's all about.' Somehow, we've got to switch to an entirely different way of thinking. Not that the ordinary way is wrong—I'm not giving up the idea that this is a flat floor, but that doesn't mean that the world isn't round."

Many members of the scientific community have begun to show great interest in Pribram's work. Yet, inevitably, when a theory of this magnitude is proposed, it takes years, sometimes even generations, for it to gain widespread verification and acceptance. Nevertheless, in under a decade Pribram's holographic model has already made deep inroads into scientific thought concerning such fundamental processes as memory and perception. It has suggested new ways of looking at everything from social relationships to particle physics, and, in time, it may even shed light on some of the most intangible aspects of the human spirit.

"All of a sudden these things are no longer mere wisps of imagination," Pribram told us with a smile. "They turn out to be, mathematically, precisely describable ideas."

Pribram is a modest man, but his enthusiasm for his model comes forward in a confident and forthright manner. As we prepared to leave, he said, "I think the hologram notion is in fact a real change in our scientific paradigm. It makes studiable by scientific tools all the things that have been dismissed as mystical and subjective and so on. In other words, here is an explanatory device that turns the corner."

11 The Law of Experience

Just as no man lives or dies to himself, so no experience lives or dies to itself.

—John Dewey,
The Need of a Theory of Experience

WE LEFT STANFORD confident that Karl Pribram's revolutionary holographic model of the brain offered our investigation the new window we had been looking for into the subjective world of human awareness. Through it, one could see the human mind in a way it had never been viewed before, no longer clouded by the paradoxes of information and experience that once posed insurmountable barriers to understanding. The brain's lightning speed and versatility, taken for granted by the layman, became much more compatible with the laws of nature and modern physics. The miracle of memory, so effortlessly accomplished, and the mystery of perception dropped into new positions in the context of the puzzle we were working.

No longer was the term "information" simply a lifeless engineering concept, a procession of signals, a tally of messages directing the performance of computers and other robots. With the aid of the hologram, we could at last understand the meaning of information in its fully human form. In the brain, information bursts alive in vivid projections of the sense impressions that create our experience of the world, superimposing on one another at many different levels or frequencies. Intermingled with those projections are the private sensations of thought and feeling, what Pribram called "introjections," that make up our experience of ourselves as human beings. Following the direction set by Pribram's insights, it became possible for us to start drawing together the separate elements of our own perspective and, cautiously, begin sketching an overall picture of the mind in communication terms, a mind that became even more amazing when viewed as a living product of information.

As we had come to understand it, the human mind was not some abstract concept, some inaccessible phenomenon, or even the subjective "ghost in the machine." It could be depicted as an *organic, holographic information mix*, the living whole of billions of interacting perceptions, sensations, thoughts, and feelings coming together not in a computer store of discrete neural pigeonholes but throughout the rich and interwoven structure of the brain. Within this compact but infinitely complex arena, an individual may focus his attention on any portion or detail of his mind in a manner characteristic of the hologram itself. He may approach the overall perspective from many different windows or points of view, or he may zero in on any particular focus of thought, feeling, memory, imagination, or perception. In holographic fashion, it became possible for us to envision every purported state of consciousness, from everyday awareness to those altered psychological or mystical states, not as disconnected "realities" but as alternative slices of each individual's holographic reach and flexibility.

However, in order to complete the communication framework essential to a full interpretation of snapping and the alterations of awareness that may follow from it, we found it necessary to go further still. We had to integrate the insights gained from Pribram and the other scientists we interviewed with our own understanding of the role of experience in human development. Finally, the last pieces of the puzzle began to fall into place. In our emerging perspective, the monster of "experience," the beast that had come charging into our culture in the sixties, devouring the traditions of psychology and loosing an epidemic of sudden personality change in the seventies, was, if not yet mathematically exact, at least precisely describable in information terms. And slowly we began to see how information alone—whether in the form of an overwhelming physical experience, a grueling weekend retreat, a rush of intense emotion, or simply an earful of the right words—could have the power to shape and alter human awareness and personality.

Whether you call it "consciousness," "ego," "psyche," "mind," or, in the last analysis, "the human spirit," the organic whole of human awareness, as we have come to understand it, is a living thing. Each moment the brain receives and processes billions of bits of experience in the form of minute electrical impulses. This torrent of multisensory information flows through the brain's 10 billion living cells called neurons, sparking slowly through the minute fibers of the synapses, the winding, tangling junctures of weblike interconnection that link each brain cell to many others. It is in these synapses that the brain's most important information-processing activities occur, for here information mixes freely, creating a teeming pool of mental activity that takes place at many conscious and unconscious levels. It is a kaleidoscope of visual images, a rush of sounds, and an endless parade of sensations, from direct impressions, such as a punch in the face, to the most subtle textures of human awareness, such as the veiled signals each individual picks up and gives off via "body language." In holographic fashion, this barrage of information is actually spread out and distributed throughout the brain and nervous system. Feelings of sadness and loss may come to rest in the pit of an individual's stomach. Shocking news may stab him in the chest, knocking the wind out of him—just as an awesome spectacle may leave him breathless. In this way, the things we as human beings experience deposit traces of information throughout the body, literally informing a person's life from that moment on.

The process may be compared to the way in which the body digests food. The powerful chemical and biological machinery of the digestive system breaks down the food we eat into its basic nutritional components, which are then made available to the rest of the body. In this same sense, the brain can be said to *metabolize* experience, through its natural capacity for transformation, converting its rich diet into information which it then uses to fuel its other complex communication operations. Like the other organs of the body —the heart, which runs on blood, or the lungs, which run on air—the human brain, the seat of awareness, thrives on information.

This analogy is not simply a vivid organic metaphor; experiments in sensory deprivation offer a taste of what happens to the brain when it is starved of information. The effects go far beyond the spiritual moments described by Sargant. In sensory deprivation tests, subjects are suspended in sightless, soundless tanks of water which produce an effect of weightlessness, the water warmed to body temperature to nullify all impressions of heat and cold. No physiological stress need be applied (adequate oxygen is ensured), yet when all information is cut off, the operation of the brain is totally disrupted. Disorientation results almost immediately. After about twenty minutes, visual and auditory hallucinations begin to occur. The alterations of consciousness that have been widely noted generally follow, ranging from high states of ecstasy and joy to deep realms of cosmic bliss and spiritual transcendence. After a point, however, prolonged periods of sensory deprivation may cause irreversible damage to the nervous system. Insanity, violence, or complete withdrawal may result—not from chemical or physiological causes such as drugs or a lack of food or sleep, but from a simple lack of information. Apparently, man's hunger for order is not merely a poetic notion. The body's basic need for information is an explicit physical demand. Deprived of information, the brain ceases functioning normally; starved to extremes, it goes altogether haywire. Yet this life-supporting information does not merely fuel the brain as gasoline fuels a precast auto engine. In human terms, information plays a much more vital and fundamental role.

Of all the organs of the body, the brain is without a doubt the most miraculous, for unlike the heart, the lungs, or the stomach, in performing its natural duties the brain does not proceed according to some genetically determined program. The most recent bio-information findings reveal that human awareness does not spring full blown from the biological machinery of the brain. Before it can begin to organize the world, the brain must first organize itself, yet this is a feat it performs brilliantly and automatically, like everything else it does: from experience.

For all practical purposes, the size and structure of the human brain is genetically determined. The number of neurons in the brain is set at birth and does not increase appreciably from then on. The intricate synaptic connections between and among those neurons, however, the information-processing pathways that determine how an individual's experience will, in fact, become ordered and interpreted, are only minimally organized at birth. The fundamental workings of the mind—the so-called wiring of the human computer —are determined by experience. During the first years of life, the infant brain establishes the basic information-processing pathways that govern its perceptions throughout life. What an individual sees, hears, senses, etc., the manner in which he or she experiences the world, is determined by these first experiences. Yet even as these basic perceptual faculties are developing, the child's awareness is being shaped by his parents and others in the modes of perception of his culture. Different cultures perceive the world in different ways, seeing different shapes, distinguishing different colors, and ignoring different things as well; and a child's awareness can only expand within the social context of his first shared experiences and relationships. Later, more complex and sophisticated capacities evolve, such as thought, language, and imagination, all of which grow and develop in response to further childhood experiences. If these basic capacities are not tapped and nurtured in the child's early years, they will not develop on their own. If he never uses his powers of imagination when he is young, when the brain is in its most ambitious period of organization and development, the capacity will not be there when he grows older. In direct contrast to earlier thinking on the subject, in recent years the prized quality called genius has been shown to be as much as 90 percent a product of experience, a result of the active cultivation of an individual's primary mental capacities during his most impressionable years.

This capacity for learning, for growth and development through experience, is unparalleled among other species. Experience literally *creates* the workings of the human brain, transforming the raw material of billions of neurons into a triumph of communication. And, in our perspective, experience also shapes the individual patterns of thought and feeling that underlie that larger human form, personality.

In contrast to the rest of nature, human beings have evolved into a general and infinitely adaptable species. Unlike animals, our genetic code contains almost no specific instructions for behavior, but rather an economical set of rules for developing individual patterns of response. These patterns form information-processing pathways in the brain which make up our individual capacities of thought and feeling. Long before the ability to communicate through language is developed, these fundamental patterns of thought and feeling, the base on which personality rests, are forged in the intimate relationship between parent and child. A mother's touch, the sound of her voice, the warmth of her skin, provide the child's first experiences and shape feelings that will influence him throughout his life. Later, as the child grows and ventures into the world, he is introduced to new forms of action, expression, and relationship, experiences which further shape his individuality and inform his budding social nature.

All this information, virtually everything an individual experiences, becomes a permanent part of the organization of the brain, but the extent to which it shapes personality throughout life, or at any one moment, is not fixed or predetermined. As we have come to understand it, an individual's personality, like his awareness itself, is fluid and ever-changing, a mix of resonating bits of information and experience, past and present.

This idea that information is, in a very real sense, metabolized and stored in basic patterns of thought and feeling throughout the brain accounts for the classical Freudian notion of personality as a product of a young child's earliest experiences as well as many aspects of the Skinnerian concepts of behavioral conditioning and environmental control. But in our view, this organic and uniquely human shaping process is ongoing throughout the lifelong course of personal growth. At any time in an individual's life, new and intense experiences may leave deep and lasting impressions on fundamental information-processing pathways in the brain. Also, in holographic fashion, thoughts and feelings from some past experience may be regenerated by new experiences of a similar nature, giving rise to images and emotions which spring up, we may surmise, in rough proportion to the intensity of the combined old and new experiences. As cited in a well-known example, exotic smells may call up long-forgotten memories and their associated feelings. In another widely noted phenomenon, long after a person has reached adulthood, the overwhelming pressures of job or career may unleash feelings of anxiety and panic reminiscent of exam periods in high school or college—sometimes even triggering explicit dreams of those bygone days. Under other circumstances, marital problems, for example, may evoke feelings of insecurity and rejection that date back to earlier romances and love affairs. In an individual's later years, the aging process may be accompanied by a flood of past impressions stirred by present thoughts and feelings; for while an individual's memory of recent events usually deteriorates with age, the earliest experiences have been shown to become *more* salient. And, finally, at death, in a phenomenon that has been endlessly reported, the entire storehouse of the brain may be illuminated simultaneously, causing the complete record of an individual's experience to flash before his eyes—and pass through every other sense as well.

Despite proof of this copious activity in the lifelong metabolism of information and experience throughout the brain, the tacit assumption among many scientists, psychologists, and the general public is that the heart of each individual's personality, his human awareness in all its multicolored variety, is an unfading flower that grows out of childhood experiences, environmental conditioning, and the rock-hard structure of his genetic code and that, once formed, it remains indelibly fixed, maintaining itself effortlessly throughout life. Our investigation of snapping has convinced us that this assumption is invalid. In the natural course of human development, experience does indeed shape individual awareness and personality. But, as we have come to understand, this shaping process is organic and in a state of constant change. An incessant flow of experience is needed to actively create and sustain our individual information-processing capacities. And as our research reveals, that same life-giving flow of information can be used to alter or destroy those capacities as well.

This prospect was first suggested in the early fifties by a British engineer, W. Ross Ashby, a seminal figure in communication science. Ashby made the first comprehensive application of communication principles to the machinery of the human brain. In two brilliant technical works, *Design for a Brain*, published in 1952, and *An Introduction to Cybernetics*, published in 1956, Ashby developed mechanical and behavioral models to describe how a sophisticated cybernetic device like the human brain could organize itself from experience, and how new experience could alter that organization at its most fundamental levels. From these models, Ashby derived the basic principle of communication that underlies both technological and human information processing. He named this principle the Law of Experience.

In proving the Law of Experience, Ashby verified that new information entering a cybernetic system destroys previous information of a similar nature. We can cite countless examples of this phenomenon in the activities of the human brain. In the brain, once a pathway of information processing has been established, whether a pattern of speech, a bad habit, or a generally accepted concept (for example, the once widely held belief that the earth is flat), that information, that way of experiencing the world, will prevail unless new information comes in to destroy and replace it. A pattern of speech may be consciously changed or corrected, a bad habit may be forcibly broken, or a new concept of the universe may gain popular acceptance. In each case, the new experience supersedes the old.

Other familiar instances demonstrate the obvious applicability of the Law of Experience to larger, more complex patterns of thought and feeling. A traveler may have an image of a place in his mind, the French Riviera, for example, and a number of feelings associated with it, such as fun, excitement, adventure, and relaxation. That image and those feelings, however, may be utterly shattered when he finally arrives and finds rundown hotels, polluted beaches, high prices, and abominable weather. The overall impact will be to destroy and replace his previous feelings with new information that is a proper reflection of his experience. In another common example, a rider who falls off a horse is traditionally instructed to get back on as soon as possible. His first feelings of pleasure and safety have been destroyed, and fresh, new, positive information is prescribed immediately to erase the trauma of his fall.

In human terms, the Law of Experience describes an organic process that does not require our conscious attention or active participation. It is a natural function of our human capacity for communication that works automatically. This fundamental principle of communication also applies to the larger forms of human awareness and personality, establishing patterns of thought and feeling where there are none and granting priority to new experiences over old.

In *An Introduction to Cybernetics*, Ashby gives this brief example of the Law of Experience in everyday life that demonstrates its larger implications for the development of personality: "Perhaps something of this sort occurs when it is found that a large number of boys of marked individuality, having all been through the same school, develop ways that are more characteristic of the school they attended than of their original individualities."

As Ashby described them, the changes were subtle; as an engineer his focus was unwaveringly upon changes in behavior. In contrast to our own investigation of experience, Ashby was not concerned with the impact of experience on human awareness. Although he acknowledged that consciousness was "the most fundamental fact of all," he declined to discuss it because it could not be demonstrated or scientifically verified.

Yet in our research, which has benefited greatly from discoveries made since Ashby's inquiry, we gathered a wealth of evidence which confirmed for us that the Law of Experience is enforced across the entire spectrum of human awareness, from primary processes of perception to the whole of personality. In interviews with neurophysiologists and bio-information scientists, we heard about exciting new discoveries concerning the brain's active response to experience which, to us, clearly described the communication process of new information superseding old. In some cases, new and intense experiences may sever long-standing synaptic connections; in others, new patterns of thought and feeling may simply bypass or be superimposed over previous ones. Science has only begun to understand the dynamics of these infinitesimal yet immensely complex organic processes, processes that may involve only the slightest shift in the electrical resistance of a tiny portion of a neural cell, or change only the most subtle chemical configurations of what are believed to be minute memory molecules. Yet most new research in the field appears to confirm the spirit of Ashby's law, suggesting that the basic processes of the human brain are in an endless state of growth and reorganization.

And, indeed, few activities in nature are as striking to behold as the interplay that takes place in this living world of communication. We experienced one of the most inspiring moments of our research, in fact, when we were shown action pictures of brain cells, magnified many times, in which we could actually see the neurons waving their tentacle-like fibers, branching outward toward other neurons, seemingly making and breaking synaptic connections with each successive moment's measure of information and experience.

Today, however, it is not necessary to use a microscope to view the Law of Experience in action. Many dramatic examples are visible in America's religious cults and mass therapies. Like an electric shock, the information an individual receives from some massive physical, emotional, and intellectual experience may be powerful enough to destroy deep and long-standing information-processing pathways in the brain. Our talk with Jean Turner revealed how the overwhelming experience of her encounter with her est trainer apparently destroyed patterns of feeling that had been a source of intense pain in her legs since childhood. Similarly, after our interview with Lawrence and Cathy Gordon, it seemed to us that, in the course of their weekend retreat among the Moonies, the constant repetition of Unification Church doctrines destroyed and replaced the couple's fundamental spiritual beliefs. In this instance, presumably, the incessant bombardment of information received in lectures, discussion groups, and personal confrontations—combined with the physical impact of the weekend—was powerful enough to bring about the couple's conversion.

But these powerful experiences, like all experiences, cannot be separated from their holographic nature and effects. Jean Turner's miracle cure was not simply a healing scalpel that excised the pain in her legs and left the rest of her body unscathed. On the contrary, as she testified, her concentrated est encounter summoned up a wrenching emotional convulsion. She felt it in her legs, her wrists, and throughout her entire body. And the next weekend of the training, it "came up like a ball," temporarily dismantling the structure of her personality and leaving her in a state of disorientation and emotional disarray. The Gordons, as well, underwent far more than a simple transformation of belief during their weekend among the Moonies. Their physical appearances changed noticeably—their eyes, their posture, their tone of voice; indeed, they seemed to become totally different people. Furthermore, their sweeping inner change also transformed the way the couple experienced the world around them. On their return, as Lawrence recalled, the everyday world seemed strangely alien and sinister. In response to the new information they had absorbed, the specter of Satan seemed omnipresent, even in the worried appearance and genuine concern of Lawrence's mother.

Like all human information processing, the Law of Experience is holographic. As these examples confirm, it is not possible to tamper with one element of an individual's awareness without endangering his personality as a whole. In many religious cults and mass therapies, the sudden injection of experience may destroy some specific pattern of thought, feeling, or belief, but it may also alter the entire focus of consciousness, shifting the window of individual awareness or changing the landscape altogether. In our investigation, we have found every reason to believe that these intense experiences effect physical changes in the organization of the brain. In some instances, they overlay new patterns of belief, behavior, and awareness that take precedence over old; in others, they actually destroy the fundamental pathways of thought and feeling that make up an individual's personality. Once these changes take place, as Ted Patrick's deprogramming and rehabilitation procedures demonstrate, the former sense of self can only be restored by breaking the tenuous new connections of the individual's cult personality and then slowly, consciously, rebuilding the deeper underlying personality by reconnecting the individual with his past experiences and relationships and with the world around him.

The principles of the hologram and the Law of Experience are cornerstones in the foundation of our understanding of snapping, tools from the communication sciences and neurophysiology which we have endeavored to use to overcome the limitations of the robot model of psychology. Now we can address the subject of how our individual personalities are shaped and altered by experience and examine the impact of that experience on the information-processing capacities of the brain. From this new perspective, we can look directly at the moment of sudden personality change, at the abrupt snapping of human awareness from one level to another.

12 The Snapping Moment and Catastrophe Theory

In time to come it will often be difficult, perhaps, to decide whether an advance in knowledge represents a step forward in physics, information theory, or philosophy, whether physics is expanding into biology or whether biology is employing physical methods and approaches to an ever greater extent.

—*Werner Heisenberg,*
"The End of Physics?"

OUR FRAMEWORK COMPLETE, the separate pieces of our investigation came together to form a comprehensive picture of the phenomenon of snapping. All the elements were there: the intense physical experiences of religious ritual, such as singing, dancing, drumming, chanting, prayer, and meditation, along with the physiological stresses reportedly used by many of the cults and groups, such as exhaustion, poor diet, isolation, and other forms of sensory deprivation.

Under the proper circumstances any of these experiences, or some combination, may produce an intense, overwhelming peak moment which may, in turn, be followed by a precipitous plunge into physical or emotional collapse. However, not even all of them in concert need set off the moment of snapping, which we have distinguished from a brief spiritual or emotional high as the sudden drastic alteration of an individual's entire personality.

An altogether different kind of information is usually needed to trigger this extraordinary human response. It consists of the potent rhetorical ploys, individual and group techniques, and mass-marketing strategies that make up America's technology of experience, everything from fervid lecturing and earnest personal confrontation to slickly packaged appeals, from casual conversation to active role playing and guided fantasy. It is this set of instruments which may be systematically orchestrated to engage the entire range of an individual's communication capacities, from the most rudimentary and automatic biological functions to the highest reaches of human awareness. This all-encompassing verbal and nonverbal assault, charged with challenging new beliefs, suggestions, and commands, may build up profound and often conflicting feelings—feelings of fear, guilt, hatred, anger, humiliation, embarrassment, and alienation—which may prompt the individual to seek release from a troubled past or from more immediate and pressing problems. Then, often in a sensuous, seductive, or totally foreign environment, or surrounded by an atmosphere of love, warmth, acceptance, openness, honesty, and community, the individual may yield to some call, either from within or without, to surrender, to let go, to stop questioning, to relinquish all hold upon the will. And more than anything else it is this act of capitulation that sets off the explosion we call snapping.

In that moment, something quite remarkable may happen. With that flick of a switch, that change of heart and mind, an individual's personality may come apart. From our perspective, this phenomenon can now be identified as an overpowering holographic crisis in the brain.

The experience itself may give rise to a rush of physical sensation: a blinding light, a floating feeling, momentary paralysis, breathlessness, a flood of tears, a coursing of blood throughout the body, or a strong tingling sensation that showers downward from the head with the surge of an electrical discharge. The immediate impact may be felt as awe, ecstasy, amazement, a quiet peace—or complete collapse. In the aftermath of this moment, a person may feel a whole new sense of being, not one of enlightenment, but of something on the far side of that spiritual crest. This is the moment when the individual falls off the precipice and crash lands with the distinct impression that somehow, somewhere, something has changed, either internally or in the outside world. Just what that change is usually remains something of a mystery at first, but the unmistakable sense is that whatever has happened is irreversible.

It is this sharp break in the continuity of awareness that the term snapping so vividly depicts. In the course of our interviews and conversations, we were amazed to find that so many people were fully conscious of this exact moment when "something snapped." For some, it was as if the massive assault of information "blew out" their existing personalities and their unquestioned perception of the world around them. In many instances, this snapping moment took people by storm, creating a deluge of new sensations and dredging up a slurry of buried images and emotions from the past. For these individuals, the experience seemed directly analogous to the familiar description of dying: we heard from more than one person that when it happened his whole life flashed before his eyes. Afterward, however, the individual may be faced with more than a simple sensation of being reborn. Many people we spoke with were indeed brought to a new and heightened state of thought, feeling, and awareness, but suddenly and inexplicably, in a manner that was jarring and led to panic and disorientation.

For the individual who experiences it, the snapping moment may pose terrifying dilemmas. He may find it impossible to integrate the keen, clear presence of his new sense of being with some vague notion of his former self which he is no longer able to locate or define. In some instances, the individual may feel catapulted across a one-way threshold that was more than he ever bargained for in his search for self. He may find himself completely severed from his past, thrown into an emotional and intellectual tailspin.

In this condition, a person becomes critically vulnerable, for in the aftermath of this shattering break, the brain's information-processing capacities may literally become "disorganized," not simply leaving the mind open to new ideas and information, but in fact rendering it receptive to a whole new plan of organization. Someone whose sense of self has just been detonated in this way may seize upon the first available interpretation or explanation of his experience. If he is told that his overwhelming ecstasy was the Holy Spirit visiting his mind and body, he will very likely believe it. If he is told that his feeling of detachment is a state of "cosmic oneness with the universe," in all probability he will find that not merely acceptable but absolute truth.

It is important to recognize that this state of vulnerability to suggestion does not represent a physiological malfunction of the brain. In its holographic nature, the snapping moment evokes a purely cybernetic crisis. As we learned from bio-information scientists, the brain's sturdy machinery is virtually indestructible except under the most extreme physical attack. Following the snapping moment, it keeps on performing its natural functions, striving to regain some semblance of organization. In fact, in this state of surrender and disorganization the human brain becomes capable of amazing feats of imagination. Under one set of circumstances, an individual may hop out of a water-filled "rebirthing" tank and begin barking like a seal, just as a person who relinquishes his self-control to a hypnotist may become firmly convinced that he is a chicken! A more common example is the mature adult who emerges from a marathon encounter group reconstructed or, in psychiatric terms, "regressed" to the emotional level of a young child or rebellious adolescent. If he receives no help in dispelling this notion, that may in fact be the way his personality becomes reorganized.

In almost every instance, the resolution of this crisis in the brain depends on the course of action followed in its immediate aftermath. If the individual returns to his former surroundings and actively restores his former relationships, the effects of the snapping moment will in all likelihood dissipate in a relatively short time. If, however, out of fear and panic he withdraws into himself, he may linger in this precarious state of mind for a period of weeks or even months, trapped in its mind-boggling aftereffects and extreme vulnerability to suggestion. Alternatively, if he remains in an alien setting with little or no connection to his former life and relationships, his personality will almost certainly be refashioned in the image of his new surroundings, and his awareness will fall into line with that of the people around him.

So far in this book we have presented a selection of instances of the snapping moment in contexts ranging from private, personal experiences to large public gatherings. In the examples that follow, we will look at some of the more unusual and startling instances of the phenomenon that we uncovered in our research, with the purpose of demonstrating how certain intense experiences may lead to the snapping moment and the condition of vulnerability that generally follows.

———————

In our investigation, the Hare Krishna cult emerged as perhaps the most practiced at inducing the snapping moment that brings about sudden changes in personality. Formally known as the International Society for Krishna Consciousness, this worldwide Hindu cult has thousands of full-time members in the United States. They are frequently seen dressed in bright orange devotional robes, chanting and singing on street corners in almost every major city in America, but they also dress more conventionally to engage in fund-raising activities, which include the selling of incense and brilliantly illustrated copies of the Bhagavad Gita in airport terminals coast to coast. Some of the most bizarre tales we heard of physical and emotional breakdowns concerned Krishna members, yet until now the cult's rituals and techniques have remained obscure.

In one of our most revealing interviews, a former Krishna devotee discussed the seductive nature of an ancient Hindu ritual the cult draws upon in its regular devotion. For this individual, the experience took place on his first visit to a Krishna temple.

"They have a ceremony called *artika*," he told us, "where they offer a candle to their deities. They jump up and down and they dance and sing. I think it was probably the most far-out feeling I'd ever had in my whole life. It was the first time I'd heard anybody chant like that—very loud, the *Hare Krishna* mantra. Then they opened the doors and there were these deities, six of them. The wooden ones on the right didn't attract much attention, and three yellow ones on the left didn't either. But there was one deity in the middle which was supposed to be Krishna that I recognized from the books and literature I had been reading. It really came out at me. The statue was stark white and very colorfully attired. He was sort of in an s-shape, standing very casually playing the flute. That was when I had this incredibly bizarre experience. All at once, while we were dancing and chanting, there was something like a flash of light, except that it didn't really happen. It wasn't on a rational level at all. The deity seemed to move. I was dancing around and getting along in my chanting, and I focused my attention on this deity and it seemed to fill my mind completely. I stared at it for a minute, and it seemed to bore right through me. Physically, I felt separated from my body—it was really strange. I felt like I was completely there and my body had been washed away. There was just sort of a link-up between me and the statue, as if everything else had vanished."

For this devotee, the snapping moment came up fast and hit hard. Its impact was overwhelming.

"The whole thing lasted maybe three seconds," he said. "I really have no idea because I lost all track of time. It was a new experience and I didn't know what to do with it. I didn't know if I wanted it or not. I was trying to resolve it, trying to analyze it and figure out why it happened, what it was."

Finally, he drew the same conclusion as those around him.

"The whole thing was very intense," he said, "and I interpreted it as a powerful spiritual experience. That seemed like such a big thing; it was the main reason I joined the temple."

Another Krishna devotee we interviewed revealed the difference between a simple peak experience and the powerful *artika* ritual used by the Hare Krishna to bring about conversion. She described her ecstatic snapping moment in a similar ceremony at another Krishna temple halfway across the country.

"I was with these devotees who were all the way they get in the *artika*," she said, "and I got all caught up in it just like everyone else. I was closing my eyes hard, trying to get that bliss and make it come; and it did, more or less. I felt like I saw a white light. I felt like I was going to explode. I guess you can relate it to a sexual thing, like a climax or something. Your mind has to be in a certain state of willingness to achieve it, then the chanting and the music and the incense and all those things just help to bring it on."

Looking back, this young woman told us how the entire *artika* setting—the bright-colored statues, the incense, and the chanting—put her mind in the proper state of readiness for her intense snapping experience. She reflected on the way the cult leaders orchestrated and exploited the group frenzy.

"Right at the peak," she said, "the person who was leading the ceremony blew the conch shell; then everyone fell to the floor and started reciting their little prayers. Afterwards, everyone was really high. Some people were in a trance state. Others became very quiet. Then we all sat down and received a lecture. When we were totally drained, they poured in all the indoctrination."

The comprehensive sensory assault that culminates in a moment of snapping filled with ecstasy and bliss is only one cult method used to bring about sudden conversions and transformations of personality. Other cults use less obvious methods to create a completely different type of information environment, yet their impact may be equally bewildering and profound. A former member of the Divine Light Mission explained to us how that Hindu cult combines fatigue, darkness, and ancient scripture in its solemn ritual of initiation.

"The initiation was held at three in the morning and none of us had had very much sleep going into it," he recalled. "The room was pitch black as the *mahatma* read from the scriptures of the Divine Light, emphasizing that the light referred to was not allegorical but real light and that all religions have been based on the same mystical experience. He told us to concentrate on a point in our foreheads where our third eye was located, and he would come and channel the divine energy into us. He came swishing through the darkness. I felt his fingers on my eyes, and I saw a light that seemed to stab down from the outer darkness. It came from somewhere behind me and created a figure eight of pure, white light. It lasted for a brief period of time and I was blown away by it."

Afterward, this new disciple of the Perfect Master experienced some disorientation. Even as it was occurring, he sensed that something ominous had happened to his mind.

"After the initiation I went through a period of five or six hours in which I felt I was not really controlling what I was doing or saying," he remembered. "I felt like I was being spiritually controlled, like a marionette of some sort. It was very strange."

One of the most puzzling aspects of the snapping moment is that, very often, it is not some overwhelming experience that sets it off but some tiny thing, a seeming irrelevancy that sparks a chain reaction of thought and feeling. A number of est graduates and encounter group veterans told us about some long-forgotten and inconsequential event that came stampeding to the forefront of their awareness at the prompting of their group leader. Many others pinpointed the start of their snapping experience as the moment they focused on a tension headache that developed in the course of their weekend ordeal. Still others, like Sally Kempton, told of a passing phrase or idea that set off a depth charge of emotional response.

There seems to be no limit to the number of settings in which the snapping moment may occur, from religious rituals to encounter groups, from public, stressful ordeals to private, stressless moments of relaxation and repose. We spoke with a suburban housewife in her mid-thirties, who described the disorientation she experienced in the privacy of her isolated New England home the first time she tried a meditation technique she read about in a book.

Here, as in other cases cited, that curious white light switched on at the precise instant of snapping.

"This particular technique recommended that you go into a closet," she said. "I put a chair in there and I sat up straight, trying not to think about anything. The idea was that if a thought came into your mind, you should just watch it, just see it come and let it go out without fighting it. Pretty soon, I found that time had disappeared. I came out of the closet and saw that two hours had passed, and it really blew my mind. I had a feeling that I was something other than my body, but other than my mind, too. I felt very light, and I remember after that being in the kitchen and reaching for some equipment and it seemed as if a big light suddenly flashed on in front of me."

This sense of timelessness is perhaps the most telling feature of the snapping moment, for to us the flash of images and rush of sensations that may take place seem clearly to describe a holographic process. Many of the people we talked to did their best to relate this burst of simultaneous experience which took place apart from their normal groundings in space and time. Yet in direct contrast, others told us of a snapping moment that was not instantaneous but drawn out. We heard from many individuals who, like Jean Turner after her second est weekend, came floating out of some cult or group on a magic carpet of bliss, only to experience a plunge into profound unhappiness and alienation after a period of several days, even months. Another ex-Krishna devotee described this delayed snapping response to us in vivid terms.

"When I left the temple that first night I went home and I was feeling really high," he told us. "I woke up Monday morning still feeling high. It was a little bit like a dope high or champagne. I was light-headed, tipsy, but still in control of my faculties. I was really feeling good, and it lasted all morning, but about noon it just went *boom!* I just crashed. I was in school and I hit the pits. I'd never been so depressed in my life. Everything just went *bang*. I was disgusted. I couldn't do any work. I was completely out of it."

This young high school student's depression kept up all week. Throughout the period, he told us, he was confused and disoriented, once even losing control of his motorcycle on a ride down a familiar road. The following Sunday he went to the temple to attend the next Krishna feast.

"That whole evening is very, very blurred," he explained to us, straining to remember. "I had expressed my interest to somebody, and they immediately put me in a room with a couple of other devotees. They talked to me for about an hour, expounding about this and that, and I said that I really thought I should stay outside the temple, where I could make quite a bit of money. Then one of the leaders said, 'Don't worry about the money; somebody else can get the money. We want you inside the temple.' I went wild then, thinking, *Wow, these people don't care about the money; they'd rather save my soul.* It was a subtle thing, though. I noticed they had convinced me, and I was really sort of surprised. I'd had no plans to stay. I'd even parked my car in a no-parking zone."

The delayed response of so many individuals is yet another dramatic indication of how some intense experience, emotion, or new idea may work its way into the organic whole of the mind. Across the spectrum of religious conversion, from the Christian Born Again moment to the Hindu rituals described in this chapter, snapping may be an instant and conscious change. Or, as in the Unification Church, an individual may be transformed over the course of an intense weekend, without ever experiencing that sudden break in the continuity of his awareness. Despite the differences, there are no contradictions among the various forms of snapping. Whether jolting and instantaneous or imperceptible and in slow motion, they may all be understood in our communication terms of information and experience, and each indicates a similar surrender of thought and will.

Until recently, there would have been no way to sift through the variety of personal accounts of snapping we have gathered together in this investigation. There was no formula available to explain how an infinitely complex convergence of physical, emotional, and intellectual experiences may build up, cresting in a comprehensive holographic crisis in the brain and resolving into what appears to be a whole new system of personality. In our attempt to grapple with this problem, however, a number of scientists pointed us in the direction of an exciting new method of interpretation. They suggested that it might help us picture the dynamics of these varied sudden leaps in human awareness and evaluate their significance in relation to one another.

Within the past few years, a new mathematical perspective called catastrophe theory has been introduced and debated across a broad spectrum of scientific disciplines. Catastrophe theory is concerned with events that take place abruptly—by fits, jumps, and starts, as one advocate expressed it. Throughout nature this type of occurrence is abundant. The physical world offers many examples of sudden or discontinuous transformations: earthquakes, cloudbursts, waves breaking on a beach. The movements of man take place with equal outbreak and surprise: stock market crashes, prison riots, and, of course, religious conversions. These events represent the abrupt resolution of conflict between steadily interacting and opposing forces. In seeking to understand the dynamics of this type of discontinuous change, René Thom, a French mathematician, developed the math and logic of catastrophe theory.

The precise "topological" mathematics of catastrophe theory would be nearly incomprehensible to the layman. Thom's basic model, however, may

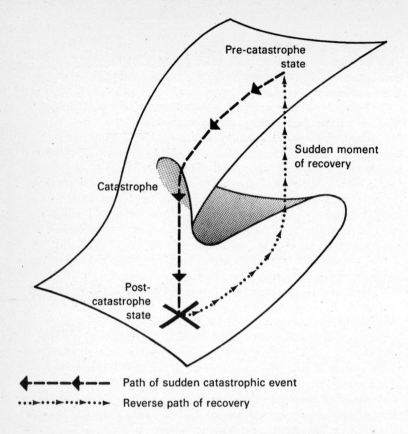

Figure 1: *Simplified version of Thom's elementary catastrophe curve*

be described, and even pictured, with little difficulty. (See Figure 1, a highly simplified depiction of the folding wave-shaped form, showing the curving surface smoothly continuous at the far side and then appearing to break in a wavelike manner on the near side; the "catastrophe" or breaking point is where the path plummets downward over the crest.) The images of an earthquake or breaking wave are basic catastrophes of nature. They are products of dynamic forces—migrating land masses, flowing water— moving in direct opposition to each other. When the opposing forces of water meet and build up on a beach, for instance, with water both flowing toward the land and slipping back into the sea, they converge gradually, adding, subtracting, canceling each other out, until they cross a complex threshold of opposition and give way in the sudden, drastic breaking of a wave. On another scale, an earthquake too is the abrupt product of opposing forces, as the unseen pressure of moving and resisting land masses builds up to an obvious breaking point. That breaking point, the final push, is no stronger than the forces that have gone before, but the change in activity, the earthquake, is sudden and discontinuous, wildly out of proportion to the tiny event that set it off.

This sudden, drastic change is an event of nature called a "catastrophe." Another example would be the straw that broke the camel's back.

When it was first introduced, the idea of a *theory* of catastrophes caught the fancy of the media and the general public, many of whom hoped it would provide a method of predicting natural and economic disasters. As it turns out, however, Thom never intended catastrophe theory to be a tool of prediction, but rather a mathematical model and visual image that offers a way to understand the incalculable complexity of natural occurrences and living things— exactly what we were looking for in our attempt to grasp the complexity of snapping.

As we began to explore catastrophe theory, several scientists cautioned us that it was a highly technical and controversial innovation. As we spoke with other scientists, however, and closely examined the underlying principles of Thom's work, we became more certain that catastrophe theory does indeed have its valid applications. One application in particular convinced us that catastrophe theory may be of genuine use in understanding the dynamics of snapping.

The most ambitious and promising applications of catastrophe theory to human affairs have been made by Professor E. Christopher Zeeman of the University of Warwick in England. In one model, Zeeman and British psychotherapist Dr. J. Hevesi offer a demonstration of catastrophe theory in action that is strikingly similar to the experience of snapping. Zeeman makes use of Thom's concept of catastrophe to study the affliction known as anorexia nervosa, or obsessive fasting, an emotional disorder found most frequently among adolescent girls who may be struggling to reconcile conflicting personal needs, family problems, and the normal social pressures of growing up. Anorexia usually begins as simple fasting, not extraordinary for a figure-conscious young woman. Unchecked, however, or taken to extremes, this harmless dieting strategy may cause a total degeneration of appetite, leading to states of profound emotional disturbance, starvation, and, on rare occasions, death. In its advanced stages, anorexia may also produce a violent counterreaction in which the individual will undergo periods of what Zeeman calls "obsessive gorging."

Zeeman likens the experience to one of Thom's elementary catastrophes, plotting the progressive stages of the disorder on Thom's basic three-dimensional model. On the folding, wave-shaped form depicted in Figure 1, the appetite may be systematically plotted as the product of opposing forces of hunger and restraint. As these forces draw the anorexic individual toward the crest of the catastrophe wave, the appetite may jump from more or less normal to, paradoxically, practically nonexistent; then some time later the individual may turn to compulsive gorging. Zeeman cites a sudden experience many sufferers of anorexia call "the knockout," when feelings of exhaustion, disgust, and humiliation sweep over them and cause them to crash abruptly from a mounting level of hunger to no appetite at all.

In treating this disease, Dr. Hevesi developed a form of trance therapy in which he offers his patients reassurance, reduces their anxiety, and gradually brings their appetites back to normal. In an article in *Scientific American*, Zeeman describes the observable moment of Dr. Hevesi's cure. It parallels the sudden snap of deprogramming (or in Figure 1, Sudden Moment of Recovery):

> After about two weeks of therapy and in about the seventh session of trance the patient's abnormal attitudes usually break down catastrophically and the personality is fused into a complete whole again. When the patient awakens from this trance, she may speak of it as a "moment of rebirth."

Thom's catastrophe theory provides a near-perfect model of the entire anorexic experience: the abrupt change from dieting to fasting, the contradictory jump from fasting to gorging, and the miraculous two-step cure from anorexia through trance to "rebirth." It also supplies a graphic, three-dimensional image for the vivid terms in which victims of anorexia describe the experience of their illness, such as "knockout," "let-go," and "rebirth." The correspondence is startling between the catastrophic jumps that occur in anorexia nervosa and the abrupt changes in personality that take place in America's religious cults and mass therapies. The sudden changes in appearance and behavior and the instant transformation of lifelong patterns of thought, feeling, and relationship all suggest the catastrophic resolution of opposing physical, emotional, and intellectual forces. Moreover, the folding, wave-shaped catastrophe curve offers a three-dimensional image of the sudden, sweeping shift that characterizes the snapping moment when the flow of new information rises and crests to destroy and replace the old. In the face of the mounting catastrophe, these two natural and generally complementary processes of change and resistance are brought into direct opposition with one another. Obvious examples of this are an intense group encounter, a religious ritual, and a head-on personal confrontation. This battle of moving and resisting thoughts and feelings may end in a dramatic upheaval in the brain. In the snapping moment, we may presume, long-standing patterns of personality that have developed since childhood—constituting one established, resisting whole

—may suddenly give way to an entirely new personality of sorts. This personality is made up of the mass of new information the individual has received in the comprehensive assault of alien and intense experiences impinging upon him with an immediate and overwhelming force. Old pathways in the brain may become disconnected and destroyed, or new pathways may be formed which suddenly override the old.

Not long after we became acquainted with catastrophe theory, we spoke with a young woman we will call Pam Mitchell who, in the early seventies, spent over a year in the Hare Krishna cult. As she described it to us, her dramatic experience in the cult and her precarious re-emergence during deprogramming seemed to map onto Thom's elementary model with full precision, describing two completely distinct yet fully interacting systems of personality.

Like most cult members, Pam Mitchell slipped gradually into her Krishna state of mind, just as most anorexics slip gradually into their state of uncontrollable fasting. Her boyfriend introduced her to the group, and she grew increasingly familiar with the doctrines and rituals of Krishna life. In the beginning, Pam attended several Sunday feasts at the Krishna temple and experienced repeated snapping moments during *artika* ceremonies. Before long, she moved into the temple and became deeply involved in the daily life and practices of the cult, sliding into the state of reduced awareness common throughout America's cults—a state she referred to as being "dumbfounded." She performed numerous temple chores and duties for several months while in that state of mind and assumed the traditional Krishna woman's role of subservience. Pam tried to hold onto some thread of her old identity as she balanced the opposing forces of fear, guilt, confusion, and exhaustion building up within her. Her modern feminine consciousness opposed the Krishnas' lowly attitude toward women, her body reacted to the restricted diet and interminable fatigue of cult life, and her nervous system actively resisted the boredom and inactivity of hour after hour of chanting. Finally, her strained emotions crested and gave way in a classic catastrophic moment.

"It slowly worked to the point where I was existing on such a low level," she recalled for us, "that finally I cracked. I walked into the room and started laughing hysterically. Then I had a real breakdown. I just collapsed for about a day and a half.

"I guess you could say I snapped in a way," she told us, without prompting. "I snapped to the point where I wasn't fighting anymore."

For the next three months, as she described it, Pam's anxiety and frustration "went inside." The tensions she had been feeling disappeared, yet before long they began manifesting themselves in physical ways. Her hands and face broke out in eczema, and she gained weight dramatically. Concerned over her appearance, the temple president refused to let her go home to visit her family.

Then one day she experienced another catastrophic change in awareness.

"It was a snap thing," she said again. "I was just talking to another girl who was working in the kitchen with me, and I went, *I've been brainwashed! What has happened to me?*"

In keeping with Thom's model, Pam's sudden moment of reawakening —not a snapping into but, in this case, a snapping *out* of her cult state—was not the direct result of any intense or abrupt experience. Instead, it was a realization, sparked by a passing impression, that had been building up for some time. Although it happened in an instant, she remembered the dynamic nature of the experience.

"I felt alive again. I felt like I was thinking again," she recalled. "It was kind of gradual at first, like when you're slowly waking up and gradually becoming conscious. I started to talk and become more and more excited, feeling, sensing more as I talked about what was happening to me. Then I got real excited and all of a sudden I looked at what I was doing and it hit me. It was like a connection."

Pam's description of the experience could easily be traced on the catastrophe curve.

"I felt like I had jumped off a cliff six months ago and I was just back up on the plateau I was on before," she said. "It was like I had gone backwards in my own development, but I knew myself again. It was me, not that other person. How can you explain how it feels to be alive?"

Soon after her awakening, Pam left the Krishna temple and made her way back to her hometown. But in a manner reminiscent of Kay Rambur's experience in the Children of God, Pam's self-styled deprogramming was incomplete. For the next few weeks, she struggled in that peculiar state of limbo known to deprogrammers as floating.

"I was unable to relate to anybody," Pam recalled. "Within a week I was going back to the temple because I couldn't assimilate back here. Everyone else seemed crazy, and since nobody was aware of what had happened to me, I just couldn't make it by myself."

When Pam began returning to the Krishna temple, however, her mother knew that her daughter was still in trouble. She made arrangements to have Pam deprogrammed properly.

"They told me I was going for a job interview," said Pam, recalling the irony of her floating state. "But as I was walking up to this house, I saw the deprogrammer standing in the doorway. Then I realized what was going on and I started to fight. Even though I had left the cult a week before of my own free will, I fought him. There was a big violent scene at the door, yelling and screaming. I started chanting *Hare Krishna* as loud as I could."

Paradoxical as it may seem, Pam Mitchell's peculiar reversion fits neatly into the catastrophe model, in the area of the fold in the middle of Thom's elementary catastrophe curve. In this limbo region, which may be depicted as more or less stable depending on the particular catastrophe model, a cult member's awareness may lurch about at random. As Ted Patrick describes it, in the floating state the cult member may go either way: toward full recovery or toward what he calls "backsliding," another term that aptly describes a path on the catastrophe curve.

"I was crazy, going nuts," Pam Mitchell told us. "I was at that insanity point people talk about when they know they're crazy but can't do anything about it. It was an uncontrollable thing. I couldn't make the transition back, even though I wanted to really bad."

But the deprogrammer succeeded in bringing her through the crisis. He talked to her and played tapes of other ex-cult members describing similar experiences, until Pam finally experienced the sudden moment of reawakening.

"It was like a realization," she recalled, "and my old self fell right back into my body. I was totally exhausted, but the skeleton of my personality had come back."

Pam Mitchell's deprogramming was a complete success. Her final reawakening was another catastrophic jump. In direct contrast to the snapping moment of dissolution, however, this abrupt transformation returned her to a healthy state of full awareness and self-control. Afterward, she spent the next few months learning to think for herself and feel again, rebuilding her values and relationships, easing herself back into the world.

Is this catastrophe model of snapping valid? René Thom's theory has come under heavy fire within the mathematics community. Many prominent American scientists have charged that proponents of catastrophe theory have rashly applied it to natural and social phenomena that cannot be verified by traditional scientific methods. Furthermore, critics claim, other mathematical formulas already exist that deal with sudden change, albeit with far less glamorous names such as "bifurcation theory," "shock wave theory," and "thresholds."

In an effort to better determine whether our application to snapping of Thom's controversial theory was, as we believed, valuable and responsible, we made a special trip to Berkeley to confer with Dr. Hans Bremermann, professor of mathematics and medical physics at the University of California there. Bremermann is highly regarded in the world of science for his development of one of the most fascinating concepts in the physics of computation, referred to by many scientists (among them, W. Ross Ashby), as "Bremermann's Limit" on the amount of data—in strictly physical terms—any information-processing device is capable of handling. His work, in effect, delineates what mathematical problems and computations fall within the bounds of physical "reality." A brilliant and far-reaching scholar, Bremermann was one of the first American scientists to hail the arrival of catastrophe theory, in his review of Thom's book written for the American journal *Science* in 1973.

We met in Bremermann's office, crowded among overflowing cartons of manuscripts and academic papers, and began by asking Bremermann if his enthusiasm for Thom had dampened in view of the recent barrage of criticism. Speaking in a soft voice with a slight German accent, he was quick to point out that despite the controversy surrounding catastrophe theory, no one has been able to find fault with Thom's mathematics. It is in the application of the theory, Bremermann cautioned, that all the trouble arises.

"I think the consensus in the mathematical community is that Zeeman, as an expositor and publicizer of catastrophe theory, has been a bit *too* successful," Bremermann told us. "I think that some people are worried because the name, which really is a technical name, has such powerful associations. They fear it may be misunderstood in popular articles."

Since it first appeared, Bremermann revealed, he has felt, along with Thom himself, that catastrophe theory is not so much a scientific theory as it is a new mathematical *language*, a scientific metaphor. As such, he said, it offers a way to talk about complex natural phenomena that would not be possible using ordinary scientific language and concepts.

"A biological organism is a phenomenally complicated mathematical entity," he said, elaborating on the dilemma from his own scientific point of view. "Look at a single bacterium. If you put it under a microscope, you can hardly see it. It's so small, only a few light waves in size. It's very close to the visible limits of light, and you can't see any of its rich structure. But there are thousands of genes in it. There are several thousand different kinds of molecules in it, plus intricate spatial structuring. This complexity is way beyond what any mathematician, even reinforced with a computer, can resolve, predict, or compute."

At the human level, Bremermann went on, the enormous complexity of nature becomes even more awesome—and incalculable.

"When you take human beings interacting and bringing about cultures, socieities, and civilizations," he said, "it's even more complex. You cannot look at the individual parts and try to figure out what the whole organism is going to do. You run into impenetrable physical barriers of computation. There are lots of things we simply cannot explore."

According to Bremermann, catastrophe theory provides a possible way out of this labyrinth of complexity.

"Okay, in come Thom and Zeeman," declared Bremermann, "and they say that if we can't fully explore complex things, we can still look at them on another level. If you have a dynamic system, maybe you don't even need to know all the details. You can look at the states it settles down to and say something about the occasional and sudden transitions that it makes. That's what catastrophe theory is."

Like Pribram's holographic framework, catastrophe theory offers a new way of picturing the world. To Bremermann, its promise lies in its potential to provide a special way of using mathematics descriptively (rather than deductively, as has been the custom in his field).

"The conceptual machinery that has served us more or less well for so long is breaking down," said Bremermann, speaking with the same urgency that characterized our conversations with John Lyman and Karl Pribram. "It is not quite adequate to deal with the enormous phenomena that we face in the world. Our poor brains can't follow the dynamics of modern society. The monster has developed, it's there, but we really don't understand it. The politicians don't know how to control it. Nobody has an intellectual penetration of the dynamics that are at work."

We asked Bremermann how well this approach to complex phenomena could be applied to our study of sudden personality change in cults and groups.

"Now we are talking about a very specific phenomenon," he said, "and I think we are on much firmer ground to try to fit it into the catastrophe framework than we are in simply discussing catastrophe theory in general."

As we laid out some of our findings, Bremermann was impressed by the similarities between snapping and other catastrophes, but he acknowledged the difficulty involved in applying the theory to human personality.

"In this situation there are lots of things which impinge upon the mind," he said. "To fit it into this folded surface and to single out specific control parameters would have to be carefully done. Instead of focusing on the mathematical theory, why not look at it simply as a model that allows us to see these different phenomena in the same frame of reference and draw comparisons? Here is a concrete problem. We have this phenomenon: on the one hand, the Moonies, say, or the Krishna; on the other, say, what happened to Patty Hearst, for example. If enough people get hit by things like this in their homes, I think they will begin to understand that there are strange phenomena that require new concepts for understanding."

As we presented some of the testimony we had gathered, Bremermann nodded.

"These deprogrammers have found something," he said. "These states of rapture and depression. It really fits the catastrophe model much better than I would have imagined, and one could draw comparisons with some other kinds of breakdowns, such as anorexia."

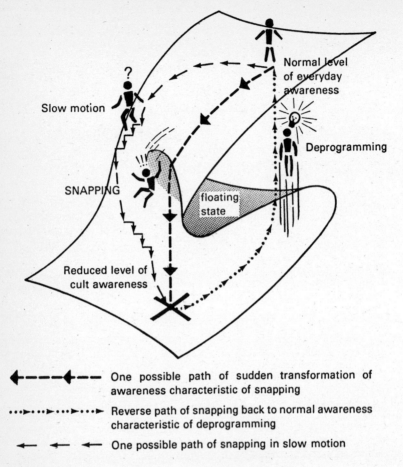

Normal level
of everyday
awareness

Slow motion

Deprogramming

SNAPPING

floating
state

Reduced level of
cult awareness

◄━━━◄━━ One possible path of sudden transformation of
awareness characteristic of snapping

••►•••►•••►•••► Reverse path of snapping back to normal awareness
characteristic of deprogramming

◄━ ◄━ ◄━ One possible path of snapping in slow motion

*Figure 2: Snapping as plotted on simplified model of Thom's
catastrophe curve*

Toward the end of our discussion, we asked Bremermann about the
numerous instances we had come across of snapping in slow motion. We told
him that many cult members, in fact, talk of a gradual descent into their cult
states of mind. During deprogramming as well, some cult members re-emerge
in a smooth progression rather than a sudden snap. We asked Bremermann
if this more continuous experience invalidated our catastrophe model. On the
contrary, he said, he found it perfectly in keeping with the finer points of
Thom's work.

"Catastrophe is just a term that applies if you want to understand a
dynamic phenomenon where something changes suddenly," he explained.

"But mathematically, all the ingredients *are* continuous. They're smooth, and then all of a sudden something jumps, but you can move from one point to the other in slow motion, by a different path if you like.

"In other words, instead of falling down a cliff," he said, "you can walk down slowly, in a roundabout way, and reach the exact same point."

We came away from our talk with Hans Bremermann fully apprised of the pitfalls of proposing any application of catastrophe theory, but more convinced than ever that our use of the model was appropriate. As only one tool among many new and controversial scientific theories we were drawing upon, catastrophe theory gave us a final handle on snapping in its varied forms, filling out and completing our initial picture of the phenomenon. In our informal application, it brought us to the point where we could trace any path of snapping and deprogramming on the simplified catastrophe curve shown in Figure 2. (In fact, a more detailed and accurate model of snapping could be drawn on one of Thom's more complex catastrophe curves, a slightly modified version of the wave shown here.)

We drove northward out of California, heading up to Oregon for a few months of solace in which to transcribe more interviews and analyze them in the light of our latest findings. A growing understanding was rapidly drawing us toward a somber conclusion, that in some cases, although certainly not all, the phenomenon of snapping as depicted on the catastrophe curve may lead to a new and frightening form of mental disorder. Left unremedied, or reinforced over time, the sudden alteration of the mind characterized by our term snapping may deteriorate into a lasting affliction of consciousness, a physical impairment of human awareness. With our new understanding of how experience in the form of information is metabolized—broken up, distributed, and reorganized—throughout the brain and nervous system, we were now able to grasp how this natural, organic process may become subject to disease, not in the medical sense, but an affliction, nonetheless, of the physical organization of our human information-processing capacities.

In the pages that follow, we will present in detail the afflictions of the mind we have found to plague victims of some religious cults and mass therapies. We now understand these afflictions to be physical impairments of thought and feeling, protracted alterations of awareness and personality that can be diagnosed, in the strictest sense, as varieties of *information disease*.

13 Varieties of
Information Disease

Where is the Life we have lost in living?
Where is the wisdom we have lost in knowledge?
Where is the knowledge we have lost in information?

—*T. S. Eliot,*
"The Rock"

NOW THE FOCUS of our investigation shifts to the terrain beneath the precipice as we draw a distinction, for the first time, between snapping—a term that up to this point we have used in a very broad sense to indicate any sudden, drastic alteration of personality—and information disease, which we now define as any of several distinct although often interrelated states the mind may settle down to in the aftermath of the moment. We identify information disease as an alteration through experience of a person's fundamental information-processing capacities. When these vital capacities become altered or damaged, the resulting change is not simply one of behavior. When snapping turns to information disease, it represents a lasting alteration of human awareness at the most basic level of an individual's personality. The disease is not physiological in nature; it does not damage or destroy the sturdy biological machinery of the brain. Nevertheless, as we have come to understand it, information disease represents a physical alteration of the complex organization of the brain.

America's religious cults and mass therapies offer an abundance of victims of information disease, individuals beset with severe emotional disturbances and states of reduced awareness, delusion, detachment, and withdrawal. Undoubtedly, throughout history, similar afflictions of awareness have occurred from natural stresses or at random. Now, however, they are becoming increasingly common consequences of America's runaway technology of experience.

Norbert Wiener first proposed that some forms of mental disturbance could be attributed to problems of human information processing. In *Cybernetics: Control and Communication in the Animal and the Machine*, Wiener discussed the information-processing aspects of some traditional forms of mental illness. He wrote:

> Psychopathology has been rather a disappointment to the instinctive materialism of the doctors, who have taken the point of view that every disorder must be accompanied by material lesions of some specific tissue involved. . . . There is no way of identifying the brain of a schizophrenic . . . nor of a manic depressive patient, nor of a paranoiac. These disorders we call *functional*, and this distinction seems to contravene the dogma of modern materialism that every disorder in function has some physiological or anatomical basis in the tissues concerned.
>
> This distinction between functional and organic disorders receives a great deal of light from the consideration of the computing machine. As we have already seen, it is not the empty physical structure of the computing machine that corresponds to the brain—to the adult brain, at least—but the combination of this structure with the instructions given it at the beginning of a chain of operations and with all the additional information stored and gained from outside in the course of the chain. This information is stored in some physical form—in the form of memory.
>
> There is therefore nothing surprising in considering the functional mental disorders as fundamentally diseases of memory, of the circulating information kept by the brain in the active state, and the long-time permeability of the synapses. . . . Even the grosser disorders . . . may produce a large part of their effects not so much by the destruction of tissue . . . as by the secondary disturbances of traffic.

Wiener's theory of "diseases of memory" and "circulating information" pertained primarily to psychopathology, and many of the fine points of his proposal have since been validated through medical research (although some instances of schizophrenia and manic depression have been shown to correspond to specific conditions of chemical imbalance within the brain). In 1948, however, when Norbert Wiener wrote *Cybernetics*, there was no such thing as a "consciousness movement" in America, and the only religious cults were long-established sects that posed no glaring psychological or legal dilemmas. In his concern for what is human in human beings, Wiener foresaw the dangers of automation and runaway technology, and he sought to use his insights to protect man's most cherished capacities. It wasn't until after his death in the early sixties, however, that new forms of experience began to threaten Americans with startling new kinds of "functional" disorders.

In the broadest technical sense of the term, information disease may result from a variety of experiences. Some may be intensely physical. As Wiener pointed out, fundamental changes in information-processing capacities may result from injury to the nervous system. Poor diet, too, especially lack of protein, as is common in many cults, has been shown to alter the overall function of the brain. Prolonged lack of sleep, as well, may weaken or impair the brain's ability to perform vital information-processing functions. But information disease may also result purely from intense experiences that abuse an individual's natural capacities for thought and feeling. The most dramatic examples of this type of information disease result from the concentrated experiments in thought, feeling, and imagination practiced by many cults and therapies; simple techniques of encounter, guided fantasy, and meditation that are in widespread use today. These communication processes are no less powerful than immediate physical experience in their potential to disrupt and impair the brain's information-processing capacities. By tampering with basic distinctions between reality and fantasy and between past and present, or simply by stilling the workings of the mind over time, these practices may result in the breakdown of vital faculties of discrimination and destroy fundamental pathways of human awareness.

We can identify three distinct varieties of information disease in America today, each of which may follow from the snapping moment, although they do not necessarily depend on the occurrence of a single intense experience of drastic change. The most prevalent is the *sustained altered state* of awareness. This altered state is not one of enlightenment or "mind expansion." On the contrary, it is the state of narrowed or reduced awareness clearly visible among many of America's young cult members, and in our view it represents the first stage in the reorganization of personality. Another form of information disease is more extreme. As we have come to understand it, it represents a lasting impairment or destruction of a vital process of the mind. This is the *delusional phase,* characterized by an absence of feeling and emotion. It may result in vivid hallucinations and in irrational, violent, and self-destructive behavior. This form is prevalent in many cults and is present in a number of mass therapies, and in recent years, in our view, it has been the cause of some of America's most startling news headlines. A third type of information disease takes the form of *not thinking* or shutting off the mind and may result in the complete dissolution of personality. This state is common among cult members and practitioners of many self-help therapies. In our opinion, it is the most damaging form of all. In keeping with the dynamics of the catastrophe curve, each of these varieties of information disease may come about suddenly or in slow motion; in their extremes, two or all three may occur in combination.

On the basis of our research, we feel that it is reasonable to suggest that hundreds of thousands of Americans may have been caught in the throes of information disease in this decade—and that millions have experienced some of its symptoms. In the pages that follow, we will examine these varieties of information disease one by one and present testimony that illustrates the personal nature of each. With these examples in view, we hope that other individuals may come to understand how their own afflictions were brought about—and realize that they can happen to anyone.

The Sustained Altered State

In the wake of snapping, after an individual surrenders or lets go, whether in a sudden moment or gradually, he may possibly slip into a level of reduced awareness in which the disorientation and confusion that follow the snapping moment become part of his everyday manner of experiencing the world. This trancelike limbo state represents the suspension of a person's response as an individual and is the first stage in the reorganization of personality.

This is the state of mind that has befallen so many of America's cult members. In this sustained state, the individual's fundamental abilities to question and to act suffer dramatic impairment. At the same time, he becomes almost wholly vulnerable to suggestion and command, and so emotionally dependent on the cult and its leaders that, in many instances, it can indeed be said that the cult member can no longer be deemed responsible for either his action or expression.

Once an individual's freedom of thought has been broken in this manner, most cults then add a torrent of new information in the form of direct indoctrination. In lectures, discussion groups, and personal confrontations, the new convert receives the values, beliefs, doctrines, and stiff regulations of the cult.

One of the most important factors in creating and maintaining this sustained altered state is the severing of the cult member's personal relationships outside the closed world of the cult. By cutting off contact with parents, friends, and other social connections, the cult strips the convert of his most vital sources of self-reflection. Isolated in this way and cut off from all external sources of information, an individual may easily be remade by the cult in their own tightly controlled image. Then, once firmly established, this new state of mind becomes self-sustaining.

A former Krishna devotee described to us how he experienced the beginning of this process.

"The temple leaders talked in a soft voice, smiling, in a kind of I-don't-care tone," he said. "There was something strange about it, because I completely forgot about everything. In a period of about two hours they convinced me to call my parents and say that I was moving in. They had everything figured out; they knew exactly what my mother was going to say. They said, 'She's probably going to ask you if you have a toothbrush, and you just tell her that we have everything here.' Then they said, 'Don't tell her that you're moving in right away, because she'll get upset. What you do is tell her that you're going to stay here for a couple of days to listen to a seminar.' So I called my mother and said, 'Hey, listen, I'm going to be staying here overnight to listen to a seminar.' And she said, 'But you don't have a toothbrush!' And I said, 'Yeah, they've got everything here.'"

For this new convert, the intense group pressure made him feel physically helpless.

"I got the feeling I couldn't leave," he told us. "Like there was no way I could get out. I don't know what that was. I had the feeling that it was God calling me, and that the whole outside world had sort of vaporized."

Once the individual has been cut off from the world in this manner, the cult's ritual practices tend to ensure that he will not return to it on his own. Initiation into the cult usually involves a change of appearance. In Krishna, for example, the new devotee's head is shaved and his clothes and money are taken away. As in many cults, he receives a new name as well, usually during a solemn ceremony. Definitions of basic words such as "love" and "family" may be changed in accordance with the teachings of the cult. In some cults, parents become agents of Satan, and their expression of love is defined as a desire to kill the one true God. Bible scriptures are often reinterpreted to exclude from care, concern, and communication anyone who isn't a member of the cult. These alterations of the outside world, each in itself a small or subtle change, succeed in creating an impenetrable barrier between the cult member and his former identity.

One of the most comprehensive programs of manipulating language is carried out by the Pacific Northwest cult called the Love Family, or Love Israel. We spoke with one young woman whose story demonstrated the innocent manner in which most young people begin their descent into the cult state. While traveling through a town in Washington, she told us, she sought overnight lodging in a safe Christian community. Directed to the Love Family house by some local townspeople, she was immediately impressed.

"They had a sign on the door that said, *Anyone who wants to worship Jesus is welcome here,*" she recalled. "I was struck by how clean and orderly the house was. No two people ever talked at the same time, and everyone seemed so self-assured. That really got me. They just had a certain air that they were important people."

At their invitation, this young woman remained at the Love Family house for four days, she told us, growing increasingly attracted to their humble lifestyle and warm hospitality. The women in the house all wore long skirts, and every meal was considered a communion, complete with sacraments of bread and wine. Discipline was severe, but the family life appealed to her. Before long she made a decision to join the family and, as she acknowledged, "give up everything for God." At that point of surrender, the Love Family introduced her to their private world of thought and language.

"Everyone was given biblical names or virtue names," she said, "like Strength, Courage, or Serendipity." (Or Logic—see chapter 6.) "When you joined the group, you were baptized into the Love Family, not the church or Christ. They used the word 'Christ' interchangeably with 'the Family.' They had different names for everything. The days of the week were named after the seven churches in the Book of Revelation; the months were named after the twelve tribes of Israel. Even their calendar was slightly different: each month had thirty days, with the extra days at the end for a Passover celebration. We also had different ages, which were computed according to the book of Matthew."

After she joined the Love Family and adopted their new vocabulary and schemes of organization, this young woman began to see that the inside of the cult was not as wholesome as she had been led to believe. Inhalation of tuolene, a powerful cleaning solvent, was incorporated into cult rituals, and experimentation with various hallucinogenic plants and chemicals was a part of daily life. Activities were rigidly controlled, and members were never left alone, with the elder males in the cult dominating an unyielding social and sexual hierarchy.

"There was no possibility of seeing or understanding what was really happening," this young woman told us. "You knew who your boss was, you had your chores, and you were expected to be doing something at any given time. But there were always surprises. They changed the rules at random without warning, and the propaganda was always being drummed into us. Their beliefs and information came at us from outside, and there was never any time to sift through it. There was never any time to step back and look at it and see if any of it fit together. The Family would always say, 'What's inside your mind is lies. We are your mind. The group is your mind.'"

In the Love Family, as in most cults, women are given roles of complete subservience. No cult, however, is more blatant in its discrimination against women than the Hare Krishna, as one former devotee testifies.

"I always said in the beginning that the way they treat women was one thing I would never swallow," we were told by an attractive young woman who had long since turned in her Krishna robes, "this never looking the man in the eye, always looking at his feet, and never being alone with a man. But sooner or later, all the women fall into their little thing, walking two steps behind the man—the whole bit."

While the women are hard at work within the cult temples or family houses, the men in most cults are sent out into the world to solicit donations and new members. Before the cult member may enter a larger environment, he is first instilled with guilt and fear, to keep him from questioning his participation in the cult and to negate the criticism of outsiders. Members of the Unification Church and other allegedly Christian cults have the fear of Satan drummed into them. Among the Hare Krishna, as in other Eastern cults, members are told to shun outsiders, all of whom are reputed to be in a state of "maya" or alienation from God, a kind of spiritual contamination.

An ex-Krishna devotee recalled for us his excursions into the outside world.

"Everyone got dressed up in their robes and shaved heads and we'd go out chanting in public," he said. "We'd dance in the streets and hand out flyers and in general attract a lot of attention. All of a sudden, here we were in the middle of this bustling city, and we were the only people doing this stuff and everyone looked at us like we were crazy. There was no way out of it. You felt really solemnly religious like you were supposed to, as if you were doing these people a fantastic favor because every time they heard the words *Hare Krishna* they were supposed to make tremendous spiritual advancement. There was a kind of facelessness about the whole thing, though. We got used to the idea of feeling very foreign. And the more you got used to being there like that, the more accustomed you got to being in the cult."

For this young man, journeys away from the temple only intensified his identification with the cult.

"I had to put up a mental barrier shielding myself from the world," he admitted. "I'd have to hold everything out, because it was all hanging over me. The whole street atmosphere, the entire outside world was sitting there, just waiting to fall on me—and I used Krishna as a protection from the whole thing. I didn't realize I was doing it, but if I didn't do it I would have gone crazy for sure. One time there was a group of devotees going out on a bus, and I remember getting this tremendously threatened feeling as we were driving through the city. I knew I'd left that world, and I really couldn't go back because it looked so terrifying."

Another former cult member described for us his very physical reaction as he slipped into his cult state of mind.

"I got a distinct sense of things actually getting dark as I was going into this thing," he recalled.

"It seemed like everything was getting a little bit darker, as if the weather had gotten really overcast, but this bleakness was only perceptual. At the same time, I started to notice more dark things around me, outside, in my room, sort of a heavy, gray mood."

Whether this darkening was actual or metaphorical is difficult to establish, although researchers have found evidence of a reduction in the peripheral vision of cult members. The effect, however, gives an inside view of a quality that has been reported by many who have had contact with cult members. As the individual enters this sustained altered state, the appearance of his eyes may undergo a dramatic change, taking on a glassy look, a cloudiness, giving the impression that the person is "not really looking back at you." This change in the eyes, more than anything, would seem to indicate an alteration in the individual's capacity to receive, process, and communicate information.

In our interviews we heard many versions of the physical transformations of cult members' eyes. One mother in the Midwest swore to us—and observers confirmed—that during a confrontation with her daughter, who was in a Christian cult, she actually saw a beam of red light shoot out of the girl's eyes. Even the young cult member herself was stunned by the phenomenon.

A former Krishna devotee recalled the effect his altered state had on his childhood friend, the family dog.

"Our dog wouldn't have anything to do with me for days after I joined the cult," he told us. "I came home and the dog didn't like me at all. He would growl at me and then bark as if I were a stranger. It wasn't because of smells or my looks or anything. When I first came back home I still had my hair, but it didn't make any difference. Then when I came back after I left the cult, I didn't have any hair at all, but he recognized me just the same and we were pals again."

In addition to changes in appearance, cult members may be affected by a number of other physical changes in their sustained altered states. Quite often, their voices change markedly. The pitch rises and the tone becomes more shrill, an alteration many believe to be a reflection of mounting tension within the individual. Entire speech patterns may change dramatically as well, and posture and mannerisms may be transformed beyond recognition. With each new day the cult member may drift further out of touch with his former thoughts, feelings, and personality, as the cult environment pours in new information to destroy and replace the old. In this state, the individual may be virtually incapable of genuine communication or relationship. His speech becomes a mindless parroting of cult doctrine, his thoughts never deviate from what he has been told by his superiors. Now his alienation from the outside world and his former self reaches its maximum, and his identification with the cult becomes all-encompassing and self-sustaining.

During this time, when long-standing pathways of information processing in the brain are being destroyed and reconstructed, it is still possible to deprogram an individual and restore his freedom of thought and feeling. This condition may persist for months, or even years—perhaps throughout the individual's involvement in the cult. At some point, however, as we have observed among a number of veteran cult members, the individual's impaired thought processes become less noticeable, and eventually the telling signs of his altered state may disappear. Then, the transformation complete, he is, to all but those who knew him before, quite undetectably a new person altogether.

The Delusional Phase

This second and more advanced form of information disease concerns reality and illusion and an individual's ability to distinguish between the two. In addition to the fundamental processes of perception that bring information to the brain, the human brain also possesses the remarkable capacity to create information of its own. This capacity is generally referred to as *imagination*.

Man's power of imagination would seem to provide still more evidence of the holographic nature of the brain. The fusion of apparently unrelated components into new images—dreams offer the most vivid example—suggests an almost obvious projection of information within the brain. But more importantly, our human capacity of imagination demonstrates the brain's organic ability to recombine the metabolized components of experience, merging people, places, objects, and symbols into new images and forms. The reach of imagination is limitless. Every physical sensation can be matched or superseded by an imagined one. Each image and idea can be instantly transformed into another. The human brain, with its enormous information-storage capacity, its incomparable powers of association, and its consummate playful nature, is capable of conjuring up all kinds of visions and sensations in superabundant detail.

For most people, the ability to distinguish between reality and imagination, between fact and fancy, is so basic that it can be taken for granted. At times, an individual may be so awestruck by the sharpness or novelty of an experience as to question whether he is awake or dreaming, but on those rare occasions a quick pinch is usually enough to set matters straight. In fact, this elementary form of verification is the best of all possible arbiters, for the ability to distinguish between perception and imagination is inseparably dependent on our ability to feel. Feeling, as we have come to understand it, is the ultimate human response, the champion of all information-processing capacities, precisely because it is the most comprehensive activity human beings perform, representing the fullest integration of body and mind.

Yet, powerful and primary as the capacity for feeling may be, it is a surprisingly simple and straightforward matter to weaken or destroy it. A direct attack on human feeling may leave an individual stunned and numb, momentarily incapable of any emotion. A more concentrated and prolonged assault may bring about a lasting alteration of this capacity and, in doing so, break down the individual's fundamental ability to distinguish between reality and fantasy. This is the delusional phase of information disease, a direct consequence of the destruction of human feeling.

Scientology defines itself as "the study of knowledge in its fullest sense." The Church of Scientology, founded in the 1950s by a science-fiction writer named L. Ron Hubbard, consists of two major branches of activity: the "pandenominational religious philosophy" contained in Hubbard's books and the practices of the church and the "applied philosophy," which is defined as "methods which enable the individual to attain a higher state of existence through personal processing." Since its early days, Scientology has grown to include church organizations and processing centers on every continent. It now claims to be the largest "self-betterment organization" in the world.

It may also be one of the most powerful religious cults in operation today. The tales that have come out of Scientology are nearly impossible to believe in relation to a religious movement that has accumulated great credibility and respect around the world in less than twenty-five years. It has also gathered an estimated 3.5 million followers. Nevertheless, the reports we have seen and heard in the course of our research, both in the media and in personal interviews with former Scientology higher-ups, are replete with allegations of psychological devastation, economic exploitation, and personal and legal harassment of former members and journalists who speak out against the cult.

To most Americans, however, Scientologists are known for the aggressive street encounters in which they attempt to recruit customers for the organization's self-betterment program. The course, known as Dianetics, employs a technique called "auditing," ostensibly to raise an individual to higher levels of being. Halfway up the ladder of Scientology, after the individual has passed through roughly eight levels of auditing, is the level of "clear," a state of existence in which the subject is supposedly capable of transcending all the quirks and pains of his past. At the top of the Scientology ladder, about eight levels above clear, is "O.T." or "Operating Thetan," which Hubbard defines as "The person himself—not his body or name, the physical universe, his mind, or anything else—that which is aware of being aware; the identity that IS the individual" (Hubbard's punctuation and emphasis).

Participants in Scientology's self-betterment program pay for auditing by the hour. The cost of attaining the level of clear, which may require several hundred hours of auditing, has been known to run into tens of thousands of dollars. Some individual payments for Scientology techniques have been reported to exceed $100,000.

But for the casual customer choosing among a vast assortment of currently available techniques for self-betterment, the Scientology procedure is well-known, attractive, and inexpensive to begin. The auditing process takes place in private sessions between subject and auditor, in which the subject's emotional responses are registered on a device called an E-meter, a kind of crude lie detector. The subject holds the terminals of the E-meter in his hands, and the rise or fall of electrical conductivity in response to the perspiration emitted from the palms is explained as a measure of emotional response to the auditor's course of questioning. The average response registers in the normal range on the meter, with abnormal indicating an overreaction, "uptightness," or sign of trauma on the part of the subject.

The goal of auditing is to bring all the individual's responses within the range of normal on the E-meter. Using a technique that bears only superficial resemblance to the popular method of biological regulation known as biofeedback, the individual watches the E-meter and follows precise instructions given by the auditor to learn how to reduce his emotional response to the auditor's questions about past and painful experiences. When the individual has mastered this ability, he becomes eligible for admission to the elite club of Scientology clears.

We met a number of Scientologists in our travels, among them students, housewives, professionals, and even some respected scientists. All the individuals we talked to fell into one or the other of two categories: those who had just begun the auditing process or who were only occasional customers of Dianetics, and those who had become active members of the church or gone on to the advanced levels of auditing. While visiting a large city out West, we were introduced to Karla Kraus (not her real name), a housewife in her late thirties whom we found to be an expressive representative of the novice Scientologists we interviewed. When we met, Karla Kraus had been undergoing Scientology's auditing process for almost a year. She understood it to be a concentrated course of study and one-to-one therapy. She was attending auditing sessions several times a week and looking forward to the higher levels of existence she saw before her.

As we sipped coffee in her living room, she explained to us the motivation behind her excursion into Dianetics.

"In Scientology you confront past experiences until there is no charge left on them," she said. "Then, once you get all the charge off that painful instance, it will never be a source of any aberrant type of behavior."

She spoke matter-of-factly, careful not to misrepresent the auditing process.

"I hope to become a clear," she told us avidly, adding, "To the casual observer, this new terminology can sound almost like *1984*, but these are simply new terms that have not been identified before."

As Karla Kraus understood it, "Clear means that your active mind is clear of all aberrational behavior, and all psychosomatic illness disappears." After two or three hundred hours of auditing, she said, she hoped to reach a permanent level of clear existence. Already, after less than one hundred hours, she had had glimpses of what that powerful state of being might be like. She recounted one of her most significant insights.

"One time during auditing I was returned to a prenatal experience," she said. "I heard my mother's voice just as clear as a bell. I've always had a vague feeling of not belonging, but I heard my mother say, 'I don't want babies.' I experienced pain and pressure, which my auditor told me was my mother sneezing or having intercourse or morning sickness. Through auditing they have determined that the fetus actually experiences and remembers these things."

Karla Kraus also revealed that her developing ability to control her emotional response to traumatic events in her earlier years was changing her ability to experience her present life in the everyday world. She viewed the change as positive.

"There are some residual effects to auditing," she told us. "Things get charged up while you're auditing which spill out onto your daily life. I can feel a change in my state of being, in my level of awareness. Where things used to cave me in, now there's nothing. Most disciplines give you ways to deal with negative emotions after they occur. This is something that I can go through which prevents those negative emotions from occurring in the first place."

She saw her potential for achievement in Scientology as infinite. She didn't know whether she would have the time or money to work her way up to the highest levels of Scientology awareness, but she looked with envy upon those who had the dedication to stick with it to the top. She offered us her perspective on life at those higher levels.

"It's really superpowerful stuff," she said. "For instance, individuals who are Operating Thetans are able to exteriorize at will. They can actually go into another person's body and find areas of disturbance and disease."

It is this level of O.T. to which devout Scientologists aspire. "When you are O.T.," she said, "if you believe something and really *know* it to be so, it *will* be so! Scientology leads you to a level of consciousness that is beyond faith. These people are into certainty. They *know.*"

In our opinion, however, Scientology does not lead people beyond faith to absolute certainty—it leads them to levels of increasingly realistic hallucination. The crude technology of auditing is a direct assault on human feeling and on the individual's ability to distinguish between what he is actually experiencing and what he is only imagining. The bizarre folklore of Scientology is a *tour de force* of science fiction. Many people at its highest levels are confident that trillions of years ago they all knew each other on other planets, that they have the power to see at submicroscopic levels and leave their bodies at will. As we delved deeper into Scientology the evidence we gathered suggested to us that, more than anything else, this combination church and therapeutic service trains people in hallucination and delusion.

We gained an inside view of Scientology in a long telephone interview with a young man we will call Howard Davenport. During five and a half years as an active, dedicated Scientologist, he became a Dianetics auditor and moved freely within the highest levels of the organization.

Howard Davenport had been recruited by street encounter, the same manner of solicitation used by almost all religious cults. At first, however, the Scientology appeal was neither religious nor psychological. Like many other cults which have turned to indirect recruitment methods, Scientology's come-on was purely social. Davenport, a shy young man in his mid-twenties, recalled the moment of initial contact.

"I was alone at the time and pretty depressed," he told us, "and a very good-looking girl gave me an address and said, 'Be there at seven thirty.' I asked her what was there and she said, 'Just a bunch of groovy people.' I envisioned this big party, but it turned out to be a Scientology meeting. We heard a lecture and saw the introductory movie, which was narrated by Stephen Boyd, the movie star. It started out in a planetarium and he was standing there as if Scientology had found the stars or something."

After the movie, Davenport continued, the Scientology leaders brought out an E-meter and demonstrated how it worked. The guests were given an opportunity to try it out, and the Scientologists interpreted their readings.

"They put me on the thing and I registered way off the dial," he said. "They told me it meant that I was in an extremely messed-up state of mind, and they convinced me to take a fifteen-dollar 'communication' course. This very good-looking girl took me into a little private room. She got up close to me and said she could see that I was depressed, that my life was in very bad shape, and that if I just took this course all my problems would be solved. I felt a great uplifting, like, *Wow, finally here's someone who can take care of my problems!*"

Soon afterward, Davenport began his journey into Scientology via a series of highly structured, pseudoscientific drills, trainings, and processes. The first one, called TR-0 or Training Regimen Zero, was part of the basic communication course designed to develop the subject's ability to interact with others.

"On the first night, they sat me down across from this other guy. They told us it wasn't staring, but it was simply staring at each other—two hours that first night. They take two novices and put them together, because they want you to feel like you're working at the same speed. At first it was very uncomfortable. We sat with our knees touching and we weren't allowed to blink. We were told, 'You don't think, you don't move, you don't twitch, you don't giggle. Just be there with the other person.' "

Davenport recalled the confusion that resulted from his first evening of "communication."

"After I had sat there for two hours, I couldn't figure out what the purpose was. I thought it was to help you learn how to look somebody in the eye when you talk to them, but it took me a couple of years in Scientology before I grasped the purpose of that drill. It was to teach you how to be able to look really *high.*"

From this initial course, Davenport went on to begin the auditing process. During auditing, he explained, the close personal contact continued.

"Each auditing session is run exactly like the last one," he said. "They're supposed to be two and a half hours long, but they can vary. The auditor sits in a little room that is decorated in a certain way so that they're all alike and interchangeable. Then he puts you on the E-meter and all you can do is look at each other, because there's not enough space in the room to look away. The auditor is not permitted to say anything except certain standard lines that are part of an exact script every time. You walk into the room and he says, 'Are you well-fed and rested?' and you say, 'Yes.' If he sees a reaction on the meter, he says, 'What did you think of there?' If there's no reaction on the meter, he says, 'Okay, that's good!' "

According to Davenport, the auditor continues to ask a series of questions about the person's past and present and waits until the meter shows no sign of a reaction. Emerging from several hours of this intense process may be an exhilarating experience, in some instances even a snapping moment of sorts.

"That's when you feel the highest," Davenport explained, "when your thought processes finally break and you go, *Wow, I feel good!* There's a feeling of peacefulness about it."

Continued auditing can bring on a condition that resembles the reduced awareness in the cults, complete with the accompanying changes in appearance and demeanor. In Scientology, however, there is a special technique that may disguise the changes.

"They have a drill to make your eyes look natural," he said. "You have someone sit three feet away from you, and you sit there and look at each other. Then one person acts as a coach and the other as the student, and he'll say, 'Start!' and if you blink your eyes in an unnatural way, he'll say, 'Flunk! You blinked in an unnatural way. Start!' He coaches you for hours like that. He'll say, 'Flunk! You're starting to smile. Start!' Like robots."

Almost all Scientology drills consist of similar set patterns of repeated commands and responses that continue for hour upon hour. According to Davenport, other Scientology drills are practiced with less innocent objectives in mind. Number three, for example, teaches the subject how to gain control over other people, a primary focus of other cult sales and recruitment techniques. The Scientology method, however, has no religious or spiritual pretentions.

"Training Drill Three," said Davenport, "is nicknamed Do Fish Swim? The whole drill is spelled out; its purpose is to get your question answered. It teaches you the various things a person can do to avoid answering your question, and it gives you a technique which you later use in counseling other people. You can force them to talk about anything at all, even if they don't want to talk about it."

The technique of Training Drill Three deals with control through communication.

"In this drill," Davenport continued, "if I were the coach and you were the student, you would look at me very naturally and say, 'Do fish swim?' You couldn't sound strained or in any way unnatural. Then you would have to acknowledge me for answering you."

Looking back, Davenport still recognized some of the practical value of these initial Scientology techniques. They gave him peaceful, relaxed feelings, he said, and they actually did improve his ability to communicate and assert himself socially. But he went on to explain what he considered the danger of the process.

"This is the thing," he stressed. "If people just took the communication course and then left Scientology for life, it would not be such a bad thing, because the beginning course does help you out. But then the technique itself sucks you into further and further courses. The counseling never ends."

As Davenport became more deeply involved in the auditing process, he also grew more dependent on the organization. Unlike most other cults, Scientology does not require that its members live in communal settings. But as people become more involved, they often tend naturally to associate more and more with other Scientologists. Davenport told us about one surprising experience that drew him further into the organization.

"When I first got in, I was with a friend whom I met in the course; we were talking to one of the guys who was way up in the organization. My friend asked him, 'Is it anything like drugs at those higher levels?' and he said, 'It's just like acid, man. I see colors all around just like particles flowing across the room.' "

Before long, Davenport began to experience those higher levels for himself, as he progressed to drills designed to teach him how to leave his body and travel through space. Looking back, he observed that in all likelihood the events never took place as described.

"They have drills that create images of things in your mind that do not exist," he said, "and they have drills that even change your image of what does exist. For instance, if I see this door that I'm looking at as being the way it is, Scientology would talk about it in such a way that I would see it in another light, *their* light."

This transformation of awareness seems to be accomplished by a specific and highly refined Scientology technique.

"It happens in degrees," he said, "and it may take years to achieve, although some people can do it in a matter of weeks. First you start just looking at something the way it is. Then they tell you that you can actually see all the molecules flowing through it—that's just one example of something they would tell you that you should see. So you start looking for the molecules, and you try all these different ways to imagine it. At first you know that you're just trying to imagine it, but then suddenly you'll have this experience. You'll be sitting there and one day you'll look over at the door and you'll just see the molecules. It's a hallucination, but you actually see them, and the leaders of Scientology say, 'How do you know it's just a hallucination?' And they have a point."

The point is that by that time it may no longer be possible for the individual to distinguish what is real. Once this barrier is broken through, a person's sense of reality may seem wholly arbitrary. His daily life may become intermixed with vivid hallucinations. Davenport experienced this state of mind as well.

"One day I was walking around convinced that I was controlling the weather," he said. "I was out selling burglar alarms door to door to make money to pay Scientology so I could buy their higher levels. It looked like it was going to rain all day long, and I felt I was using my own thought to hold the rain back. Another time, as I was going to bed, I wanted to talk to a friend, so I thought to myself, *I'll go exterior,* and I started getting into these things about leaving my body and visiting people. The next day if they didn't say anything to me about it I would say that they weren't aware enough to have seen it."

Davenport told us that he was reluctant to call all his strange experiences hallucinations, especially in the light of the wealth of popular testimony concerning astral travel and telepathy. What he denied, however, was the validity of Scientology's fantastic world view and cosmology, despite the fact that many of the Thetans he worked with in the organization were strict adherents of Hubbard's sci-fi philosophy.

"People would remember experiences on other planets, or marriages from three or four lifetimes ago," he recalled. "They'd talk about people from

Xerkeson who flew down to Earth in doll-bodies and drove around in long black limousines observing the people on our planet. When you use the techniques, finally you start seeing these things, too. And you say, 'Yeah, he's right. How come we were never aware enough to see them before?' "

The delusional phase of information disease may result from a variety of techniques. In our opinion, Scientology has refined the most reliable methods for bringing it about, but it makes its appearance elsewhere across the spectrum of America's cults.

Similar techniques are also employed in many of today's popular therapies and self-help techniques. One method, called guided fantasy, is a clearly identified technique for using the power of the imagination to bring about changes in consciousness and personality. Another method, called psychodrama, is also one of the most potent and widely accepted techniques of modern psychiatric therapy. Psychodrama takes the imagination one step further than fantasy, engaging the individual in the physical dramatization of his psychological problems and past traumas. The power of this method lies in the conflicting patterns of information it gives rise to in the context of intense group interaction.

We spoke with a number of individuals who reported experiencing overwhelming discomfort, anxiety, and even intense snapping moments during role-playing and psychodrama. The experience left some in a state of disorientation for several months, during which they found themselves constantly struggling to test the reality of their perceptions. Others admitted to being virtually paralyzed by the specter of images and emotions that defied validation. Only with the passage of time and the support of people close to them were they able once again to mark off the boundaries between what was genuine and certain and what was not.

Symptoms of the delusional phase of information disease can also be identified in another highly developed and controversial outgrowth of the human potential movement, Fritz Perls's Gestalt therapy, which was refined at Esalen during its heyday of experimentation. Among the many techniques of Gestalt, one toys directly with basic mechanisms of perception. A former participant in this therapy told us about a jarring moment in her training.

"I had only been in Gestalt for about a week," she said, "but they had this technique where you had to find a two-colored thing and stare at the two colors until they reversed. I spent a whole day trying to do this, looking at this two-colored pillow. Then suddenly it happened. I looked down at this pillow and the colors switched around. I jumped back and went, *Whoa!* I'd never had anything like that actually happen, and I guess I was a little shocked by it. I tried to do it for the rest of the day, but I was never able to do it again."

And then there's est, which claims to borrow a little something from every branch of the consciousness movement but which in many ways is a direct offspring of Scientology. In the early seventies, Erhard had what is described as a brief flirtation with Scientology, and he now acknowledges that many of his est "processes" derive from Scientology's drills and regimens. Est appears to produce its own form of the delusional phase of information disease. There have been documented instances of est graduates suddenly coming to believe they could walk through panes of glass, breathe naturally under water, or perform similar feats in defiance of nature. Est's greatest challenge to the imagination, however, and perhaps its most compelling feature, is what we consider the grand delusions it fosters at the intellectual level. Its most controversial premise is its interpretation of self-responsibility; est training emphasizes that the trainees are responsible for their own fates and that, in fact, the individual "creates" everything that happens to him. In est sessions, trainers drive home the implications of this lesson. Est graduates report hearing that rape victims desire to be raped, that Vietnamese babies created the napalm that fell on them in the war, and that the Jews of Europe wanted to die in Hitler's concentration camps.

We spoke with a nationally prominent est graduate who found it only slightly uncomfortable to accept this line of reasoning.

"Yeah, now that's one thing where with my head I believe it," he told us, "although I haven't quite gotten my body to feel it yet. But I think it's true. I've talked to people about that, people who had parents in Germany who got destroyed, and I said, 'Would you accept the possibility that that's what they chose to do? They *wanted* to stay there and get destroyed?' The next day, one particular woman came back to me and said, 'I remember, they both had tickets to Argentina and they didn't use them.'"

During the ordeal of an est weekend, these perversions of logic make as much sense as anything else after a while, and they sink in along with the physical and emotional experience of the training. Once planted, however, this information takes root and, as we observed, becomes highly infectious, spreading into other areas of an individual's thought and understanding. This particular est graduate was quick to point out that the implications of est's philosophy of self-responsibility are enormous.

"If you really understand self-responsibility," he told us with unwavering conviction, "it means that nobody has to die unless he chooses to; all deaths are suicides, and there are no accidents. And you can fly if you allow yourself to know how."

Not Thinking

By far the most widespread and frightening threat to personality posed by America's cults and mass therapies is the impairment of an individual's most fundamental capacity of mind: quite simply, his ability to think, not just to think for himself, but to think at all—to make sense out of the information he receives from experience and to use that information in a way that will best serve his survival and personal growth.

Almost every major cult and group teaches some form of not thinking, mind control, or, as it is often called, self-hypnosis as part of its regular program of activity. This process may take the form of prayer, chanting, speaking in tongues, or simple meditation. Initially, this quiescent state may provide physical and emotional benefits, feelings of inner peace and relaxation, or a calming of nervous tension. After a while, continued practice of the technique may even bring on various forms of euphoria: an emotional high, a feeling of bliss, or lightness of mind or body. In this state, an individual may have sensations of being in intangible realms or alternate realities. He may see divine visions, receive spiritual communications, or experience breakthrough moments of revelation or enlightenment.

With the extended cessation of thought, however, the cumulative effects of inactivity may wear upon the brain until a point is reached when it readjusts to its new condition suddenly and sharply. When that happens, as we have discovered, its information-processing capacities may enter a state of disruption or complete suspension, producing individual states of mind that incorporate all the other forms of information disease: disorientation, detachment, withdrawal, delusion, and the trancelike, altered state visible in the cults.

In America today, aware, intelligent individuals of all ages are being persuaded to stop thinking voluntarily. While many do so in their escape from the real world through authoritarian cult religions or extravagant psychological fantasies, an even larger number stop thinking with no immediate religious or psychological goals in mind. Their intentions are, instead, quite down to earth and practical as they pursue training in simple techniques for reducing brain activity that may produce immediately desired and beneficial effects. What they do not realize, however, is how the brain responds to that experience: positively, at first, but after a very short time the benefits may drop away as the brain readjusts in a catastrophic manner. When that happens, not thinking becomes the norm, and with it there is a reduction in both feeling and awareness. Moreover, once a person's brain enters this state, the individual may be incapable of coming out of it.

This can be the cumulative effect on personality of the experience known as meditation.

To gain a close-up view of meditation, we turned to a veteran—and an insider.

A man we call Barry Robertson practiced Transcendental Meditation for four and a half years, for nearly two of which he earned his living as a beginning instructor in the popular technique. Transcendental Meditation is the largest and most successful self-help therapy in America. Transported from the Himalayas to the West in the late fifties by its developer, Maharishi Mahesh Yogi, TM has been hailed in the United States as an instant, non-chemical tranquilizer for the relief of nervous tension. The basic meditation technique costs $125 to learn, and in 1977 the TM organization reported that in the United States alone 30,000 new meditators were signing up for the introductory course each month. According to a recent Gallup poll, 4 percent of Americans have become involved in Transcendental Meditation.

At the beginning of our talk, Barry Robertson cautioned us that his experiences in TM would come as a shock to most casual practitioners of the technique. This was because, according to him, most American meditators never succeed in actually *transcending.* Most, he said, only use their twice-daily sessions of meditation for simple rest and relaxation. Robertson, an energetic and resolute young man in his late twenties, slim, fair-haired, and eager to be heard, explained in detail why the transcendental form represents a particularly hazardous technique among the varieties of meditation.

"There are four basic types of meditation," he began, "and there is a major difference between TM and the others. First, there's *contemplation,* in which you take a sentence or a parable and you think about it. You just go into your mind and close out the outside world and you think. A good example which I find very funny is one the Zen Buddhists use: 'What is the sound of one hand clapping?' They think about it, they meditate on it for hours, and they come out with nothing. That's contemplation.

"Contemplation is similar to another type of meditation that I would classify as *Christian meditation,*" he continued. "This consists of studying the scriptures and pondering God and thinking about how you can use that scripture to give meaning to your life. The third type of meditation is simply *concentration,* where you concentrate on one spot on the wall or on your navel or on a spot in the middle of your forehead. You concentrate on one thing and you try to get the ability to hold your thoughts there. If you find yourself wandering off into other things, you bring your mind right back to that one point."

As Robertson saw it, however, Transcendental Meditation is none of the above.

"In TM you *empty* your mind," he stressed. "You don't concentrate on anything because that would take up mental energy and make you control your mind. TM is switching your mind into neutral. You have no control over it; you try not to have control over it. You try to let your mind just go flat, with no thoughts whatsoever. When you concentrate on anything, you have at least one thought. TM attempts to go beyond that."

According to Robertson, to achieve this emptying of the mind, each student of Transcendental Meditation is given what is said to be his own custom-tailored *mantra*, a Sanskrit word which the Maharishi has defined as a meaningless sound with a "vibratory effect" that will help the mind reach a quiet state. According to the TM organization, the various sound qualities of particular mantras have been known for over five thousand years.

"To do TM," Robertson told us, "you repeat the mantra over and over in your mind, and as with anything, if you hear a steady noise over and over again, eventually your ears won't hear that noise anymore. For instance, I live by a railroad track, and when I first moved there the noise was terrible. Now I don't even know when the trains go by. My ears have been turned off to that sound."

Unlike a passing train, Robertson said, TM mantras are pleasant sounds with no harsh vibrations or side effects. As the mind becomes accustomed to a particular one, the meditator's awareness begins to change.

"You start the mantra in your mind, saying it over and over," he explained. "Then all of a sudden it gets quieter. At first it's a voice in your head, you're subvocalizing it in your mind. Then your mind just kind of floats on this nice sensation."

As Robertson described it, the first effect of TM is a soothing emotional high brought on by the brain's response to repetition. But for the new student of TM, achieving this state of relaxation may require concentrated and laborious effort. He must close his eyes, sit in a quiet place, and actively undertake to still the normally busy faculties of the mind. With time and practice, however, the individual acquires the ability to keep the mantra present without difficulty. Then, slowly, as the mind adjusts to the repetition, the sound of the individual's "inner voice" becomes quieter still. At this level of relaxation, the technique can be beneficial, a kind of tranquilizer, relieving stress and providing the "restful alertness" TM claims to offer.

"A lot of people do experience these positive effects for a long time," said Robertson. "A certain amount of relaxation and clarity of mind results when you reach this mental state."

Robertson noted, however, that for some reason, after about six months at this level of achievement, almost half of all Transcendental Meditators stop practicing the technique. Despite its immediate benefits, the initial high wears off quickly, and the twice-daily, twenty-minute meditation periods become a chore.

"People stop because they find it boring," he said. "Those who go into TM because they're uptight can't stick with the technique, and those who become involved in it for spiritual reasons usually drop it for something else."

According to Robertson, those who stay with meditation for any length of time become vulnerable to its long-range impact. He described his impression of the cumulative effects of TM in startling terms.

"To say that TM is a technique of rest is like saying that shooting off a forty-four magnum is just exercise for the forefinger," he said. "At first the new student has to work very hard at meditating, but eventually the mantra will just take over the mind. As you get better at it, your mantra is just there all the time. It gets to be like an impulse, something very subtle happening in your mind. It's not even a sound, it's just a kind of rhythm. Then it gets to a place where it's very, very still, and then, finally, nothing."

Robertson went on to describe some of TM's roots in Hinduism and Tantra Yoga, stressing what he saw as the Maharishi's intention to keep the "unenlightened classes" ignorant of TM's religious underpinnings. Then he explained why he believes that among Western meditators the mantras may have a particularly destructive effect.

"Pretty soon your mind gets to a place where it no longer associates meaning to anything," he said. "You just have this sound going on in your mind, and you get to a place where there's no longer concrete meaning. You're just abstractly experiencing nothing. You would think that a person would become afraid in this emptiness or vacuum, but this happens to your feelings, too. You reach a state where you're not feeling anything either. By the way, this is the state the Maharishi calls *bliss.*"

As Robertson described it, the TM state of bliss is not a state of profound pleasure. It is a level of awareness devoid not only of all thought but of all feeling and, by default, of all pain.

"At first you don't even know that you're experiencing this transcendental consciousness," he said. "You can't remember it, you can't grasp it. But as you do more and more meditating, you become aware that you are aware of nothing. Then you have arrived at what is known as the *fifth state of consciousness*, where you are able to experience that nothingness, that emptiness. You can peer down into it."

This fifth level of awareness is what TM calls Cosmic Consciousness. In this state, according to Robertson, the individual experiences the world around him from a peculiar orientation.

"You can experience everything around you in Cosmic Consciousness," he said, "but you're totally detached from the world. It's like being at a movie theater when you're watching a boring movie. You're not really part of it. What you are doing, your personality, your emotions, your thoughts are no longer important to you. You can watch yourself do things, you can even watch yourself sleep! You actually—it's hard to explain—*dissolve* would be a good word."

In 1973, Robertson told us, after he had been a casual meditator for a couple of years, he traveled to Spain to enroll in the Maharishi's training course for beginning TM instructors. There he found the course of instruction to be rigorous and methodical, consisting of lectures which had to be memorized word for word, individual training, class-time practice, and meditation for periods of up to ten hours a day. During that period of official instruction, Robertson first experienced the TM state of Cosmic Consciousness.

"I only had glimpses of it," he admitted. "I never had a steady flow. I'd be driving a car and all of a sudden my arms would be holding onto the steering wheel and I'd be sitting back watching it happen. My body seemed more like part of the car than part of me. But again, there were no feelings involved with it. There was no fear, no joy. It was neutral, just happening."

When Robertson returned to the United States and began to pursue his new career as a TM teacher, his ongoing state of bliss and Cosmic Consciousness made life in the everyday world a bit bizarre.

"I was sensing all kinds of telepathic things," he remembered. "I would see energy surrounding people, little thin auras of different pastel colors, and bigger egg-shaped ones made out of huge spirals. It was weird, trying to associate in the ordinary world when you're seeing all these things happening around people."

During this time, as Robertson described it, he became trapped in his state of Cosmic Consciousness. Yet, while he continued to teach TM and advance the cause of the Maharishi, he was beginning to grow disenchanted with the organization.

"I was sold on it," he said. "I honestly believed that the Maharishi was the world's spiritual leader and that TM was going to usher in a new era of mankind. But the constant hassling for customers got to me eventually, and some of the Maharishi's teachings started rubbing me the wrong way. Deep down, I knew I was lying to the public. I was lying when I said that TM wasn't a religion. I was lying about the mantras—they weren't meaningless sounds, they were actually the names of Hindu demigods—and about how many different ones there were—we had sixteen to give out to our students. I felt the Maharishi's goal was to bring about his particular bent of religious belief and get everybody into it, but I objected to the way he was going about it. He gives them a little tidbit and they have a certain experience. Then he gives them a little more, until they're lured into it and caught. When I say caught, I mean that a person's brain reaches this place where it's humanly impossible to come out of it."

Indeed, Robertson was unable to find any direct way out of his predicament in Cosmic Consciousness. Visions of auras and other uncanny telepathic experiences continued to plague him. Finally, he found his personal alternative solution.

"Once you get your brain to the place where you're seeing yourself as nothing, the only way anybody can get delivered from that would be through something of God's doing," he said solemnly. "So I asked the Lord, 'If you want me to be able to see that kind of stuff, halos and all that, I'll do it; but if you don't, take it away.' And then Jesus cleared my mind of all that stuff, and now I no longer see everyone glowing or perceive other people's thoughts."

Barry Robertson discovered an unlikely—but not all that surprising—route from the world of TM's veiled Hinduism to everyday life in the United States. This final episode of Robertson's TM adventure brought him to an almost comical split spirituality.

"I started reading the Bible on the sly," he confessed, "and teaching TM the rest of the time. Then one time I added a prayer to God between my breathing exercise and my meditation. Then finally I got serious with myself, got serious with God, and asked him to reveal Jesus Christ to me. He did in a personal way and I became Born Again. I was alone, supposedly meditating, and I said, 'Jesus, I want to know who you are.' All of a sudden, deep down inside of me, I guess I had what you could call a divine revelation. It was a very strong, powerful experience. The whole thing happened in a second, and I surrendered myself to Him."

After Robertson's personal encounter with Christ, he continued to teach TM until the conflict of interests became too much for him.

"Two weeks later, I was getting ready to give a TM initiation ceremony, where we go through a Hindu ritual. The person was standing right there with his shoes off and he had his fruit and his flower and his handkerchief on a tray before the picture of Maharishi's master. The incense and candles were burning, and I started going through this chant in Sanskrit. But I was only pretending to go through with the ceremony. I was actually praying all the time, praying to Jesus that he wouldn't let it have a bad effect on me. And it was at that moment I chose to chuck my existence as a TM teacher and follow Christ. That's how I got out of it."

In the beginning of our investigation, we openly approved of TM. Among America's mass therapies, it was the only one that seemed to be completely beneficial, having amassed a wealth of medical and scientific support which had been widely circulated and the subject of several best-selling books. And, although neither of us had ever enrolled in a TM course, we both had close friends, even family members, who were Transcendental Meditators.

Robertson's view of TM wasn't the only one that surprised us, however. We had several in-depth conversations with another TM instructor who was currently active in the inner circles of the organization. His own dependence on the technique startled us, for we had known him before he became involved in TM. We had difficulty understanding his fanatic devotion to the Maharishi, his growing detachment and lack of emotion, and his unquenchable desire to advance to the TM world headquarters in Switzerland—until we talked with Robertson. Then other random impressions of TM we had gathered began to line up with our understanding of snapping. There was the young professional we had met in the Midwest who told us that she was selling her home to take an advanced course in meditation, that she too was seeing auras around people, that she felt her life was "being controlled." Many other people we spoke with in connection with other mass therapies or cults began their searches, like Jean Turner, with a casual jaunt into TM. Finally, we went back and examined the mass of scientific data that had been published. We were surprised to discover the amount of questionable research that had been reported as fact and published by the TM organization, and the extent to which TM used the sciences of biology and physics to build its argument for "inner energy" and "creative intelligence."

Perhaps most disturbing of all, we were struck by the way TM repeatedly called on alleged scientific facts to prove that only the explicit sound of its own secret mantras would produce the beneficial effects of meditation. TM has claimed that, unless the meditator takes the course and purchases his own specially tailored mantra, he will be vulnerable to "severely deleterious effects."

TM, however, is not the only organization in America that could be said to abuse the practice of meditation which, when used properly and in moderation, may indeed be beneficial. Nearly every cult employs some version of the technique in ways that in our opinion may impair their members' ability to think.

A former Krishna devotee told us how the Krishna ritual of chanting the familiar *Hare Krishna* mantra may have succeeded in maintaining and deepening his sustained altered state.

"The chanting puts your mind on hold," he told us. "You totally concentrate on the words and listen to them and say them and don't try to think about anything else. It's very difficult at first, because your mind has a much higher capacity than just chanting for hours on end. Of course, we aren't told at the time that we're putting our minds on hold. It's just part of the program of activity, and it does reduce our anxieties because we aren't thinking about things while we're chanting. All I remember is that it would make the mornings go tremendously fast. You could go through the whole two and a half hours of chanting and the time would just fly by."

Remembering the many snapping moments he experienced during his frequent periods of chanting, this young man looked back at them as indications of his domination by the cult.

"I don't know when I lost control of my mind," he said. "Once in a while when I was chanting, I'd have little boilings of emotion, shivers and intense shudders, like a sort of mini-convulsion. Everything would just go *boom*, as if I'd jumped into an icy pool. All my muscles would contract, and I'd feel this sudden tensing and release, like a *bip* in my emotional state. I have no idea what it was. They explained it as a spiritual experience."

For the new devotee, chanting is the principal activity of Krishna life, in our view a way to kill not only time but thought itself. Cult members are constantly being sold on the value of the activity.

"They always tell you that chanting is the answer to everything," he said. "I remember one Krishna leader saying, 'I know the cure for cancer.' And I said, 'You know the cure for cancer! What is it?' And he said, 'Chant *Hare Krishna*.'"

During his deprogramming, this Krishna member snapped out of his cult state instantly and completely. For months, however, he felt the aftereffects of his endless days of chanting.

"It took me a long time to get back to using my mind," he said. "It took me six months to get back to studying, but slowly I felt myself getting more and more together, feeling more and more aware of myself, knowing what my mind was thinking and why it was doing these things."

Ironically, from their backgrounds of education, affluence, and lifelong good fortune, many young people remain ignorant of the happiness they already know.

"I was twenty years old and I had no idea what happiness was," this young man said. "I'd been happy all my life, but if you've never been down in your whole life you don't really know what happiness is. So the cults come along and say, 'Here is the way to get the ultimate happiness.' First they convince you that you're unhappy, then they tell you that they've got the answer. They tell you all the nasty things you're doing and feeling, then they tell you how to right them: you chant *Hare Krishna*."

The Divine Light Mission is apparently even more direct in its manner of transcendental seduction. A former member told us about the straightforward appeal that attracted him.

"They had obtained my name from an organization I belonged to," he said, "and they sent me letters explaining that they were teaching meditation techniques free of charge. At the time, I had had contact with a number of people who had found TM beneficial, but I couldn't afford TM's initiation fee."

As he became involved in the Divine Light Mission and had the first free lessons in meditation, he felt a weakening of his own mental abilities.

"I found myself becoming increasingly dependent on other people's judgment," he recalled, "and increasingly willing to follow whatever course they laid down in order to be initiated. As I became more and more caught up in that, I noticed a decrease in my degree of attention and my force of will."

In contrast to the emptying of the mind that takes place in TM, the Divine Light Mission style of meditation was what Barry Robertson would call concentration. As this former member explained the differences, the similarities also became apparent.

"The meditation Maharaj Ji was teaching involved intensity, not depth. The intensity was the concentration with which you focused on, say, the sound of your own breathing. As such, it was simply a technique for jamming the mind, in the sense that the Russian government might jam Radio Free Europe by broadcasting sounds of railroad collisions on the same frequency. It gave me a certain absence of feeling. It eventually reached a point where, when I had doubts, guilt, or other uncomfortable emotions, I would immediately react by meditating. After a while, any significant thought I might have was immediately obliterated by meditating."

When he was finally deprogrammed by Ted Patrick, he found himself unable to refrain from meditating.

"After my deprogramming, it took several weeks before I was able to maintain a train of thought and make two sentences go together without having the whole thing erased," he said. "Meditation had become a conditioned response. My mind just kept doing it automatically."

Immediately after his deprogramming, Patrick showed him ways to break the spell.

"I was sitting there with this dazed look on my face," he remembered, "and I came to the conclusion that it might be a good idea to try experimenting with not meditating. Then I discovered this conditioned reflex and it was very difficult to stomach. It was very scary, depressing, and I asked Patrick what I could do to stop meditating. He suggested that I pick up a book and start reading aloud to keep a train of thought going. So I picked up a copy of *1984* and reread it with a completely blown mind. Now I understood very well what Orwell was talking about."

It took this former Divine Light Missionary months to rebuild his capacities of thought.

"After I finally broke the reflex of meditating, I found I was going through another stage where my thoughts were like a very weak telephone signal," he said. "Normally, when you're thinking, you're with your thoughts; they're right where you're talking from. In this case, however, my thoughts were like way off over there, way out yonder, very faint. I really had to pay attention to them to hear them at all."

The Eastern religious cults are not the only ones that employ techniques to put the mind on hold. The international Christian cult called the Way uses the Pentecostal practice of speaking in tongues. A young woman who spent several years in the Way explained the cult's highly developed method of teaching its members this technique of spiritual "possession."

"The first class is twelve sessions long," she said. "It's a whole buildup to get you to the point where you believe you'll be speaking in tongues. You go to their fellowships and they call on people who have already had the classes to speak in tongues and then interpret and prophesy. It's like kindergarten. When you hear it enough, you finally learn how to do it. When I finally started to do it, there were no ecstatic moments. I had been told for twelve sessions what it was, so it was no bolt of lightning. I could control it. I could start it and stop it. It's kind of funny, now that I think back on it."

Her instruction in tongues appeared to be a more methodical version of the learning process Marjoe described to us. However, once she mastered the basic sounds and patterns of speech that made up, in this instance, something resembling a Middle Eastern nonsense language, the leaders of the Way issued a familiar command to this young woman and other followers.

"We were told to do it 'much,' " she recalled. " 'Speak in tongues *much*,' was the phrase, and that meant as much as you could, whenever you weren't talking or reading the Bible. It wasn't out loud, it was in the mind. It was no more than a silent chant, like the Krishna mantras, only we were just babbling in tongues. Toward the end of my involvement with the Way, I was doing it all the time without being aware of it. I would forget every once in a while, but as soon as I caught myself not doing it, I would make myself do it. It's weird; it's something that gets out of control. The only real thinking you do in the group is about God and the things you are taught, but all your thinking automatically goes together with speaking in tongues."

After her deprogramming, this former member still experienced difficulty with the tongues habit.

"When I got out of the group it was still going on in my mind. I couldn't go to sleep without saying it. When I tried to stop myself from speaking in tongues and couldn't, I knew I was in trouble. Finally, I developed my own way of breaking it. When I listened to someone talk, I formed their words in my mind. I'd concentrate on every word that came out. I'd make mental images and spell their words out to keep from straying. It took me a good six months before it was completely gone."

The Unification Church has also developed its own form of meditation. It is called "centering," a process that corresponds closely to Robertson's category of Christian meditation.

A former Moonie described for us how centering focuses on the specific teachings of the church to the exclusion of all other thoughts and feelings.

"Centering is centering yourself on Moon's definition of God as the church gives it to you," he said. "You're instructed to concentrate on the thinkings of the church at all times and take the upper hand in any threatening situation. You are to assume dominion over the people you're around, because you're the enlightened one."

Instead of jamming the mind by endlessly repeating mantras and chants or focusing on their breathing or heartbeat, Moonies control their thought processes at a higher level of mental activity. Every person who is not a fellow cult member, and every social, religious, and political institution that lies outside the cult's domain, is portrayed as a representative of Satan's world. Moonies focus on this belief, along with other church doctrines, to the exclusion of all other thought. In this way, centering may achieve two purposes at one time: it may neatly prevent the individual from thinking independently, and it may add a larger element of intellectual and social control to an already airtight web of domination.

Like most cults, Erhard Seminars Training attacks the process of thinking head on. Over the course of the sixty-hour training, est leaders focus on thinking as the cause of their trainees' problems. Est's lectures and processes provide trainees with alternatives to thinking as it is customarily defined, using basic techniques that still the activity of the mind. Throughout the training, est keeps up its own form of indoctrination, urging individuals to refrain from the activity that is causing all their problems and, instead, to simply "experience" life itself.

We spoke with a recent est graduate about this curious distinction between "experience" and thinking.

"Thinking is the enemy," he said flatly. "Thinking is absolutely the enemy to me because it is a barrier to experience. Thoughts are not based on truth; they're based on tapes, things from the past. People are such machines, they let their thoughts run their lives rather than their experiences."

As this man, a professional in his late thirties, explained it to us, est appears to view the process of thinking essentially as tape recording. It declares the mind a storage vault of troublesome tapes that clog the essence of pure

By most standards

experience. Erhard's pop philosophy works like a charm for individuals fleeing their pasts, as it does for those whose route to pleasure is simply ignoring the things that trouble them. Ironically, the est process of "encountering" seems to do exactly the opposite, bringing the trainee's entire past to the fore until his or her "tapes" become strained to the point of snapping.

With est's philosophy of pure experience, we come full circle in our interpretation of information disease, through the techniques of chanting and meditation, religion, and therapy back to the starting point of experience itself. Est trainees seek a state of raw, unmediated experience which they consider the healthiest level of human existence. By most standards, est is not a cult, but it offers the best example of the pervasiveness of America's runaway technology of experience. Est brings the process of not thinking to its logical conclusion. By slickly packaging concepts and techniques that have been roaming loose in our culture since the sixties, it offers its participants a fully rationalized, legitimized self-defense for shutting off the mind.

What are the long-term effects of this widespread process of shutting off the mind? The best information available to us is found in the Krishna cult.

Late in our research, we interviewed a former Krishna *brahmin,* a temple executive. As we talked, he gave us his view of how, in the early seventies, the once penitent International Society for Krishna Consciousness turned into a full-time book-distribution operation. Extravagant hardbound copies of the Bhagavad Gita, he said, complete with beautiful full-color engravings, were handed out to devotees of Krishna for public sale, and experienced salesmen traveled to Krishna temples around the country instructing devotees in the techniques of salesmanship. According to him, in their unthinking state, the devotees remained perfectly willing to solicit up to twenty hours a day; but there were some who, over time, were no longer able to do so.

As our contact described it:

"There were two vegetables at our temple, people who were really bad off from chanting. We'd have to spend about two hours a day chanting our rounds to Krishna, but they would take four or five hours to get through them. There's not a whole lot of work to do around the temple, so we would just let them chant all day. Eventually these people deteriorated to the point where they couldn't get their chanting done. They would become slower, and we couldn't get them to work or do anything. They were basket cases."

According to him, over time, extended chanting may lead to complete dissolution of the mind.

"The vegetables are amazing," he said. "Once they get to a certain stage they can become very destructive. The guy who brought me into the cult was a college graduate in philosophy, and he used to teach classes every day. He went nuts, started saying weird things, and began screaming at the women all the time. The last I heard of him, he'd gone to the Krishna commune in Africa."

In the course of his official duties, this former brahmin spent several months at a Krishna communal farm in West Virginia. A meeting place for Krishna leaders, from his description, it appears that it may also house members who are among the cult's worst casualties.

"There are people cracking all the time," he said. "Either they become vegetables or crack violently."

After more than a decade, the Krishna cult no longer attracts much attention in America. The public and the media have become inured to the Krishnas' strange appearance and practices, preferring to focus on the newer and more sophisticated cults. Nevertheless, according to reports from around the United States today, Krishna members continue to crack. Amidst the current epidemic of snapping, they are perhaps an intimation of what lies ahead.

"There were a couple of nuts in our temple," recalled another ex-Krishna we interviewed. "We had a crazy girl there who would go nuts occasionally and start throwing knives at people. Some people would have attacks and become very violent. Others would suddenly just turn on you and scream and yell. After a while you just accept it. You accept insanity as a matter of course."

14 Snapping in Everyday Life

Consciousness is a social product.

—*B. F. Skinner,*
Beyond Freedom and Dignity

AND WHAT ABOUT the rest of us—those of us who have not even remotely considered participating in a religious cult or mass therapy and, in all likelihood, never will? Why should we be concerned about snapping?

The answer is, because it's all around us. The threat of snapping extends far beyond America's religious cults and mass therapies, beyond their dramatic rituals and intense experiences to the overwhelming pressures of everyday life. These forces, too, may cause profound although often less immediately observable changes in awareness, as well as sudden drastic alterations of personality. Just as moving land masses may shift gradually and imperceptibly and then give way in a massive earthquake, so, too, the sheer mass and movement of experience—of information—that has engulfed our culture in recent years may bring about changes in individual personalities, making us less aware, more vulnerable to manipulation, and, ultimately, less than fully capable of thinking and acting as human beings. Already, the forces are at work on each of us in our daily lives, and they are mounting.

A great deal has already been written about how the accelerating rate of drastic change and the spread of mass production, mass marketing, and mass culture have altered our environment, our lifestyles, and our personal relationships, and how the overwhelming amounts of information each individual is called upon to process every day push his body to the limits of endurance and adaptability. Physicians have identified the various health hazards that may result from this kind of extraordinary stress: headaches, ulcers, heart disease, and possibly, as recent research suggests, many forms of cancer as well. Psychologists and sociologists have analyzed the effects of increasing personal and social pressures in terms of work, marriage, family life, and an individual's sense of identity in "post-technological," "neo-tribal" America. Culture watchers such as Alvin Toffler have even foretold the approaching menace of "future shock" and other ills caused by unrelenting change and stimulation. Throughout this decade, Americans have been warned about all these threats to their health, happiness, and prosperity. They have been offered countless recipes for living, strategies for coping, and exercises for relaxation. Ironically, this abundance of warnings and threats alike have become simply more of the same—a further onslaught of information, more experience for the brain to metabolize. On top of everything else, this stepped-up assault on our modern minds may lead to still another form of snapping, one that is much less tangible yet clearly observable in America today. It is a form we call snapping in everyday life.

Everyone, without exception, is susceptible to snapping. The pace and stress of life in the seventies is enough to do the job. The physical stress which has been singled out as the potent tool of "brainwashing" in cults is so much a part of our daily lives that its impact on each individual's ability to think and feel may be easily overlooked. What with job, family, travel, and entertainment, most of us can go for days, even weeks, and save scarcely a moment for reflection. Yet, an individual who simply consumes each experience in this way, like junk food or candy, may over time become inattentive, passive, and totally open to the barrage of intellectual and emotional propaganda that comes at him daily. This propaganda urges him to surrender to the seductive enticements of our consumer society, to the manipulation of his opinions and beliefs, and to the overpowering weight of new and traditional images, roles, and rewards which, in the seventies, make promises of fulfillment that our society cannot keep.

This flood of information and experience makes up the constant, comprehensive assault on human awareness that confronts most Americans each day. Yet, the more experience an individual consumes—the more information he tries to process—the more confused he may be, causing his mind to become disjointed, scattered, unguarded, and vulnerable to suggestion. Many cults make use of this principle when they concoct exotic ritual environments combining strange music, lights, incense, and foreign languages that may confuse and control the potential convert's awareness. This same principle of distraction, however, can be identified in countless everyday forms: in television commercials that use beautiful models and actresses to confuse the viewer's desires, as well as extravagant supermarket displays that bombard the senses with dozens of competing brands of the same product. These effects are deliberately subtle, yet they represent a few little ways in which our individual awareness is divided and conquered every day, dazed just long enough to slip some message or suggestion past our normally more attentive decision-making processes.

In every area of our daily lives, other distractions can make us even more vulnerable. Perhaps the most common threat occurs when the driver of a car becomes lost in conversation or reverie and can drive for city blocks or country miles completely oblivious to the road ahead. This familiar form of "highway hypnosis," like the sudden attacks of vertigo that are not uncommon to long-distance drivers, may in fact be responsible for thousands of accidents each year. This modern peril, like the other examples cited, is not caused by the sheer quantity of massive "information overload" but by the brain's constant need for variety, for change and stimulation—but only within manageable limits. In contrast to these threats of boredom and repetition, information *too* varied, too new and foreign, experience for which the brain has no previously established or related patterns, may also take an individual completely by surprise. Shocking news—the death of a loved one or some accident or tragedy, for instance—may evoke many of the symptoms of the snapping moment, and a further quite harmless but unusual experience in that context can be seriously disorienting. A man who has just learned that he has lost his job, for example, then comes home to find his living room flooded with water, might have a massive snapping experience if, say, a lost partygoer appeared at his door in a gorilla costume. In a more serious example, one truly baffling element introduced into an otherwise ordinary environment, a vacationers' chartered airliner being hijacked by a group of armed terrorists, for instance, might leave many passengers stunned, groping for a response—and also extremely suggestible, and open to mass hysteria and individual withdrawal.

Today such threats of increased vulnerability to suggestion are ever-present. Yet mere stress, shock, and surprise do not tell the complete story of snapping in everyday life. Here, as in many cults and groups, the attitudes of the sixties and their development in the seventies play leading roles in the drama. Everyone is now capable of imagining a richer personal life. People have been given new models of awareness, wholeness, fulfillment, completion, and the realization of their human potential. They have been exhorted to discover their capacity for joy, to have fun, to indulge in play, to nurture their innate spontaneity and creativity. Many have learned how to express private feelings and share their most intimate fears. The consciousness explosion, which is already past history, has left its mark on every aspect of our society. Even if some people were not directly touched by that cultural upheaval, even if they managed to isolate themselves from the civil rights movement, rock music, long hair, psychedelic drugs, antiwar demonstrations, and women's liberation, these changes have affected them through the mass media, the arts, fashion, and America's shifting political climate. To a great extent, the sixties' famous "generation gap" has been bridged. Yet in the seventies a new rift, a kind of "sensibility gap" that cuts across all age groups and social classes, is also being spanned, as each day more Americans become aware of new possibilities for experience. Even for the most tradition-bound individuals and communities, the search for happiness and fulfillment within the traditions of work, marriage, and family that comprise the base of American life is no longer enough. Today, people want to *feel* their satisfaction. They want to consciously experience their happiness. To compound the challenge, most Americans still strive to incorporate their growing awareness into the fabric of their daily lives, to cultivate a new state of consciousness without destroying everything that has gone before.

Furthermore, many traditions and institutions that once gave stability to people's lives have themselves collapsed under the weight of new experiences and information. In a sense, these time-honored values and institutions—such as the nuclear family, the work ethic, and organized religion—formerly served as shared modes of information processing for our entire culture. They set patterns of thinking, feeling, and living that reduced potential chaos to social order. As these institutions crumble, however, even in the name of equal opportunity and long-overdue social justice, many of the resulting changes and social benefits only serve to increase personal confusion. Without established roles and expectations, without guidelines for making new choices, individuals in a shifting culture are forced to improvise, to test a variety of alternatives before selecting one that they hope will be the best method of going forward. In a rapidly changing society where time-tested patterns of living can no longer be recycled from one generation to the next, new lifestyles, experiences, and opportunities, however promising, may lead unforeseeably to disaster.

And disaster does seem to be overtaking many Americans in the seventies, as the awareness that fired our culture a decade ago has been tempered into reluctant trade-offs on every level—personal, social, and political. Despite that increased awareness and the cornucopia of new material goods and experiences that have become available to almost everyone, the demands of America's monstrously complex and globally interdependent technological society still overshadow the needs and aspirations of the individual. Among the people we talked with in our travels, those of all ages expressed new hopes, new dreams, and new goals. But many who were dedicated to creating truly meaningful lives for themselves and their families also seemed to be confronted with a growing sense of exhaustion and an impending conclusion that the ideals they had been striving for just might not be attainable, considering the serious problems of energy, economy, and environment which cannot be ignored. To us, it seemed that people in every walk of life across the country were edging toward a confrontation with the mounting pressures and conflicting emotions of modern life: individual awareness versus social responsibility; immediate pleasure and sensation versus long-range planning and some larger and less tangible form of happiness. We heard people express the feeling that they were simply pushing themselves to the point of futility. They said they feared that everything they had been struggling for in their personal searches and practical plans would have to be reconsidered in the light of an even newer awareness which might be called "realism" or "pragmatism," but which they sensed would spell the surrender of their ideals and their dreams. In this way, the grim realities of the seventies seem to be drawing so many Americans to the brink of their own personal catastrophes.

———

We have watched the forces building in people struggling to avert an impending crisis in their jobs and careers. They know that the "grind" is self-defeating, that the rising cost of maintaining even the most modest lifestyle and standard of living means that, in all likelihood, their work will be all-consuming. They also know that even their hardest efforts will be offset by inflation and steeper taxes. Yet they are aware that they must save some time for their families, their friends, and their community—not to mention their favorite sports and hobbies and their own private needs. For America's growing number of working women, as well as its working men, the immediate trade-offs of everyday life pose challenges of potentially catastrophic proportions. The consciousness explosion and the women's movement have shattered the myth of the carefree, happy housewife. Yet few women, married or single, are capable of juggling the multiple roles of wife, mother, lover, companion, housekeeper, and career woman many of them are now expected by society to play. Some women manage to play them all for a while. Some men reap the best of both worlds, home and office. A growing number of individuals, however, are finding it impossible to pursue a career, a family, *and* meet their new demands for personal development. Caught in this bind, many members of America's emerging singles class, both young and old, have become the nation's most avid searchers, often declining the rewards and responsibilities of marriage and family life in favor of their need for independence and the promise of a full life down the road. Yet in many ways theirs can be the hardest life of all, lonely, disconnected, and, like their more traditional counterparts, poised for some unforeseen and possibly catastrophic resolution.

When that catastrophe occurs, it may take a variety of forms. In keeping with the principles of catastrophe theory, some tiny change may set off a sudden drastic reaction. A man may quit his job, leave his family, kill himself, go crazy in any number of recognized forms of mental illness—or, in the manner of snapping, undergo a complete and inexplicable transformation of lifestyle and personality. Or, following the path of gradual catastrophe, a professional or businessman or woman may simply withdraw from his or her friends, family, and the outside world in a quiet struggle to suppress negative emotions and disturbing thoughts. A housewife may do likewise, sinking into depression, running away from home, or timidly embarking on a personal search for a higher level of existence. Young single people may go further, being free from commitment and in the most likely position to seize upon— or be seized by—some novel alternative. It is these individuals who, even in adulthood, may slip into religious cults or devote their lives to becoming teachers or volunteer laborers in paternalistic mass therapies.

Then there are those who, from all appearances, have simply given up and stopped worrying altogether. These are the legitimate titleholders of snapping in everyday life: people who have confronted their own potential and rejected it for something less. Like cult members, the victims of snapping in everyday life have gone to great lengths to suppress their negative emotions and still their minds to all doubts and questions. Their manner of snapping may take innumerable forms, both glaring and subtle. There are those who dive into grueling work routines or feverish physical activity to keep back their doubts and fears. Others achieve the same end by plunging headfirst into idle fancies and diverting pastimes, much the way ardent meditators slip into the still pool of their senseless mantras.

The temptations of the American marketplace cater to this form of snapping in everyday life, beckoning the individual to become totally absorbed in each new consumer craze. No CB radio, digital watch, or "recreational vehicle," of course, carries within it any inherent germ of snapping. Yet amid our current cultural confusion of new goals, shifting values, and collapsing traditions, it is not inconceivable that an insignificant consumer item could become the narrow focus of some wider and deeper discontent. Like any manner of not thinking, the simple preoccupation with gadgetry so flagrantly promoted in our society may itself constitute a socially approved form of distraction, a way to still the mind to all larger questions by filling it with small concerns. Taken to extremes, however, over time these popular patterns of not thinking may become ingrained, and the larger whole of an individual's personality may begin to reflect both the experiences with which it has been filled and the thoughts and feelings that may be lacking.

In this way, the dominating force, not simply of our consumer society but of its entire system of values, raises much broader questions of snapping in everyday life. Today, American business and advertising have at their disposal the latest and most comprehensive body of knowledge concerning the manner in which human behavior can be manipulated by means of strategically targeted messages, images, and suggestions. This well-oiled machinery of mass persuasion functions on the strictest principles and assumptions of the robot model of man, pouring out a constant flow of information to the American public designed to stimulate the consumer's guilts, fears, weaknesses, insecurities, and fantasies—and then reward each individual in immediate physical and emotional terms for succumbing to them. This simple ploy is carried out repeatedly on Americans literally hundreds of times each day, stunning them with a barrage of false promises, distorted values, and jumbled personal priorities, then urging them to give in to every wish and impulse.

What happens to an individual who is subjected to an endless stream of such scientifically conceived and vividly produced appeals? Our perspective on snapping suggests that this all-engrossing experience—combined with the other mounting pressures of modern life—must have some cumulative effect on personality. The cults provide the symptoms to look for in a world of constant stress, artful distraction, and endless propaganda. People become passive, vulnerable to suggestion and command, and incapable of thinking for themselves. In our opinion, these symptoms have become widespread throughout our country.

It could be that in subtle ways these stresses and techniques which shape our modern lives have started every American down the sloping catastrophe curve of snapping and information disease. Our individual capacities of thought and feeling may have already become impaired. Many people, in the rush of daily activities, appear to have relinquished their ability to form an original point of view, paying little more than token consideration to the real issues and events that influence their lives. The majority of their opinions on world events are shaped by mass media. Their attitudes toward pressing matters of politics or the economy are determined less by reason than by persuasion. Our current popular attitudes toward the energy crisis, for example, reflect the possibility that America as a nation may be snapping collectively, for despite the ominous statistics and dire predictions, many Americans now seem incapable of long-range thinking and planning.

But even more important than the urgent issues of energy, the environment, and the economy are the intimate personal questions that many people also seem incapable of confronting and thinking through on their own. Despite our rampant national quest for personal growth and spiritual fulfillment, most Americans ignore their inner thoughts and feelings until they hit some emotional impasse or crisis. Only following a divorce, the loss of a job, the death of a loved one—or when frustration and boredom become unbearable —do many people sit down and sort out the painful feelings and negative emotions they generally harbor at all times. The popular turn in the seventies toward authoritarian cults and therapies that offer easy answers seems to confirm that hundreds of thousands of Americans can no longer reason their way through the complexity of their personal problems. They are unable to recognize the happiness they may have already found and feel compelled to buy emotional guidance from all kinds of spiritual and psychological suppliers.

Last, but not least, there is television, the all-powerful convergence of our American experience and daily communication habits that may be our culture's primary contributor to snapping in everyday life. The most efficient, effective, yet subtle tool of mass communication and persuasion, television has drastically altered American life in less than three decades. It has reshaped our eating habits, our sleeping habits, and our family and social relationships. It has become the predominant purveyor of news, the molding force of public opinion, and the principal source of our collective images, dreams, hopes, amusements, and desires.

As important as the content of the information that television puts out, and its widespread social repercussions, is the manner in which it may affect personality—not simply an individual's actions and behavior but the way he or she perceives the world. Like any intense or prolonged experience, the electronic experience of television does indeed have the power to shape and alter human awareness. Like TM, TV stills the mind through repetition, not in the form of meaningless sounds but in the larger assault of momentary images upon vision, the dominant sense in the nervous system. Like both Transcendental Meditation and Scientology's auditing process, television also may be a potent neutralizing force of human thought and feeling. Its incessant transmission of information physically trains an individual to hear and observe without stopping to think, to switch from one set of sounds and images to the next without pausing to reflect or digest the information that has been consumed. Advertisers have long known that this rapid-fire kaleidescopic manner of consumption may make television viewers more vulnerable to their suggestions, but only recently have even more potent side effects of this communication technique come to light. In its unique way, television teaches an individual to experience scenes of terror, anger, shock, and tragedy—purely as entertainment.

Within the last few years, our society has begun to acknowledge the disquieting fact that an entire generation of Americans has now been molded in the image of television—shaped by the combined impact of both the medium and its messages. It may be no coincidence that this generation is the same one that has been drawn en masse into religious cults. According to A. C. Neilsen, by the time of graduation from high school, today's typical teenager has spent more·than 15,000 hours before the tube. By the age of seventeen, the teenager has been exposed to 350,000 commercials and watched 18,000 dramatized murders. The net result, many concerned investigators are finding, is that today's youth has suffered markedly from the shaping experience of television.

Television watching may have profound physical effects on the nervous system of a young child. Every minute the child spends sitting motionless before the tube—for a total period of inactivity that rivals sleep as the major experience of childhood and adolescence—is time that is not spent working, reading, playing, or engaged in other molding activities of the early years. During this period in which fundamental patterns of thought, feeling, action, and expression develop, television provides a singular mode of experiencing the world, and its cumulative effects may touch the basic organization of the brain. As the nervous system adapts to great daily doses of experience received with no initiative or effort, the child may, in fact, become physically passive and intellectually lazy. Furthermore, reading tests of young television watchers confirm that their imaginations may have become permanently stunted. Educators report that heavy TV watching destroys the natural ability of children to form mental images from what they read or hear. With too much TV, the growing child's basic capacity of imagination, like an unused muscle, never reaches a level adequate for performing even the most elementary creative acts.

Our educational systems are powerless to counteract these formative effects, for few methods of instruction have the impact and attraction of the information avalanche of TV. Few teachers can rival television's power over the individual, cultivated from infancy, that gives the medium its hypnotic hold on a young child's attention and trust. Yet the medium is not wholly to blame, even for these fundamental ills. The quality of programming and the kind of information television disseminates could undoubtedly, with increased effort and concern, be used to make human beings more sensitive and more imaginative (TV triumphs like *Sesame Street* and, on a culture-wide scale, "Roots," are obvious examples). For the most part, however, the overall effects of America's television programming and viewing habits seem to be inseparably linked to a new and growing form of personal malaise.

And in the seventies, it is America's young people who appear to have been the most deeply affected by the combined stresses, ploys, and techniques of modern life. Their intelligence test scores have declined markedly, while their suicide rate has risen to almost double that of a decade ago. This generation's collegians have become once again politically mute and narrowly, intensely career-oriented. They are also proving dangerously vulnerable to suggestion and spiritual seduction. In a few years, they may become the legitimate heirs to a world in which people have stopped considering their lives and the other people in them, stopped feeling the conflicts of their discrepant values; a world in which people have studiously avoided long-range planning and stopped thinking about the future except in fantasy and science fiction. This legacy America appears to be leaving to future generations is a heritage of snapping.

Today these numbing effects of modern life are even more ironic. They have come to light at a time when our culture has finally discovered how to experience feeling good. In this decade, American business and religion have mastered the art of shaping people's choices by positive rather than negative means, while self-declared experts and spiritual pioneers have developed skills which tap the power of man's innate capacity to change the way he thinks, feels, and experiences the world. The only thing we in America haven't learned in the exploitation of our indomitable faith and trust, and in the refinement of our dazzling technology of experience, is how to use these new tools responsibly. In the sixties, we set out to help people become more fully realized human beings, and now, with the understanding and ability to accomplish that goal at our disposal, we seem hell-bent on turning ourselves into robots and lesser things.

15 Snapping and Punishment

A population subjected to drastic change is a population of misfits—unbalanced, explosive, and hungry for action.

—Eric Hoffer,
The Ordeal of Change

YET, NO MATTER WHAT, it remains an impossible task to turn a human being into a robot. In their infinite flexibility and adaptability, human information-processing capacities may, in fact, be altered to make human beings behave like mechanical men. But our investigation has shown us that even in a mindless, desensitized, automatic state, these people are still processing information—and even under conditions of impaired awareness, delusion, and domination, there is always the possibility that they will snap out of it. After years have passed, these robots may still regain their freedom of thought; their responses as individuals may be restored, and the skeleton of their personalities may drop back into place.

Who, then, is responsible for the actions of people who may have snapped and become imprisoned in a less than fully human state? The individuals themselves? Their parents? Their cult leaders? Society in general? And who is to be punished when those deeds are serious crimes—even murder?

In the last ten years, a number of horrifying crimes have been committed by young Americans, men and women in their late teens and early twenties, all unlikely candidates for the crimes with which they were charged. In none of these cases, however, was the individual proven to have a Jekyll-Hyde split personality. Rather, all had, in the period preceding the commission of their criminal acts, undergone complete and drastic transformations of personality, if not in a sudden moment, at least over a relatively short, identifiable span of time.

The three most notorious and perplexing cases were mentioned at the beginning of this book: the Tate-LaBianca murders committed by members of the Manson Family in 1969, the armed bank robbery and other acts committed by Patricia Hearst following her kidnapping by the Symbionese Liberation Army in 1974, and the series of random street murders in New York City allegedly committed by a young postal worker named David Berkowitz, apprehended in August, 1977, and charged with being the .44-caliber killer who called himself the "Son of Sam." In its own way, each of these cases continues to confound traditional psychological and legal interpretation.

Our investigation of snapping, however, has provided us with a new vantage point from which to view and understand these crimes. We examined the information made public concerning the circumstances of these events and studied the material we were able to gather in private interviews and confidential communications. It seemed to us a worthwhile and potentially important contribution to see if these cases and the questions they raised could be further illuminated from our perspective on snapping and information disease.

Without exception, we found that they could. The sudden changes in personality common to the people who were recruited by Charles Manson into his Family, to Patty Hearst, and to David Berkowitz, as well, are all traceable to specific intense experiences, techniques of manipulation, or systematic and sustained changes in the individual's general information environment. The result was a recognizable alteration or shift of personality from the individuals they were before to the individuals they were at the time they allegedly committed their crimes. We offer the following interpretation of these notable instances of sudden personality change as an alternative to the various psychological, legal, and media explanations that, in our opinion, have proved to be of limited value in informing courts, juries, and the public of the overriding significance of these human tragedies.

———

Although it is public knowledge that Charles Manson was deeply interested in Scientology before he formed his Family (though he never joined the church), the possible resemblance between some Scientological practices and Manson's methods of controlling his band has never been fully explored. We do not believe or intend to imply that there was any formal or informal connection between the Church of Scientology and the murders of actress Sharon Tate and her houseguests and Leno and Rosemary LaBianca. We are, however, suggesting a similarity between the techniques used and taught by Scientology and the manner in which Charles Manson manipulated the members of his Family.

Vincent Bugliosi, prosecuting attorney in the Manson trial, made frequent mention of Scientology and one-time Scientologists with reference to Manson's life and career in his best-selling account of the case, *Helter Skelter: The True Story of the Manson Murders,* published in 1974. Bugliosi served up all the details of Manson's drifting, troubled youth—an illegitimate child, he bounced from town to town, engaging in a haphazard string of petty crimes and larcenous acts. Over seventeen of Manson's first thirty-two years were spent in jails and prisons, yet, Bugliosi noted, Manson's criminal record to that time showed no sustained history of violence.

"Burglar, car thief, forger, pimp," he wrote, "was this the portrait of a mass murderer?"

It was in prison, apparently, that Manson became interested in Scientology. According to *Helter Skelter,* in the early sixties, Manson's tutor in Scientology was another convict, Lanier Rayner, and under his direction Manson claimed to have achieved Scientology's highest level, which he described as "Theta clear." Bugliosi wrote that Manson remained interested in Scientology longer than in any other subject except music (his continuing career goal was to gain recognition as a rock musician). A prison progress report written during that period asserted that Manson "appears to have developed a certain amount of insight into his problems through his study of this discipline."

There is no way to determine whether Charles Manson actually experienced becoming a Scientology clear. It is known that not very long afterward, upon his release from prison in 1967, Manson began to formulate his grand delusionary and messianic schemes. It was also during this period that he began to demonstrate an uncanny ability to exert influence and control over other people.

There were many other influences during those years, psychedelic drugs being the most prominent, of course, along with the culture-wide impact of the San Francisco scene to which Manson gravitated during the Haight-Ashbury's famous Summer of Love. Another powerful element in that tumultuous environment was the music of the Beatles, who wrote "Helter Skelter" and many of the other songs that Manson took to be direct communications from cosmic forces. Of even greater impact was the biblical Book of Revelation, which Manson interpreted as an explicit battle plan for the coming apocalypse. He read into its prophesies hidden meanings that licensed him to initiate his campaign of mass murder. Manson's interest in Revelation may have been derived in part from another cult, for throughout the spring and summer of 1967, when Manson was recruiting members from the hippies, drifters, and runaway flower children of the Haight, his fledgling Family had frequent interaction with another ominous tribe that lived just two blocks away. This was the early religious cult called the Process, or the Church of the Final Judgment, a group who walked the streets in long black robes, preaching the imminent arrival of a violent Armageddon as presaged in the Book of Revelation. According to Bugliosi, the Process was founded by a former disciple of L. Ron Hubbard himself who broke with Scientology to form his own group after attaining an important position in Scientology's London headquarters. Bugliosi cited numerous elements in Manson's world view he believed were borrowed from the Process: distorted attitudes toward life and death, the worshipping of fear and violence, and a variety of satanic delusions and black revolutionary schemes.

Manson's activities as a pimp and forger and his years in prison certainly schooled him in the basic skills of an expert conman. But it may have been his experiences with Rayner that provided him with some of the communication tools he used to manipulate the minds of his young followers. "Undoubtedly," wrote Bugliosi, "he picked up from his 'auditing' sessions in prison some knowledge of mind control, as well as some techniques which he later put to use in programming his followers." Bugliosi also noted that one of Charles Manson's chief disciples, Bruce Davis, was heavily involved in Scientology at one time, also working in its London headquarters until April, 1969. According to Scientology spokesmen, Davis was kicked out of the cult for drug use, and shortly after that he returned to America to join the Family and participate in two brutal crimes of murder and dismemberment that preceded the Tate-LaBianca murders.

Bugliosi identified all these influences in his attempt to explain how Charles Manson formed his philosophy and recruited the Family. He declined to make any connection. however, between Manson's background and his protracted exposure to rudimentary techniques of controlling others and the almost unbelievably twisted states of mind of his followers, in particular, the three women who were convicted along with Manson for the Tate-LaBianca murders: Susan Atkins, Patricia Krenwinkel, and Leslie Van Houten.

No one knows how Manson worked each individual conversion, but as we have come to understand it, his technique was classic—and potent. In the Haight's atmosphere of psychedelics and free love, Manson approached prospective Family members, most of them young women, with the standard cult leader's ploys of affection and acceptance. More importantly, he relied on those specific suggestions to stop thinking and refrain from questioning that, if heeded, may in themselves evoke the powerful snapping moment and the condition of vulnerability that follows.

Susan Atkins, in a recently published book about her experiences with Manson, described what went on "in the storm of my mind" when she first met Manson. During a typical early Haight scene of loud rock music and easy encounters, Manson came up behind her and began dancing with her, putting his hands on her hips and guiding her body in rhythmic, sensual movements. As she remembered the scene, he also planted powerful suggestions that opened her up to his advances—both psychological and sexual.

"He whispered into my left ear," wrote Atkins, " 'That's right. That's good. . . . In reality . . . there's no repetition. No two moves, no two actions are the same. Everything is new. Let it be new.' "

From our perspective, it seems that in this simple moment of contact, Manson managed to induce a profound snapping experience in Susan Atkins.

"Suddenly I experienced a moment unlike any other," she wrote. "This stranger and I dancing, passed through one another. It was as though my body moved closer and closer to him and actually passed through him. I thought for a second that I would collapse. What had happened? Was I crazy? It was beyond human reality."

In the days that followed, Manson moved in on Susan Atkins in a total sexual and psychological assault. In their first sexual encounter, Manson took full advantage of the experience to bring her under his direct control. "You must break free from the past," Manson told her. "You must live now. There is no past. The past is gone. There's no tomorrow." The sentiment was commonplace in the sixties, a touch of Eastern philosophy and a touch of Western existentialism. Taken literally, however, in the context of the cult's world of sexual and psychedelic orgies, Manson's young followers slid easily into sustained altered states of consciousness. They totally identified with his satanic prophecies, including his claim to be Christ or the Messiah, and his plan to set off a worldwide revolution with a series of random ritual murders.

In the aftermath of the Tate-LaBianca murders, however, the trial of the four accused murderers turned into a ghastly public sideshow, complete with garrulous courtroom outbursts by the defendants and a noisy street scene outside the L.A. courthouse orchestrated by other members of the Manson Family. At the time, in the thick of pandemonium, no one in the courts, the press, or the public asked the very serious, sensitive question of what in the world had happened to Manson's girls?

Least of all Bugliosi. Riding a tidal wave of public opinion, Bugliosi, District Attorney of Los Angeles, pressed hard for the swift conviction and execution of the defendants. Calling a succession of psychiatrists as expert witnesses, Bugliosi shot down every possible contention of the defense concerning Manson's conversion tactics, the role of LSD and other psychedelic drugs, and the psychological histories of the defendants, asserting that each was mentally competent and a willing participant in the Tate-LaBianca murders. During the penalty trial to determine the sentences of the convicted murderers, Bugliosi contended that each of the accused Family members possessed some kind of "inner flaw" that would have prompted her to kill—

even without Manson's orders and influence. Bugliosi called upon the jury to "have the fortitude" to return verdicts of death for all four defendants.

"These defendants are not human beings, ladies and gentlemen," said Bugliosi in his final statement to the jury. "Human beings have a heart and a soul. No one with a heart and a soul could have done what these defendants did to these seven victims.

"These defendants are human monsters, human mutations."

The jury in the Manson trial did return verdicts of death for Manson and the three women. In 1972, however, before the executions could be carried out, the California State Supreme Court abolished the death penalty in that state by a vote of 6–1 on the grounds that it constituted cruel and unusual punishment. The sentences of all four were commuted to life imprisonment, and throughout the decade of the seventies, Manson, Atkins, Krenwinkel, and Van Houten have remained in prison, first on death row and then in isolation.

During our initial stay in California, we attempted to arrange interviews with various members of the Manson Family in order to determine whether their transformations could be interpreted from our perspective. We soon discovered that there would be little to gain from personal conversations with three out of four of them.

Manson himself turned out to be the most unreachable and unlikely prospect. "Charlie?" one official at the California State Prison at Vacaville told us. "Charlie is anyone he wants to be these days." From all reports, Manson had not changed noticeably in prison. He was said to be still shuffling his conman roles, at times appearing to play the part of a model prisoner yet, from everything we heard, showing little sign of genuine rehabilitation, refusing, as is his prerogative, nearly all requests for interviews from concerned journalists and psychological and sociological researchers (although, we were told, Manson did grant one interview to the tabloid *National Enquirer*). Because of numerous threats he has received, for the most part Manson stays away from the other prisoners at Vacaville. Nevertheless, he has not become a total recluse. He is said to keep in loose contact with his remaining followers.

Patricia Krenwinkel, we were told by those who had followed her activities at the California Institute for Women at Frontera, was still struggling to find her identity.

Susan Atkins, on the other hand, had become a self-confessed Jesus Freak, after having been baptized in a water tank in her prison yard in early 1975. From accounts we gathered, it appeared that, like many other individuals we interviewed, she had found her personal answer to an irresolvable emotional crisis in America's most widely accepted form of spiritual renewal. In her recently published book, *Susan Atkins: Child of Satan—Child of God*, she declared that Christ had come to her in her prison cell, in a scene complete with blinding white lights and swinging portals. "Susan, I am really here. I'm really coming into your heart to stay," he said, as she recalled it. "You are now a child of God. You are washed clean and your sins have all been forgiven." Following that experience, she claimed, "There was no more guilt! It was gone. Completely gone!"

Of the four, Leslie Van Houten was the only one who appeared to have emerged from her cult state of mind.

By every measure, Leslie Van Houten was the most unlikely of the accused Manson family members. A one-time high school homecoming princess, she grew up in an active, concerned home where her childhood was shared with an older brother and two younger adopted children. When she was fourteen, however, her parents separated and divorced, and Leslie was profoundly affected by the breakup. During that turbulent sixties era in southern California, Leslie began taking LSD fairly regularly with a young man with whom she had fallen deeply in love. In time, the young couple drifted apart and Leslie, barely eighteen, dropped out, became involved in the Haight-Ashbury scene, and ultimately found her way to Manson and his Family at Spahn Movie Ranch, an isolated, dilapidated old Western movie set at the mouth of the San Fernando Valley.

Unlike Manson, Atkins, and Krenwinkel, Leslie Van Houten had no part in the murder of Sharon Tate and her houseguests. She was tried and convicted along with the others of the gruesome murder of Rosemary LaBianca, but the case against her was sufficiently cloudy to justify a second trial, completely separate from the confusion and chaos of the first proceedings against the four accused. Late in the course of that original trial, Leslie's attorney disappeared mysteriously while on a weekend camping trip. (He was later found dead in what some have speculated to have been the first of the Manson Family's "retaliation murders.") In his absence, another lawyer, Maxwell Keith, a prominent and highly respected Los Angeles attorney, took over Leslie's defense. It was largely through Keith's efforts that the courts granted Leslie a retrial in 1977.

In early February, 1977, a month before the scheduled retrial, not yet attuned to any of the details of the case, we contacted Maxwell Keith in his downtown Los Angeles office, telling him a little about our backgrounds and our project and expressing our interest in speaking with Leslie. At first, Keith was leery of us, but he admitted that he was still in the process of formulating his defense and that he was interested in hearing our thinking and our findings. Making no promises, he invited us to have lunch with him, and a talk.

At lunch, Keith informed us of his conviction that his client was now a totally different person. Leslie, he explained, had completely come out from under Manson's spell. "You wouldn't recognize her," he said, contrasting her to the fanatic individual last seen publicly in 1971. In the intervening years on death row and then in isolation, Keith told us, while many women members of the Family had remained unswervingly loyal to Manson, Leslie was talking with prison psychiatrists, other prisoners, and her family—who had given her a great deal of support—in an attempt to understand the transformation that had come over her. This personality change, one of her early lawyers once pleaded to a California judge, had made her "insane, in a way that is almost science fiction."

She was back to normal now, Keith assured us, returned to a stable and healthy state of mind. Though we were impressed by Keith's sincerity, we were nevertheless skeptical about Leslie's transformation. By now we were completely willing to admit that an individual could snap out of that kind of mental state. But, according to Keith, Leslie hadn't emerged in a sudden moment of renewed awareness. The change had taken place slowly, he observed, over a period of years. From his description, it seemed likely that, not having been determinedly and skillfully deprogrammed, Leslie could still be in some kind of confused, floating state beyond the detection and comprehension of prison officials and psychiatrists. On the other hand, we both knew that if Keith's report of Leslie's re-emergence was accurate, it could not only confirm our thesis of snapping but expand it in a way we had not anticipated. Above all, it would demonstrate that even the most severe forms of information disease can be cured. We also knew that, if Keith was right, as her lawyer he would face a new and almost unfathomably complex legal challenge. Not only were there no precedents in defense of this kind of sudden personality change among traditional insanity contentions, there were no established criteria whatsoever for a jury to use in order to reach a judicious verdict. Before we could begin to offer any interpretation from our perspective, we told Keith, we would have to see and hear for ourselves how Leslie experienced her re-emergence.

The following day Keith accompanied us to L.A.'s Sybil Brand Women's Jail, where Leslie was being held while awaiting her retrial. By agreement with Keith, we promised for legal reasons to refrain from discussing the killings or the events immediately surrounding them.

It took us over two hours to get through Sybil Brand's rigorous security procedures. Finally, after each of us had passed a computerized identity check and a thorough inspection that included fingerprinting, mug shots, frisking, and electronic weapons detection, we were allowed to pass through a series of iron gates, clanging doors, and bulletproof partitions into a hot, rectangular visiting room just large enough to contain a wooden table and four chairs. After a short wait, a uniformed prison guard escorted Leslie Van Houten into the room.

She was wearing a floppy, navy blue sweater over her dark gray prison dress. Her long brown hair was neat and shiny, with bangs curving down to her eyebrows. Although slightly pallid from her years in prison, she looked almost wholesomely attractive. There were tears in her eyes. As we looked on, she greeted Keith warmly, like a close friend and confidant, telling him that she had been taken from her cell into a dim, sweltering holding room and given no information about why she was being detained. For the two hours we were being checked, she had sat in this small, barren room. It was, she explained, typical of the impersonal treatment she had come to know and expect, yet she couldn't help crying every once in a while, she said, over the boredom, isolation, and daily humiliations of prison life.

Keith offered her a cigarette and lit it for her, giving her a moment to relax before we began our interview. He updated Leslie on the latest legal developments in her case; then he introduced the two of us and told her a little about our backgrounds, our project, and the lunchtime conversation we had had the day before. Leslie seemed to grasp our mission immediately. She turned toward us openly. When we told her that we were interested in focusing on her transformation of personality, she said that she would be very interested in talking about it and that she would be happy to cooperate with our questions in any way she could.

It was difficult to match this woman we were observing with the headlines' cold "thrill killer" of nineteen who, when asked at the trial if she were sorry for what she had done, replied blankly, "Sorry is only a five-letter word." At twenty-seven, Leslie seemed sober and thoughtful, in sharp contrast to her sensationalized media image. Her eyes were soft and alive, her smile relaxed, her posture altogether natural. It seemed to us very possible that she had, indeed, broken free of Manson's spell. For the next two hours Leslie talked easily, with full awareness and composure, commenting on the significance or irrelevance to her plight of a number of experiences from her childhood and high school years. She looked back at her deep and continuing relationships with her family, especially her mother who had visited her every Sunday since her conviction. She explained to us with great clarity the paths by which she went into and came out of her nightmare existence in the Manson Family. As we addressed the question of her initial transformation, Leslie recalled the naïveté with which she first became involved with Manson. After our months of interviewing for this book, we found this part of her story extremely familiar.

"I didn't know Charlie had studied Scientology," she said. "I never realized how he manipulated our minds with all his Eastern philosophy about getting us out of the ego and not thinking."

According to Leslie, "the way Charlie did it" was through strict isolation and unrelenting intimidation. "The isolation was the major factor," she said. "We completely severed ourselves from the rest of the world." Then she went on to describe Manson's manner of capitalizing on each Family member's individual weaknesses and needs.

"I was always frightened of not being accepted," she admitted, "even when I was in school. But Charlie played on that; he saw a danger in my humor and outgoingness. He put me down all the time, and I went into a shell. The whole thing just was not me. He'd try to make me feel I was missing something. He said I didn't know what was happening and that I was really stupid."

As we talked, Leslie confirmed our suspicions regarding the role of LSD in the Manson murders. The drug issue had never been completely settled in the case. Attorneys and expert witnesses on both sides during the original trial seemed unable to determine whether the Family's frequent use of powerful psychedelics could be blamed for transforming innocent teenagers into a gang of crazed, unfeeling murderers. Even today, almost a decade later, the mind-altering power of LSD still awaits full medical interpretation. Use of the drug has been widely linked to hallucinations and distortions of perception, and there is a great deal of evidence indicating that young people on LSD may become extremely vulnerable to suggestion. Yet, despite the drug's observed physical effects, most researchers agree that if LSD has any pronounced effects on behavior whatsoever, it is not to make the user crazed and murderous but generally passive and nonviolent.

Leslie didn't discount the importance of LSD in the activities and rituals of the Family, but she stressed that like most Family members she had had extensive experience with the drug before she ever came into contact with Manson. She took "really mellow trips" regularly on weekends during her high school years, she told us, and none ever led to violence or violent impulses. A child of California in the sixties, when psychedelics were inseparable from the rest of the smog of the cultural environment, Leslie knew what to expect from the drug.

She did not, however, know what to expect from Manson.

"I felt an immediate affinity with the Family," she said, recalling her attitude in the beginning. "They lived that kind of 'acid reality' everyone was looking for at the time. It wasn't until the last four months that things started getting really weird. Then, out at Spahn's ranch, instead of coming back down after each LSD trip, Charlie would reinforce everything that was going on in the Family. He would make gestures that would take root in our minds. One time he acted out the entire crucifixion, going through contortions of pain and making really ugly faces. Then he would play card tricks, and because he was quick with his hands, we would all think we had seen a miracle performed by a very special person. But he was always so unpredictable. He would play

Beatle records over and over, saying to us, 'Can you hear it? They're talking to me!' Then he would read from the Book of Revelation and say that it was calling for us to find a hole in the desert and stay there until the race war was over. To this day, I don't know if he really believed what he was saying, or if everything he did was just to get even with the world."

Listening to Leslie, we began to see clearly how Manson had manipulated his followers during their frequent LSD trips together by leading intense role-playing sessions and fantasy games for up to eight hours at a time which, as Leslie said, "took root" in their minds. Under Charlie's direction, they played pirates and maidens, cowboys and Indians, devils and witches, in scenes replete with violent and sadistic imagery. When it came time to play Helter Skelter, life in the Family had become a game with no borders on fantasy and reality, an extended "trip" that kept up long after any chemical effects had worn off. Moreover, using the same kinds of techniques employed in many cults, Manson guided and badgered his followers into lasting states of confusion and not thinking that laid them open to every suggestion and command he gave. At all times, and especially during the Family's psychedelic episodes, Charlie's adept wordplay hammered home the final spikes of snapping.

"Being around Charlie during that time was like playing a game of Scrabble," Leslie told us, aptly characterizing Manson's method of inducing madness. "He never labeled anything as exactly like it was. He'd say, 'The question is in the answer,' and 'No sense makes sense'—things that would make your mind stop functioning. Then it wasn't a matter of questioning when things began to get bad. We'd stopped questioning *months* before."

Skipping over the period of the killings, we asked Leslie when she first started to feel herself coming out from under Manson's spell.

She thought about it for a moment. "When we were in court, I was still feeling like I was with him," she said slowly, "but toward the end of the trial he started to mess with me. He was playing his same old games, but I was starting to break away. If he said to do something, I'd do it. But my heart wasn't in it anymore."

Leslie's own description of the trial suggested to us that, had the proceedings been conducted differently and the defendants been separated from one another, she might have broken free of Manson sooner.

"I really didn't know I was under his control," she said. "In the courtroom I was only starting to hesitate and feel stupid, but just being locked up in this place was not enough to free me."

Leslie looked back on that first trial with some bitterness. "I know I was on trial for something horrible," she acknowledged, but she seemed to resent the attitude of Bugliosi and others who displayed little interest in finding out what had happened to her mind.

"Bugliosi was always saying it was 'bad blood,'" she told us, "but he never asked us any questions. One second we were Charlie's robots; the next we were completely responsible for what we did. He never looked for answers. He only looked for the conviction."

With so many factors working against her, Leslie's real "coming to," as she called it, didn't begin until after the trial, when the clamor had subsided and she, along with other Family members, was awaiting her execution.

"When they left us on death row, we were in complete isolation," she recalled. "For almost three years, I was only in touch with my parents and family. At first, when I realized how much my family loved me, I felt guilty, terribly guilty, for having hurt my mother. But I hadn't even started thinking about the crime itself. I was still thinking about the revolution that would come."

We asked her if during those years she ever felt herself awaken from her cult state of mind in what some former cult members had described to us as a sudden *"Aha!"* experience.

"Sometimes," she said, "I could feel myself on the verge of that kind of experience. But I always ran from those moments because, at the time, my mind really fought that more than anything."

It was during her years on death row, however, that Leslie did in fact snap out of her altered state, not in one overwhelming moment but in what appeared to be a series of partial deprogrammings effected inadvertently by a prison psychiatrist and another condemned prisoner. Neither of them possessed any intimate knowledge of deprogramming, but both simply talked straight to Leslie, showing their genuine care and concern and, in the process, helping her to start thinking for herself.

"Slowly," said Leslie, "without realizing it, the prison psychiatrist got me to start questioning things in myself again. Another woman on death row helped me even more. I'd be talking to her, and she would say, 'That doesn't make any sense. Explain yourself.' And I knew I couldn't. I thought, *If I'm not making any sense, then maybe there's something wrong with what I'm saying.*"

Through these informal confrontations, Leslie actually pulled herself up by her own mental bootstraps, yet she recalled the very real pain she experienced trying to break her mind free in this manner. As we listened to her and watched her, we were aware of the resemblance between Leslie's plight and that of so many other cult members we had interviewed.

"When I'd be questioned and not have any answers," she said, "I'd go blank and become frustrated, like when a machine jams and just sits there making noise. In my head, nothing was functioning. More than anything, I was trying to understand, breaking down stiff little slogans that had been drilled into me every day for months."

Eventually, the breakthrough came, and the spark that set it off was California's abolishment of the death penalty. For Leslie, the hope of leaving prison alive spurred her on to active thought.

"When they abolished the death penalty," she said, "the director of corrections brought the three of us together and said it was up to us to prove we could handle it. For me, that made all the difference in the world, when I saw that they were going to give me the responsibility for my future."

With death row no longer in existence, Leslie and the other two women were held in a special security unit constructed for them at the prison. It was during this time, isolated from the other prisoners, Leslie said, that she regained full control over her thought processes.

"In the long run I'm glad I spent so much time in isolation," she said, "because it gave me a chance to get to know myself again. I continued to receive letters from other women in the Family, but when it came time to write and talk to them, I realized that there was no relating at all. I was seeing them in their absurdity."

Like other newly deprogrammed individuals, however, Leslie had the most trouble confronting her fellow Family members, who were not making the same progress she was. Now back in Sybil Brand while her former sisters remained at Frontera, Leslie admitted to being proud of the progress she had made.

"I don't mean to be bragging," she said, "but out of everyone, I'm probably the only one who has done well."

Since her re-emergence Leslie has concentrated her efforts on becoming an active participant in prison life, serving as editor of the prison newspaper and devoting much of her time to reading and writing in an effort to prepare herself for release or parole—whenever that should come.

"I hope that after I'm out for a while," she said, trying not to sound overconfident, "once I'm used to being out there again, I can do something, not as a big cause but just to bring to light some of the things that can happen to young people. That's one thing that never came out in the trial."

Hearing her speak, we had to agree with Keith that Leslie's newfound stability appeared to be genuine. But was it really? Could it be, as a future jury or parole board might suspect, that she was simply pulling a clever con to win sympathy and approval? We weighed the evidence before us and, after our numerous interviews with former cult members, felt confident that Leslie displayed the vital signs of full recovery. We noted her poised, natural appearance, her interest and attention as we spoke, and the clarity of her understanding and expression regarding her most personal thoughts, feelings, and experiences. As our interview ended and the guard came to escort her back to her cell, Leslie's departing words suggested to us that she had not only regained control of her mind but that she had already embarked on a new and meaningful course of action.

"My coming to was slow," she emphasized, "but I've made every step on my own, and I'll never lose it. I have a complete drive to make it. I'm going to make sense out of it all, and I know I'm going to be heard."

On August 6, 1977, a California Superior Court judge declared a mistrial in Leslie Van Houten's second murder trial when the jury reported that it was hopelessly deadlocked after twenty-five days of deliberation. Five of the twelve jury members voted to accept Maxwell Keith's argument that Leslie suffered from diminished mental capacity at the time she went along on the LaBianca murder mission, but no unanimous verdict could be reached. A third trial began as this book went to press.

In the years between Leslie's first and second trials, the American public and another jury were confronted with another startling example of the sudden transformation of a young woman into a hardened criminal. On February 4, 1974, nineteen-year-old Patricia Campbell Hearst, granddaughter of legendary publisher William Randolph Hearst, was kidnapped at gunpoint from her apartment near the University of California at Berkeley and taken captive by a group of revolutionaries who identified themselves as members of the Symbionese Liberation Army. The SLA was a political cult, not a religious one, yet its leader, a charismatic figure named Donald DeFreeze who called himself Field Marshal Cinque, was regarded as a prophet by his followers and commanded total reverence and obedience.

The exact methods by which DeFreeze recruited and organized his small band of loyal followers have not been established, yet DeFreeze's extensive criminal record and his revolutionary goals bear surprising similarity to both the background and the visions of Charles Manson. Many of his techniques —including intimidation, isolation, a conman's charm, and the use of intense sexual experiences—may indeed have been the same as Manson's. DeFreeze's motivation was also similar to Manson's: through a campaign of carefully targeted violent acts, he hoped to set off an uprising of the underprivileged. And like Manson's string of ritual murders, DeFreeze's calculated plot to kidnap Patty Hearst misfired from the start. Patty's father, Randolph Hearst, in his sincere response to SLA ransom demands, hurried the distribution of several million dollars' worth of food to California's poor, setting off riotous outbreaks and a backlash of black resentment of the SLA.

In those first weeks after the kidnapping, DeFreeze also failed to exploit Patty for the purpose of freeing several other SLA members imprisoned on earlier charges. Before long he enacted an even more daring plan for capitalizing on his newly acquired and valuable asset, as he put the finishing touches on a scheme that may or may not have been his intention all along: that of making Patty Hearst a highly visible and apparently willing member of the SLA.

His methods in this effort are now well known: the conversion was accomplished by means of classic brainwashing techniques—and much, much more. For the first two months of her captivity, as she has consistently described the period, Patty Hearst was kept blindfolded on the floor of a cramped closet in the SLA's headquarters, repeatedly abused both physically and sexually by DeFreeze and other members of the group, further traumatized by never-ending threats of death if she did not cooperate with their instructions, and informed that she had been abandoned by both her parents and society. In April, 1974, Patty re-emerged from this assault as Tania, brandishing a submachine gun during an SLA bank robbery in San Francisco. For more than a year she kept up a fugitive existence, after the lies she had been told were seemingly confirmed when her six captors burned to death in a police raid on their Los Angeles hideout. Then, finally, in September, 1975, she was apprehended by the FBI.

The trial that followed, on federal charges of bank robbery, stands as perhaps one of the most contestable legal proceedings in recent American history. In what many charged to be his attempt to court the overwhelming consensus of public opinion against Patty and her family's wealth and social position, U.S. attorney James L. Browning, prosecutor in the case, called as his expert witness Dr. Joel Fort, described in the *New York Times* as a "maverick," neither a psychiatrist nor a psychologist, who had testified in over 260 criminal cases (including the original Manson trial). Fort, whose professional practices have raised numerous questions of propriety, argued that Patty was a "willing participant" in the bank robbery, that her personal history clearly established her as a "rebel looking for a cause," and that she was not raped by SLA members but surrendered willingly—if not happily.

The defense contended that Patty had been a "brutally victimized prisoner of war." But the three expert witnesses called by defense attorney F. Lee Bailey—among them brainwashing expert Robert Jay Lifton—repeatedly contradicted one another's testimony, arguing in favor of both conversion and coercion, and were so strongly opposed in their views that, as Browning told the jury, "they wash each other out." Lifton's analysis was thorough and well-grounded, comparing point by point the SLA's tactics to those of the Chinese thought reformers he studied in the fifties. But he and Bailey's other experts were unable to give the jury any much-needed insight into Patty's plight as something altogether new on the American social, political, and psychological scenes. To add to the bewilderment of the jury, attorneys on both sides of the case engaged in endless rounds of bickering. Bailey's attempt to bring Fort's questionable medical background to the attention of the jury was denied, yet one assistant prosecutor did succeed in suggesting to the jury that Lifton had a vested professional interest in finding a clear-cut case of "domestic" brainwashing.

The result was that no one, neither the jury nor the American public, ever got from either side a comprehensive and comprehendable explanation of what happened to Patty Hearst. The significance of her purported initial ordeal in the SLA closet got lost, along with the predictable impact of the techniques used by the SLA in their program of alternating brutality and sympathy toward Patty. The outcome of the trial was a verdict of guilty for Patty Hearst, and dim prospects of acquittal in an upcoming trial on eleven more counts of kidnapping, robbery, and assault.

What about Patty? From most accounts, following her capture she became something of a legal fiction herself, playing whatever role her lawyers or psychiatrists deemed most advantageous at the time. For seven months following her conviction she remained in jail, pending appeal, and then was reported to have suffered a severe emotional breakdown. In the wake of that incident, Randolph Hearst posted the $1.5 million bail that freed his daughter, only for her to become a prisoner once again, this time in her family's lavish Bay Area surroundings, guarded around the clock until her legal fate was resolved.

While on the West Coast, we attempted to contact Patty Hearst. We wrote to her father, exchanged telephone messages with his secretary, and then, finally, wrote directly to Patty herself to explain the nature and purpose of our investigation. All our efforts proved unsuccessful. Randolph Hearst was refusing all interviews, and we never found out if Patty even received our letter. Eventually, we were forced to admit that the barrier around her was impenetrable. We did, however, talk with several people who had spoken with Patty or the Hearsts (among them, Ted Patrick, who had discussed with her parents the possibility of deprogramming Patty on her release from prison, a plan that was tabled when Patrick's own legal problems landed him in jail in Orange County).

From those conversations and the paltry amount of information that has been made public concerning Patty's current state of health and mind, it seemed clear to us that the destruction of her personality, so deliberately and methodically carried out, had left her in an emotional condition that conformed with our picture of snapping in the most extreme sense of the term. As we had come to understand her condition, more than a year after her trial, following all the psychiatric care and treatment money can buy, Patty Hearst still seemed to be a troubled, unstable young woman, still wondering what had happened to her mind.

The most visible proof of her distress can be found in Patty's own words. In a half-hour interview granted to CBS News shortly after her release from jail, she spoke with surprising lucidity about some of her experiences in the SLA. When it came to her participation in the bank robbery, however, and the trauma of personality change she had undergone, she displayed noticeable confusion.

"I remember so little," said Patty of her performance during the robbery. "I remember what happened inside the bank up to—well, up to where their man was shot, and then it just all goes blank and I don't remember getting outside, getting in the car, any of it."

She did remember the SLA's death threats if she did not cooperate, and her own feelings when she watched her fellow members burn to death on television. It was then she concluded that everything her captors had been telling her was true: that her parents had abandoned her and that the FBI was out to kill her along with the rest of the SLA. Nevertheless, despite her explanation, like her original jury and so many other Americans, her CBS interviewer still sought an answer to the question of why Patty did not call home during her desperate year on the run. To us, her reply further revealed her own profound confusion as well as the degree to which she has been misunderstood. It was reminiscent of the frustration Leslie Van Houten experienced in her attempt to come to grips with her own thoughts while in prison.

"Well, you know," Patty told her nationwide audience, "I've tried to explain about the not calling home, or going home, the best I can. And I know it's really hard to understand, because it's really hard for me now to try to think of what was really in my mi— you know, how I could have thought that way, because it's crazy. It doesn't make any sense at all; and it's something that I'm still working on myself, trying to understand how I could get so twisted around in my own head."

During that interview, almost three years after her kidnapping, Patty Hearst displayed all the characteristics of a cult member who had not been properly deprogrammed. She laughed uneasily and cried sporadically in her muddled attempt to present her story to the American public. The impression she left, however, was that she was at best uncertain and at worst attempting to cover up her guilt. The one point Patty did not address in her interview, which from all recent reports her family seems bent on pushing into the shadow of her experience, was what happened to her mind in that closet during the first two months of her captivity. In our opinion, it was that prolonged and comprehensive assault on her body, her emotions, and her intellect which annihilated the foundations of Patty Hearst's personality, making her every subsequent action problematical from any traditional psychiatric view and unquestionably moot with regard to all charges of criminal intent.

In his testimony, Dr. Martin Orne, an expert witness for the defense, stated that in personal interviews with Patty before her trial, whenever he asked her about her time in the closet, "You would see an immediate collapse. A totally helpless person would appear at that time." Others who have talked with Patty since her apprehension reported similar reactions whenever they brought up the subject of this experience.

Another picture, drawn by *New York Times* reporter Lacey Fosburgh early in 1977, provides still more insight into the lasting ramifications of the SLA's all-out assault on Patty Hearst's mind. From her own observations and those of others close to Patty at the time, Fosburgh determined that Patty was in a paradoxical and unpredictable condition, one that signified to us the state described earlier as "floating"—the limbo of conflicting emotions that often follows an intense snapping experience. Friends described Patty as a "chameleon" capable of assuming a wide variety of personalities, from dutiful daughter to flirting coquette to angry, bitter, spoiled child. A year and a half after her life in the SLA had come to an end, Patty was reported to be still in a state of physical and emotional upheaval: menstruating nonstop for months at a time, her moods alternately anxious, giddy, or withdrawn, and manifesting other signs of distress characteristic of severely traumatized cult members. Fosburgh's description of Patty's appearance completed our sense of this tragically misjudged young woman. She pictured Patty as perpetually tentative, her voice a dull monotone, still tending to lapse into long and frequent periods of silence. "Her eyes are as large as plates," wrote Fosburgh, "and they are as sad as the history of the world."

Without having talked to Patty about her experiences, it is difficult for us to specifically relate her condition to our larger perspective on snapping, especially since the circumstances surrounding her transformation were so extraordinary. From our point of view, as we write, the outlook for Patty is uncertain. In view of the intensity and violence of her experience and its apparently continuing effect, and after having seen many other young Americans in comparable predicaments, we are inclined to agree with the opinion expressed by Ted Patrick that, until she is in some manner successfully deprogrammed, Patty may remain in a perpetual floating state of mind.

In that case, she will be a prisoner for the rest of her life, regardless of the eventual outcome of her entangled legal battles. Yet, no matter what she is known to have been through, the courts and the public continue to view her as a criminal. Despite her sworn contention that she was kidnapped, blindfolded, locked in a closet, assaulted, raped, threatened with death, and cruelly remolded in the image of the SLA, apparently most Americans agree with the man in the street, whose opinion was printed shortly after the jury delivered its guilty verdict, that "brainwashing can only be done by experts, not by kooks." Reading these popular and legal judgments in the light of everything we had discovered about snapping, it struck us both how desperately most people want to believe that their individual awareness is invincible, that their personalities, which they consider to be shaped once and for all in early childhood, are not subject to domination, alteration, or destruction. It also called up echoes of the appeals we heard from Karl Pribram, Hans Bremermann, and other scientists—the complexities of modern life have created an urgent need for bold new ways of looking at the phenomena of our day-to-day world.

Shortly after we returned to New York last summer, following our failed attempt to see Patty Hearst and a final swing through the Southwest and the Midwest to gather interviews, another shocking series of crimes broke into the nation's headlines, capturing attention unparalleled since the Hearst trial. On August 10, 1977, New York City police arrested twenty-four-year-old, David Berkowitz in connection with a year-long killing spree in the New York area which left six persons dead and seven wounded. The assailant wielded a .44-caliber handgun and identified himself as the "Son of Sam."

This slightly chubby postal worker bore no resemblance to the blood lusting, psychopathic figure conjured up by the media prior to the arrest. Neighbors and co-workers described Berkowitz as "quiet," "subdued," and "a loner." No one could imagine what would prompt this meek, clean-shaven, well-fed young man—if, in fact, he was the murderer—to prowl the lovers' lanes of the New York area seeking out young couples parked in cars, shoot them in the head at close range, and then flee.

Upon his capture, after what was hailed as the longest and most extensive manhunt in the history of New York, Berkowitz was said to have shown "no remorse." Throughout his arrest and interrogation, he remained placid and uninvolved, a bemused smile on his face at all times. People who saw the suspect remarked, "That couldn't be him. No way. He doesn't look mean enough. He looks so soft." A police investigator who talked with Berkowitz said that he couldn't even feel anger toward the man.

The story grew even stranger. Under questioning, Berkowitz talked easily about his neighbor, Sam Carr, the real "Sam" whose barking dog had tormented Berkowitz and, as he later declared, instructed him to begin his campaign of terror. Throughout that year, in a series of letters to local newsmen, Berkowitz spoke of himself as "Sam's creation," a cryptic reference to the owner of the howling black Labrador retriever, which Berkowitz once wounded in the leg with his famous .44 handgun and which later became the focus of his hallucinations and delusions.

The more facts that emerged, the more clouded the overall picture became. Berkowitz in custody did not conform to anyone's image of a psychopath or mass murderer. In their first round of examinations, court-appointed psychiatrists pursued traditional diagnostic paths in their efforts to establish whether Berkowitz was certifiably schizophrenic or psychotic in a way that could be linked to verifiable disruptions of his brain's normal biological activity. After a battery of medical tests, including a brain scan, doctors ruled out the possibility that Berkowitz had any chemical imbalance, tumor, or other form of physical brain damage. Further psychiatric examinations and psychological tests also failed to establish the exact form of the functional disorder from which he was believed to be suffering.

As we followed the mystery of David Berkowitz, noting the doctors' findings that the machinery of his brain was thoroughly intact, we began to suspect that Berkowitz's condition might be better understood in our new framework as a severe form of information disease. Studying all the available testimony and waiting each day for the latest reports, we were convinced within the first few weeks of his capture that Berkowitz was our first clear-cut example of snapping in its most destructive form, outside the context of a cult or mass therapy. As more on his background came to light from published interviews with former friends and letters written by Berkowitz, we came to our own understanding of how he had reached his state of delusion and emotional detachment. Berkowitz had snapped, we discovered, not through an extraordinary cult ritual or therapeutic technique but as the result of a sequence of intense experiences from his recent past.

Unlike Charles Manson or Donald DeFreeze, David Berkowitz was not the typical product of a broken home, misspent youth, or mile-long criminal record. On the contrary, his early years and his teen-age development more closely resembled that of Leslie Van Houten and, in some ways, Patty Hearst. Although adopted, he was raised by responsible, loving parents; yet he grew up in the midst of a social environment torn by the conflicting values of the youth culture of the sixties and early seventies. In our opinion, it was not in a religious or political cult but in the United States Army that Berkowitz underwent the drastic shift of personality that caused him to snap in the most extreme manner. In the army, over a period of several years, Berkowitz set off on a winding road of religion and drugs that left him, in the words of the psychiatrist who declared him mentally unfit to stand trial, "emotionally dead" —a macabre but absolutely precise description of our delusional form of information disease.

Until he joined the army, Berkowitz had led a relatively normal, if somewhat lonely and disaffected, youth. Although chided in school for being a "fat little Jewish boy," he had numerous close friends—both male and female. Growing up in a middle-class Bronx family, he was left, in 1971 at the age of eighteen, with a high school degree, little money, and few desirable alternatives for the future. So during that time of political protest and social upheaval, Berkowitz, by all accounts a straight, conservative, retiring youth, enlisted in the army and was shipped off to basic training in preparation for a tour of duty in South Korea.

Like any other rigidly structured organization with a restricted philosophy, clear-cut objectives, and its own alien, harsh environment, the U.S. armed forces have been shown to produce dramatic changes in personality. For World War II, every branch of the service turned out its breed of instant soldiers and officers. During those years, however, when the word "War!" commanded the utmost urgency and national support, American life moved at a slower, more deliberate pace. Most soldiers had numerous sources of help in confronting the emotional difficulties connected with mustering out when their tours of duty ended. Some branches of the service had specific programs and timetables for reintegrating their soldiers with society; the GI Bill offered generous benefits for continuing education and professional training; and a grateful public heaped on most returning soldiers the added rewards of a hero's welcome. Only recently, with the acceleration of American life and the wrenching controversy surrounding the Vietnam War, have American soldiers faced personal battles even greater than their military conflicts. And only since the sixties have large numbers of them discovered that making the transition back into civilian life can be a lonely, painful, and frighteningly difficult ordeal.

From our perspective, there is catastrophic potential in the conflict that has arisen between almost every young American's growing awareness and the rigorous training and intense experiences he may undergo in military service. David Berkowitz seems to have succumbed to this. Berkowitz's induction into the army marked the complete severance of the individual from his past. During basic training, America's modern prototype of depersonalization, he performed admirably and he was shipped over to Korea, where, in a clerk-typist position with considerable responsibility, Berkowitz displayed fast thinking, a good appearance, and natural ability. Few Americans who haven't been there, however, can possibly appreciate the hidden emotional hazards of the peacetime limbo existence of American troops in Korea. In that environment lurked psychological dangers which in many ways exceeded those of combat itself. From stories we had heard about life in Korea, it was easy for us to understand how a "fat little Jewish boy" from the Bronx could find himself adrift and cut loose from reality.

This is apparently what happened to David Berkowitz in Korea. During his years there he was pummeled by a barrage of new ideas, experiences, and decisions, tossed back and forth in this sealed environment until the unique configuration of personal strengths, sensitivities, and vulnerabilities that made up his personality was literally shaken apart. In a series of handwritten letters to a former girlfriend from various army posts in Korea, Berkowitz described how easy it was to "get hooked" on the LSD and morphine that were readily available to American soldiers. In this foreign, free-floating army world, Berkowitz, until then a gentle young man and a vocal pacifist, was court-martialed because of a confrontation in a chow line with a superior officer who demanded to know why he wasn't wearing a gun.

"I said I didn't bring it to the field and I refuse to bring it to the field," Berkowitz wrote at the time. "Well all hell broke out after that. They just can't tell me when to carry a gun. I explained it to them but it didn't do much good. I also explained it to the chaplain. And guess what, he's with me all the way. He never carried a gun in his life."

From the concern he expressed frequently in his letters, it seemed clear to us that the gun incident set off a crisis of both conscience and consciousness in Berkowitz. After that, he became heavily involved in the rampant drug scene among American soldiers in Korea and got caught up in the peace, love, and rock music culture that was as popular among Korean military units at the time as it was among young Americans in the United States. Like Charles Manson, David Berkowitz had his rock interests and satanic influences, and it is likely that in a suggestible psychedelic state he read undue apocalyptic significance into the lyrics of a rock album by the popular group Black Sabbath.

His army buddies were the first to detect Berkowitz's transformation. "There seemed to be a personality change," another soldier who knew Berkowitz in Korea reported. "He tried talking to me about it. He used to say, 'If it makes you feel good, do what you want to do. Don't ask me to accept you. Do what makes you feel good.' " His letters changed, too. He began writing about changing colors, dark red and purple hues, and "things" coming at him from mists. In phrases familiar to us, he described the same feelings of detachment that characterized so many victims of snapping and information disease we had interviewed.

"When I look in the mirror all I see is one green soldier staring at me," he wrote his girl friend. "I feel like a robot being told when and where I can do things."

The sentiments expressed in Berkowitz's letters suggest that drug use was at most, as with Leslie Van Houten, only an indirect cause of his later violent acts, just one factor among many new experiences and emotional pressures that made him vulnerable to distorted ideals and delusions—both paranoid and messianic. Yet it could be argued convincingly, as Berkowitz himself declared, that drugs provided him with a rare source of release from the countless tortures of military life in Korea. In that environment there is little doubt that drugs contributed to the free-for-all of reality and fantasy taking place in Berkowitz's mind. His letters of that time, rampant with misspellings and bad grammar, demonstrate the extent of his confusion.

"I must truly admitt [sic] to myself that unless I don't manage somehow to find a way to temporarily escape this lousy life, I will become really insane. So it doesn't hurt to escape [on drugs] once and awhile or often, to straighten out my distorted messed up mind. . . . 'Why dope you ask.' Because it is to damn boring here. Where all a bunch of humanoid robots, so we feel."

After everything that transpired during almost two years in Korea, like so many victims of snapping, Berkowitz was fully aware that he had undergone a drastic change of personality. The change frightened him, as did the prospect of returning to his former life in the United States. He expressed those fears in another letter to his girl friend.

"I hope they let me go home in July. You know something, I'm really scared to go. I think the freedom will get to me. . . . Do you know something Iris. I have really changed. To much I think. I don't understand what its all about. . . ."

In our view, David Berkowitz's letters from Korea provide a dramatic record of his protracted snapping experience. When he returned to the U.S. in early 1973, he was as unstable as a former prisoner of war and as desperate to find an identity as a person who has left a religious cult without being properly deprogrammed. After Korea, however, Berkowitz was assigned to another clerical position with a military combat brigade stationed at Fort Knox, where he spent over a year trying to accustom himself both to his new personality and to a new and equally foreign domestic environment. There, like so many of his fellow soldiers who may have been no more sure of their identities than Berkowitz, he settled on a final, surprising, but not completely incomprehensible course of action: he converted to Evangelical Christianity.

"I just asked him to go to church with me one day," said Jim Almond, the fellow soldier who introduced Berkowitz to that old-time religion. "He said, 'I'm a Jew.' " Almond told a reporter, "And I told him I didn't care what he was, did he want to go to church?" Berkowitz accepted Christ on his first visit to the Beth Haven Baptist Church. "Well, we went and he really enjoyed it," said Almond. "He went forward at the invitation [to accept Christ as one's personal savior from sin]. And after the service, he came up to me grinning and laughing and saying, 'Man, I'm saved.' Then we came back that same day for the evening service and he went forward again at the invitation. He told me afterward that he just wanted to make sure it took."

For a while, at least, his renewal appeared to be successful. Berkowitz spent the year after his baptism fervently attending three church services a week and reading Bible stories to little children. Fellow church members described him as "a really fantastic guy with a great personality" and "a great soul-winner" who brought a number of GIs from the base into the Evangelical fold. After over a year of Christian life however, Almond noted, Berkowitz began "backsliding"—a term used frequently among Born Again Christians. According to Almond, Berkowitz's parents were greatly dismayed when they found out that he had become a Christian, and during this time we can imagine that Berkowitz, anticipating his discharge, began to seek a new anchor for his personality, one that would serve him when he returned to his former life in New York.

But he never found it. Although we can only speculate from the sparse information available, it is very likely that David Berkowitz returned to New York in 1974 in that peculiar twilight zone of floating, poised for the even greater personal catastrophe that lay ahead. Following his return, he drifted through a local community college and a series of uneventful jobs. With his family now relocated in Florida, his former girl friend married, and his old high school friendships long abandoned, he never seemed to find so much as a thread of connection with which to mend his sundered personality.

From all reports, Berkowitz remained detached, withdrawn, lonely, and suggestible, coasting through the everyday world atop a wave that threatened to break at any moment. In that condition, the trivial but penetrating sound of a barking dog was the tiny measure required to send him over the edge. It is our belief that Berkowitz, having depleted his entire reservoir of possible alternatives—from drugs to Jesus—had only one remaining source of experience, one pattern of information, to direct his course of action: guns. So, burned-out, drifting, and alone, he slipped all the way into the fantasy world with which his mind had long ago become acquainted. He began hearing voices, receiving messages from God and Satan, and following the commands of a black Labrador retriever who ordered him to launch a reign of terror on New York as a warning to the world from the demons he perceived.

We believe it unlikely that David Berkowitz derived any satisfaction from the murders he allegedly committed. By that time, he was probably incapable of feeling anything at all, caught in the grips of his delusional frame of mind. Press reports suggest that Son of Sam committed his crimes coolly, carefully going about each adventure and, after some of them, demonstrating the ironic acuity of his twisted state by writing painstakingly neat letters to Jimmy Breslin and other New York journalists which displayed occasional glimpses of wry humor.

It is also a good bet that, if David Berkowitz were to reveal the specific experiences that so drastically altered his personality, his story would not seem all that exceptional. In America today, as Berkowitz himself has tried to explain, there may be countless "Sons of Sam" in the making, frustrated, confused, disconnected individuals who have searched in vain through fields of drugs, religion, and therapy, trying to find some meaning and direction for their lives, looking for themselves and some route to other people—and discovering only the private horror of snapping.

It is not only impossible to understand the particular transformations of personality illustrated by Leslie Van Houten, Patty Hearst, and now David Berkowitz within the prevailing traditions of psychology, it is also futile to attempt to judge and rehabilitate such people in accordance with the codes of America's legal and penal systems. No social purpose is served by their drawn-out psychiatric and legal battles, and no greater or lesser human good is derived from simply imprisoning them or sentencing them to death.

In our view, Leslie Van Houten, Patty Hearst, and David Berkowitz are not "common criminals," nor can they be dismissed as "human monsters, human mutations." If anything, their tragedies underscore the urgency of acknowledging that snapping is something new and threatening to our society. In their extremes, these cases verify our contention that no one is immune to snapping. Until we in America take steps to find out what happened to Leslie Van Houten, Patty Hearst, and David Berkowitz, to help them and us "make sense out of it all," our society will remain vulnerable to the random blows of others with similar fates.

For these criminals are victims, too, victims of something that our society does not yet fully understand. And we have a lot to learn from them.

16 The Future of Personality

> *We have to touch people.*
>
> —*Jacob Bronowski,*
> The Ascent of Man

AS WE WRITE this final chapter, a new book on the controversy surrounding the Unification Church echoes Moon's claim that all great religions go through "disruptive stages" in their early years.

The FBI recently conducted raids on Scientology headquarters in Los Angeles and Washington, charging that the cult had infiltrated both the Justice Department and the Internal Revenue Service and had stolen documents relating to government inquiries into the organization's operations. Scientology lawyers quickly took the case to court, claiming that the raid was conducted illegally, and won the return of the seized material, along with a gag order preventing the government from revealing what they had uncovered.

The once-tiny Children of God, which now claims that its 8,000 missionaries have made over two million conversions, has expanded its operations into Western Europe, the Canary Islands, and North Africa. Leaders of the cult are reportedly encouraging their more attractive women members to become "Happy Hookers for Jesus," not to raise more money for the wealthy group, the leaders swear, but solely to "show people God's love."

Werner Erhard has launched a new campaign to end world hunger in a nationwide lecture tour before audiences expected to number in the hundreds of thousands. Ticket price: $6.00.

The TM organization is now offering courses in levitation which supposedly enable advanced meditators to rise up in the air and, as many report, fly. According to one TM "executive governor," more than five thousand Americans have already learned the new TM "Sidhis"—the word means *perfection*—technique, which is taught in a series of sixteen week-long courses that costs approximately $4,800 per person. These are only a few of many signs we have observed that the groups, movements, and cultural trends discussed in this book are not about to go away. On the contrary, they seem to be gaining in both reach and strength.

Toward the end of our own travels, we were especially disturbed by our visit to a town in the Pacific Northwest. There we encountered the spread of a new mass therapy called Lifespring, that sounded to us like a high-priced replica of est and that was apparently being test-marketed on a broad local scale in this progressive medium-sized city.

Everywhere we went that week, in restaurants, barber shops, and private gatherings, we heard about and witnessed firsthand the striking effects of this powerful new mass-group technique which, according to several Lifespring veterans, a team of psychologists had refined from Werner Erhard's basic prototype. People we spoke to seemed to be in a state of perpetual ecstasy, filled with glowing praise for the Lifespring "experience," which, we were told, could run to $650 for a single weekend, depending on the potency of the particular package. "I've been high for a year and a half, and I haven't come down yet," we were told by a hairdresser in a local unisex barber shop, yet both he and the young man sitting in his chair, another happy Lifespring graduate, adamantly refused to tell us what went on in the training sessions. In a familiar refrain, the customer informed us that it was something we could only experience for ourselves. "How can you describe the taste of a strawberry," he said, "to someone who has never tasted one?" The barber at the adjacent chair concurred. Although he hadn't yet attended Lifespring, he had been on the waiting list for several months, he explained. To answer our questions, he offered us the same cryptic sales pitch he had been given by a number of Lifespring veterans, a phrase that we were to hear repeated time after time throughout that week by people who wished to assure us that Lifespring wasn't nearly as grueling an emotional experience as est was reported to be. "If est is Listerine," he said enigmatically, "then Lifespring is Lavoris."

Observing the people in this town after four years of research and exploration into the techniques and jargons used by many cults and mass therapies, we questioned whether they were just feeling good, high, or happy or whether they might have undergone artificially induced alterations of awareness that could lead to bizarre states of mind.

Quite apart from Lifespring, however, in the many forms we have seen it take, snapping is so new in our society that many vital distinctions still need to be made on sensitive, delicate questions. The seductive promise of instant resolution for personal problems such as neurosis, despair, aimlessness, and boredom—whether through cults or mass therapies—continues to pose a threat to our society, but any attempt to curb these activities raises questions of constitutional rights and individual prerogatives. Many people continue to ask, "If it feels good, why not?" and, "What can possibly be wrong, if it makes me happy?"—even if their pursuit of happiness may lead to potentially devastating states of disorientation, detachment, delusion, and withdrawal. Well aware of the controversial nature of this issue, we discussed these questions and others with lawyers and concerned citizens around the country, addressing ourselves not to the belief, psychology, social purpose, or even business practices of any particular cult or group, but solely to the methods by which human awareness may be manipulated.

How do we defend ourselves against a phenomenon as new and challenging as snapping? It is our belief that the best way to combat snapping, in cults, in groups, or in everyday life, is to understand it, to be apprised of the ways in which the mind may be subtly attacked and of the threats to each individual's awareness posed by new and intense experiences and by the extraordinary pressures of modern life. An individual who understands this will be more capable of recognizing possibly damaging patterns of experience and combinations of events and of consciously eliminating or minimizing their effects on him.

In addition, to counter what appears to be a massive, richly funded tide of exploitation of experience in our culture, we believe there is an urgent need for an equally ambitious campaign of public information and action. Further scientific research should be conducted aimed at providing the American people with detailed criteria that would go beyond the scope of what we have been able to present here for distinguishing between a valid religion and a cult and between a sound mental health therapy and a potentially dangerous form of physical and emotional abuse. Such efforts would also help clear up the confusion over deprogramming and provide guidelines for legal and medical intervention.

Undoubtedly, any action on these sensitive issues of religion and mental health is bound to cause legal battles, but the overriding imperative may be simply stated: somehow, through public guidelines, court precedent, or specific legislation, we as a nation should declare explicitly that no individual or organization may, by means of physical stress or any subtle or covert technique, impair, make captive, or destroy an individual's freedom of thought.

However somber our message has been throughout this book, our investigation of snapping has not led us to draw entirely negative conclusions. There are also hopeful signs and extraordinary promises, for if there is one thing snapping reveals, it is that our human information-processing capacities, our individual abilities to think and feel, remain almost infinitely flexible throughout our lives. Although our culture now possesses the know-how and the tools to destroy human awareness, that knowledge may also be used to enable people to shape their own personalities, to cultivate their individual powers of thought and feeling, and to enhance, rather than impair, their abilities to perceive and respond to the world around them.

Individual growth and fulfillment need not be bound by traumas from the past. Our adult lives are not necessarily determined by how we were weaned or toilet-trained; no one has to suffer unrelievedly from the shocks of childhood and adolescence. As the mass therapies demonstrate, however recklessly, Americans now have a battery of techniques at their disposal with which to annihilate long-standing hurtful emotions and self-defeating patterns of thought. At the same time, there is no reason for an individual's humanity to be swallowed up by the process of change. A person's personality need not become a passive product of whatever environment he finds himself thrust into. His life is not required to fly off on a new tangent with every "rite of passage" or intense experience he undergoes. Once each of us grasps the larger significance of our natural capacity for change, we can protect ourselves from manipulation and control our own personal development, and even beyond this—we can step into the process of our human evolution and direct the manner in which our extraordinary individual capacities of mind unfold.

Throughout the seventies some of these truly positive trends in personal growth have been overlooked or ignored. While the cults and mass therapies have been capturing the attention of the media, some of the founding figures of the human potential movement have remained faithful to its ideals and principles, nurturing the fundamental values of human development, shunning the fireworks of so many of their colleagues and disciples in favor of more thoughtful, thorough explorations of man's capacities. Amid the free-for-all, these elders of the movement, Carl Rogers, Jack Gibb, and others, pulled back from controversy, going about their own research in firm but quiet ways.

Toward the end of our stay in southern California, we stopped in to see Carl Rogers in his office in La Jolla. Rogers is perhaps the most revered survivor of the heyday of the human potential movement. Founder of the person-centered approach to psychotherapy which bears his name, and impressed by the demonstrated power of group dynamics, Rogers in the sixties had proclaimed the encounter group "the most significant social invention of the century." Now, a decade later, Rogerian therapy still holds fast to the goals of humanistic psychology.

When we called Rogers and expressed our interest in his view of the recent turns the human potential movement has taken, he granted us a few hours of his time just days after he had returned from a series of seminars in Brazil. At seventy-five, Rogers still displayed the grace of the humanist and father figure that he is. We found him tanned and healthy; thoughtful, relaxed, and pleased to share his views. As we laid out the general plan of our investigation, Rogers responded to our ideas, from the outset placing himself in firm opposition to mass therapies such as est which function on, as he put it, "intrusive" principles.

"I've never been through est," Rogers told us, "and I don't think I want to. Their goals are not too bad, actually, but their means are horrendously authoritarian. I feel that they have lost completely the distinction between means and ends.

"I've read a great deal of transcribed material of Werner Erhard's. There's a lot of rather rambling talk about how great it is to discover that you make your own reality and that you're responsible for your own life—some of which I agree with, some of which I don't—but nowhere does he mention the *process* by which you're supposed to arrive at that goal. In my opinion, that process is all-important."

The fundamental principle of humanistic psychology is that the process of an individual's experience is more important than any end-product of behavior. In contrast to est's intrusive style, Rogers described his method as "facilitative." Instead of aggressively confronting their participants, Rogers's group leaders consciously place the power and control of the group experience in the hands of each participant.

Rogers agreed with us that an authoritarian, intrusive group can produce dramatic changes in personality and that a religious revival can bring about miracles of renewal and rebirth. But from his point of view, Rogers asserted, there is much more to personal growth than can be achieved by simply overwhelming the individual.

"It comes down to a question of your basic philosophy and intention," he said. "I think people like Werner Erhard and Billy Graham—and I'm not trying to equate the two—both know how to use mass effects to bring about very potent personal experiences. But these are not self-induced, they're mass-induced. Those kinds of conversions don't last very long unless you keep the person in the group that brought it about."

While he had been traveling around the world, however, Rogers admitted he had not been paying a great deal of attention to the ways in which the principles of humanistic psychology have been exploited in other brands of therapy and in the cults.

"I guess I hadn't realized myself how much the issue has become blurred in people's minds," he said frankly. "There has been an awful lumping together of anything that is a group. I think that it is a terrible thing to unnecessarily exert power over another person. The more you move toward power *over* others, the more potential for damage there is, and the more danger there is, as in the cults, that people may get caught in something they can't get out of. I think the goal in the cults and groups is to attribute personality change to something outside the individual. It's always, 'Look what happened to me!'—whether it's because of Christ or Werner Erhard. The other kind of personality change, the kind I am concerned with, is a process from within. *I* did it. Others facilitated it, but I'm the one who did it. I'm the one who's in charge of it, and I'm the one who can determine whether it goes any further."

Rogers's insight that beneficial change rarely results from just a sudden moment of intense experience confirmed the message we had received from so many individuals who had learned that lesson the hard way.

The remainder of our conversation with Rogers was devoted to speculation along more hopeful and uplifting lines. We spoke of creativity, of trust, and of our culture's movement away from the "ultra-rational" toward inclusion of the emotional. To our surprise, Rogers's forward-looking approach to man's unfolding human potential incorporated an increasing interest in—and regard for—man's older intuitive powers. "We do have a kind of primitive wisdom that we've completely forgotten," Rogers told us, adding, "We need to get in touch with it again."

"If I were a young psychologist today and I knew what I know now," he said, "I'd probably start looking into the psychic realm. I've never had any psychic experiences myself, but I feel there's enough evidence these things can happen that it bears looking into. In the future, I think the nonrational aspects of a person will come to be more honored and will prove to be more useful than we have any idea at the present time."

As it turns out, many young psychologists, and some older ones as well, have already set out in that direction. In contrast to the popular movement's misguided turn toward "intrusive" therapies, leading figures in humanistic psychology, along with concerned scientists from a number of other disciplines, have begun delving into the intriguing world of psychic activity. In our research, we spoke with many professional men and women currently exploring one or another branch of this new arena. We interviewed prominent psychologists who were attempting to solve the mystery of "holistic healing," a secular version of the Evangelical "laying on of hands" which has demonstrated how belief alone may produce very real and lasting cures for physical ailments. We contacted physicists, biologists, and former surgeons who had begun to investigate other psychic phenomena such as clairvoyance, telepathy, and telekinesis, using strict scientific controls in an effort to satisfy the rigorous standards of their peers.

Among laymen as well, interest in psychic phenomena appears to be at an all-time high. Throughout our travels, even in casual conversations unrelated to our investigation of snapping, we heard people of all ages and walks of life recount their personal stories of "out-of-body" excursions, telepathic incidents, premonitions that later came true, and brink-of-death experiences —not all of which could be dismissed as simple hallucinations.

Despite our concern over the dangers and delusions of the cults, our extensive knowledge of the techniques that may be used to create vivid impressions of psychic events, and our inherent skepticism with regard to so many wild stories we were told, we endeavored to listen with open minds to each tale of extrasensory and psychic phenomena. From our perspective, none of the experiences described was necessarily of supernatural origin. So many of the experiences people now refer to as mystical or psychic are completely natural: they can be explained in communication terms, at least in theoretical, if not yet fully verified, accordance with our emerging understanding of the brain's holographic information-processing capacities and man's extraordinary intuitive and nonverbal communication abilities.

Researchers who for years have been questing after exotic "psi energies" and "parapsychological dimensions" only now appear to be on the verge of drawing similar conclusions. Science, however, our ultimate standard of verification in the West, still awaits a comprehensive theoretical framework and experimental method that will enable people to accept the psychic feats that each individual may be capable of performing. And slowly that framework appears to be taking shape. The new interdisciplinary sciences promise in time to explain the hidden powers of the human mind, not by means of psychology, psychiatry, or traditional physical medicine, not even in accordance with our usual notions of matter and energy, but in terms of information, a newly recognized entity in itself. Before long, we may come to fully understand information and harness it with the aid of the new scientific languages of quantum physics, neuroscience, cybernetics, and information theory.

Yet in a very real sense, it could be said that man's psychic powers are already being tapped and exercised every day by participants in religious cults and mass therapies through their extraordinary rituals and practices and their recruitment and solicitation activities. Up close, however, the uncanny powers of healing, mind control, and "on-the-spot hypnosis" used by people in these groups may be identified as nothing more than finely tuned versions of man's ordinary communication powers, "psychic" capacities which many have already come to understand in the unembellished terms of suggestion and belief, of nonverbal communication, and of the dynamic bonds of relationship between individuals that give rise to all kinds of remarkable occurrences. These natural capacities for communication are the most powerful tools an individual possesses, yet most people remain ignorant of these sophisticated powers of mind, unaware that they already use them all the time in their day-to-day lives, affecting other people as others affect them. As we come to better understand the natural power of our human communication abilities, it is very likely that the psychic skills formerly viewed as parlor tricks and miracles will become readily available to us all. Throughout history, these powers have been held for man—as if in safe-keeping—by religion. Now we can begin to bring these treasures out of hiding and place them where they belong: in the space between human beings.

Before bringing this book to a conclusion, we drew back from our work just far enough to view our own perspective in perspective, and think about the note on which we wanted to end this inquiry. After everything—the cults, the mass therapies, information disease, and the challenges of everyday life— we thought about the larger meaning of snapping in America as our culture heads into the nineteen eighties, and we came full circle to address the first question we posed at the beginning of this book: Has mankind crossed the threshold of a great new era of human fulfillment?

Yes, it's true, we agreed: in America today, mankind does stand poised at the threshold of a new age. But in our view we haven't entered that era yet; and we may never see it, because our culture seems to be embarking on a destructive new course of manipulation and escapism, of human abdication. Snapping, as we have come to understand it, may be summed up in a very simple definition: it is a phenomenon that occurs when an individual stops thinking and feeling for himself, when he breaks the bonds of awareness and social relationship that tie his personality to the outside world and literally loses his mind to some form of external or automatic control. In that sense, the moment of snapping, when the mind shuts off, remains a moment of human decision. It takes place as some invisible switch is thrown in the infinitely flexible human brain, whether voluntarily and in good faith or unwittingly and in a state of confusion, as individuality is surrendered to some religion, psychology, or other recipe for living that requires no real conscience and no consciousness, no effort or attention on the individual's part.

It seems clear to us that, confronted by the demands of a complex, ever-changing, and often overwhelming mass society, an individual cannot elect mindless happiness over everything and everyone else in his or her life. That kind of happiness is information disease, for, severed from humanity, it cannot be understood or shared. Contrary to popular opinion, our exploration has confirmed for us that there really is nothing *human* inside human beings. It's all biology—chemistry and machinery. Our humanity lies in the space between. That is why we have chosen to look at snapping from the point of view of communication, for it is this social process of communication that dictates what each individual's awareness and personality will be. This process also teaches us that an individual's sense of self can be no greater than the quality of that individual's interactions and relationships with other people. For it is only in relation to other people that the human mind finds a pathway to itself. Even the loner or recluse who believes he is self-sufficient in his private thoughts or the world of nature has been raised by someone, given a language, and taught to think and feel.

Snapping, in all its blind detachment from the world, its disconnection and self-delusion, is a product of a futile attempt on the part of millions of Americans to escape the responsibilities of being human in this difficult, threatening age. In that sense, it is an act of betrayal both of one's individuality and of one's society, for our human nature binds each individual to every other. So long as we ignore this undeniable imperative of human communication, we will remain slaves to our genes, our machines, our environment, and to those who seek to exploit our culture's rapidly expanding technology of experience.

If, on the other hand, we choose to cultivate our natural capacities of thought and feeling, respecting the fundamental values that did, in fact, emerge from the consciousness explosion of the sixties, and if we come to understand how our individual personalities are bound one to another, we may actually discover that new era of fulfillment, that great new age of enlightenment. Then together each of us will be able to step across that threshold without snapping.

Postscript: Jonestown
The Face of the Eighties

ONLY SEVEN MONTHS have passed since the first publication of *Snapping*. In that time, the phenomenon of "the cults"—considered by many to be a fad of little or no social consequence—has exploded before the public eye with a violence and horror that has shocked the nation and the world. In the closing months of 1978, a quick succession of events transformed the curious phenomenon into what more than one respected journalist called "the story of the decade." Having observed, researched, and struggled with the complexities of this story throughout the seventies, we have long been convinced of its significance, but the events of recent months have provided us with new pieces of the puzzle, sharp fragments of what we perceive to be a picture not just of the immediate past but of the near future as well.

The image taking shape is the face of the eighties, its character lines etching shadows much deeper than any single religious cult—or even the cult movement as a whole—had cast in the seventies. Its broad emerging visage reveals the specter of mind control brought home, an everyday reality in which powerful new techniques of human exploitation and manipulation may run rampant through our culture. From our view at the moment, the face of the eighties looks troubled and unruly.

The first shock wave hit in August 1978, when the U.S. government indicted eleven high officials of the Church of Scientology on criminal charges of conspiring to plant spies in government agencies—including the Justice Department and the Internal Revenue Service—breaking into government offices, stealing government documents, and bugging government meetings. The twenty-eight-count indictment alleged one of the most extensive domestic plots of government infiltration in history.

Soon after, independently, another branch of government leveled charges against a second major cult. In November, 1978, a House International Relations subcommittee chaired by Rep. Donald Fraser of Minnesota released a report urging that a federal task force be established to investigate the Unification Church for violations of U.S. currency, immigration, banking, tax, foreign agent registration, arms export control, and other laws. After a three-year probe, the subcommittee charged Korean evangelist Sun Myung Moon with attempting to establish a world government under his rule and, among other illegal acts, of attempting to become an international supplier of Korean-made M-16 rifles.

About the same time, another event took place that signaled a major escalation in the running battle between America's religious cults and the law. In October, 1978, Los Angeles attorney Paul Morantz, who had recently won a $300,000 damage suit against Synanon, the once-respected but increasingly extremist California-based drug rehabilitation foundation, was bitten by a four-and-a-half-foot rattlesnake that had been placed in his mailbox with its rattle removed. Quick thinking by Morantz along with eight vials of anti-snakebite serum are credited with saving his life. Following leads supplied by Morantz's neighbors, police arrested two members of Synanon's self-styled "Imperial Marines" commando unit and charged them with attempted murder. Later, authorities also issued an arrest warrant for Synanon founder Charles Dederich, charging him with conspiracy to commit murder, assault with a deadly weapon, and solicitation to commit murder. To those observers who have been keeping close watch on the cults of the seventies, it was the first instance of a group electing undisguised terrorism in response to its critics. Up to that point, most cult counteroffensives had been limited to lawsuits, harassment, and, at worse, mere threats of violence. With Synanon's violation of that tacit ground rule, the cult issue seemed suddenly to have been thrown into a whole new arena of controversy—and cause for alarm.

Then came Jonestown, and in one of the most staggering human tragedies of modern times, the prospect of cult terrorism was fulfilled in unimaginable detail.

The facts have become legend: On November 18, 1978, a U.S. Congressman and three newsmen were shot and killed while on a fact-finding mission to investigate charges that American citizens were being held against their will, beaten, and subjected to other physical and emotional abuses at the jungle commune of an American religious sect, the People's Temple, in Jonestown, Guyana. The victims, among them Rep. Leo J. Ryan of California, NBC News correspondent Don Harris, NBC cameraman Bob Brown, and *San Francisco Examiner* photographer Greg Robinson, had uncovered evidence confirming many of the charges made by a group of concerned relatives of temple members and had agreed to take with them more than a dozen temple members who had requested safe passage back to the United States. At the grassy airstrip in nearby Port Kaituma, as Ryan's party was boarding two chartered planes, a red tractor and trailer from the the People's Temple pulled up to the runway. Three or four men jumped off and opened fire on the group. As the wounded fell to the ground, the attackers strode forward and shot them in the head at point-blank range.

At the same time in Jonestown, People's Temple founder and leader Rev. Jim Jones signaled his players to enact the final scene in what turned out to be a well-rehearsed tragedy. Jones's lieutenants gathered at the commune's main pavilion, their automatic rifles ready. Then Jones called together the population of Jonestown and informed them that the congressman and the journalists were dead and that Guyanese defense forces were on their way to Jonestown to torture and kill the commune residents. "It is time to die with dignity," said Jones, reiterating for the last time his repeated vow that he would lead his followers in a "mass suicide for the glory of socialism." Next, at Jones's command, the temple doctor and his medical team brought forth a battered washtub of strawberry Flavour-aide laced with heavy doses of cyanide, tranquilizers, and painkillers; and Jones told the assembly that "the time has come to meet in another place." "Bring the babies first," he ordered, and his nurses shot the poison down their throats with syringes. Then the rest came forward, including whole families, each member drinking a cupful of poison and being led away by temple guards and told to lie with others in rows, face down. Within minutes, people began to gasp for air, blood flowing from their mouths and noses before the final convulsions set it. According to one witness who managed to escape, the entire ritual lasted almost five hours. All the while, they said, Jim Jones sat on his raised chair in the pavilion repeating, "I tried. I tried. I tried." Then, "Mother. Mother. Mother. Mother." When it was over, Jones lay toppled on the podium with a bullet in his head. And 912 people were dead.

The massacre and mass suicide in Guyana left the entire world stunned and groping for answers. Who was Rev. Jim Jones? What manner of religious group was the People's Temple? What was the chain of events that led to what the *New York Times* termed "one of the most shocking and extensive losses of U.S. lives outside of wartime"? Even before the final body count was completed, the real story of what happened in Jonestown began to emerge.

As it turned out, People's Temple was not a temple at all, but a scheme devised by Jim Jones to create a socialist utopian community in the guise of fundamentalist Christianity. Although he was an avid churchgoer from an early age, by the time he reached adolescence James Warren Jones no longer believed in religion. At eighteen, Mao Tse-Tung was his hero, yet he continued to espouse his Christian faith—believing religion to be the ideal tool with which to build a Marxist social group in the United States. In 1956, he formed the first People's Temple in Indianapolis, and in 1965, fearing racial bigotry and anti-Communist persecution, Jones and one hundred of his most devout followers moved to Redwood Valley, California.

Jones's temple flourished in California, attracting thousands and establishing centers in San Francisco and Los Angeles. But it soon became apparent that life inside the People's Temple fell far short of the utopia Jones depicted. Jones began making increasingly stringent demands on his followers, commanding them to make a total commitment to the temple, instructing them to break off relationships with family members outside, and urging them to donate all their money and possessions and sign over their homes and real estate to the temple treasury. Reports of beatings, violence, bizarre sexual practices, criminal activities, and death threats to former members and potential defectors led to a series of exposés in California newspapers and magazines; and in August 1977, Jones quickly removed his flock to Guyana, where he had leased 27,000 acres of land from the Guyanese government for the establishment of an "agricultural mission."

At the jungle site, its climate almost unbearably hot and steamy and its living conditions primitive, Jones managed to cut off the entire populace from the outside world. A few rare visitors and defectors brought back information on worsening deprivations and physical abuses inflicted on temple members, along with consistent reports of Jones's own progressive mental deterioration. There were also rumors that millions of dollars were being cached in secret temple bank accounts in Switzerland and Panama, and that Jones was planning a mass migration to a Communist country, possibly Cuba or the Soviet Union. Those reports and the desperate pleas of a newly established Concerned Relatives Committee prompted Congressman Ryan's mission. When Ryan's authority to conduct such an investigation was challenged by temple lawyers, and information was received that any intruders might be met by heavily armed defenders, Ryan permitted television and newspaper journalists to accompany him, convinced that full media coverage would be his best protection. The journalists, on the other hand, felt that the presence of a U.S. Congressman was theirs.

These sad details and many others surfaced in the first media inquiries into the People's Temple, and undoubtedly more information will emerge in the continuing criminal investigations and government inquests into the events that transpired: names of individuals who committed specific acts, exact balances of the temple's foreign bank accounts, and even the full picture of Jones's underlying political aims may add whole new dimensions to a tragedy already rich in grotesque subplots. But, in our opinion, one of the key factors in the equation that has been inadequately explored is the broad question of the state of mind of Jim Jones and his followers at the time of the debacle in Guyana. In its immediate aftermath, our print media and airwaves overflowed with speculation, but as the public's thirst for discussion and dissection waned, a number of serious questions remained unaddressed

—lingering issues that, we feel, merit further inquiry out of respect for the dead and responsibility to the living. Was Jim Jones from the beginning a sadistic, calculating megalomaniac, or did he begin with a sincere dream of an interracial socialist utopia? If the latter was so, what factors led him to his final blaze of infamy? What program of manipulation did he employ that led nine hundred people to take their lives at his command? Indeed, in view of the particulars of life in Jonestown—especially the presence of arms and numerous reports of beatings and other acts of coercion—can what finally happened truly be called suicide, or must it more properly be labeled mass murder?

To gain insight into these dilemmas, we undertook our own inquiry into life and death in the People's Temple. For two months we researched Jim Jones and his organization and interviewed a number of individuals with personal experience in the group. We spoke to former members of the temple, to people who had lost family members in Guyana, to representatives of the Concerned Relatives Committee who had tried to bring the threat of mass violence to public and government attention, and to staff members of the Human Freedom Center, the Berkeley, California halfway house that was established by former temple members to help others who wanted to leave the group make the difficult transition back into the larger society. Most of the people we interviewed requested anonymity, but two former members of Jones's executive Planning Commission, Jeannie Mills and Grace Stoen, permitted us to use their names and quote liberally from our conversations. Like ours, their concern was that the tragedy of People's Temple be given a full public airing, and that the lessons that may be derived from it be responsibly applied to any similar cult threat should it arise.

Our findings made deep impressions on us. With each interview we grew more amazed at Jones's crude, almost primitive manner of manipulation, and repeatedly we had to ask ourselves if his method even warranted the label of mind control. Certainly, Jones achieved an alteration of belief and behavior in his followers described classically as "brainwashing," and we could see that, by his strong-arm intimidation tactics, to a certain extent he even gained control over his followers' minds, shaping their thoughts, feelings, and desires. But, from our perspective, we found nothing in Jones's scheme that produced the kind of bedrock alterations of personality that we have termed *information disease.* Jones had no specific ritual or technique such as those used by other cults we have studied that may, over time, alter or destroy fundamental information-processing pathways in the brain.

In fact, Jones's method tampered only superficially with the fundamental structures of personality that we have been exploring throughout this book. Jones used many of the elements of physical, emotional, and intellectual manipulation that have been identified with mind control—isolation, decep-tion, indoctrination, exhaustion, poor diet, and an instilled fear of the outside world—and together these techniques managed to suppress, if not overwhelm his followers' freedom of thought. But the very fact that Jones resorted to blatant physical coercion, frequent beatings, punishments, sexual abuse and humiliation, and, eventually, the forced use of psychoactive drugs on temple rebels and dissidents suggests the profound ineffectiveness—and perhaps the ultimate failure—of Jones's attempt to gain mastery over the minds of his followers.

We found a sharp point of departure between the People's Temple and other cult groups in the dramatically different nature of its comprehensive cult experience. Where most other cults attract converts with the promise of life-changing spiritual and psychological experiences—intense moments of revelation, enlightenment, ecstasy, or bliss—Jim Jones's approach was, from the beginning, more social and political than spiritual. In this sense, it could be said that the most noteworthy element of the People's Temple experience was a legitimate social objective: the establishment of an experimental interra-cial community based on principles of shared labor and equitable distribution of wealth. This expressed goal was down-to-earth and genuinely attractive to the underprivileged blacks who comprised the great majority of temple mem-bers. It also had great appeal to the fundamentalist Christian whites who were drawn to Jones's plan from the first days of his ministry in the Midwest, and to the middle- and upper-middle-class white liberals and intellectuals who, in the heyday of sixties' political activism in California, saw Jones as a dynamic and effective organizer and agent of social change.

But where Jones's initial social intentions may have been admirable, his methods were questionable from the beginning. From his earliest preaching days, he proved to be an expert manipulator, combining the wealth of knowl-edge he had gleaned on the Holy Roller circuit with the force of his personality to tailor-make a personal pitch to every potential covert. When courting black recruits, he made moving appeals to their deep desire for a better life, both materially and spiritually. He spoke of their longing for racial harmony and sympathized with their historical plight dating back to the roots of slavery in America.

"You know, black people have suffered all down through history," a black woman who belonged to the temple for five years told us, "and he used to tell us about the slave ships and the suffering. The man laid it on heavy, I'm not lying. He knew how to talk to you. He knew how to make you feel good."

Another former temple member whose daughter died in Guyana remem-bered Jones's seductive style. "To me, he was just like a cat charming a bird," she said. "That's the way he sucked those people in. He told them to give all their possessions to the church and that the church was going to take care of them, take care of all their needs. All they had to do was live and enjoy themselves. They wouldn't have to worry about any bills, food, anything. The church would take care of everything."

Jones's social overtures to blacks were not without their spiritual elements. He was well-acquainted with the central role of religion in their lives, and in his weekly religious services he employed techniques that wowed their belief in his supernatural and divine powers. His miraculous healings and psychic "readings" were largely responsible for his illustrious reputation among blacks in California. A woman who lost five close relatives in Jonestown told us how she and her family were recruited into the temple:

"I went to the beauty shop and my operator told me about this Jim Jones, that he could heal people. That's the way he drew his crowds, telling people that he healed cancer. So my momma and I decided to go and check it out, just for kicks. We had to get there before eleven o'clock Sunday morning, and the place was packed. They had singing and dancing and people meeting other people for two or three hours before Jim Jones came out. Finally, he appeared to preach or whatever he called it. Then he picked out one person and told him that he had cancer and said that he was going to heal him. Then a nurse ran back to this person with a cup and told him to spit the cancer in the cup, and the person started gagging and spat this cancer into the cup—it was supposed to have been cancer, but I heard it was rotten chicken liver. They put it on a piece of gauze and passed it all through the church and it smelled up the whole place. Everybody jumped up and down and clapped their hands and shouted and carried on. I was hard to convince, but of course my momma believed it. She joined the temple, then she got my sister to go. Then she joined and convinced her daughter to join. Then her daughter brought in her husband and several of their friends."

Jones's healings, like other aspects of his style that gave him such power, especially over the middle-aged and elderly blacks in his congregation, were patterned on the world-renowned ministry of Father Divine, a black preacher who first appeared in the 1930s as founder of the Kingdom of Peace Movement. The ostentatious Divine, who proclaimed himself God of the universe, said he raised the dead and healed the sick in his colorful, bombastic revivals. In the late fifties, when Jones was traveling around the country observing various black and white preaching styles, Divine's technique made a strong impression on Jones, as did his fanatical obsession with maintaining strict discipline and unwavering loyalty among his followers.

Jones's trick of extracting "tumorous masses" in his healings is a classic ploy of faith healers, voodoo priests, and "psychic surgeons" around the world; and similarly, his famed psychic "readings" were carried out with great flourish and showmanship. "He used to 'call people out,' " another ex-member told us, "and when he called out a person's name that person would stand up and the usher would go up to him with a mike. Jim would ask him, 'Have you ever seen me before?' And he'd say no. 'Have I ever been in your house before?' No. 'Well, you live in such and such a place, your phone number is such and such, and in your living room you've got this, that, and the other, and on your sofa you've got such and such a pillow . . . Now do you remember me ever being in your house?' "

Grace Stoen, one of Jones's closest aides for many years before she quit the temple in 1976, explained Jones's elaborate system for gathering information that he used in these readings. "It wasn't until after I left the church that I found out how he did it," she said. "He had a whole staff of people, about six women, and when you entered the church you had to give them your name, address and phone number. Then, once the services began, before Jim came out the staff would go and call up the numbers and say, 'Hi, we're doing a survey and we would like to ask you some questions.' That's how they got the information, then he had it all handy when he called people out during the service."

The technique worked well enough to impress the majority of those in weekly attendance; and when more persuasive displays were needed, Jones frequently called upon loyal members planted in the audience to fake even more impressive cures, to testify that Jones had retrieved them from wasted lives of alcoholism, drug addiction, or prostitution, and to provide heartfelt confirmation of Jones's extrasensory abilities. But always, despite his grand theatrics, Jones's most powerful ploy was the direct appeal he made to each potential convert. "He had a different faith and a different message for everyone he dealt with," said one observer. "He was able to hook in with each one in an individual way."

Grace Stoen recalled the breadth of Jones's preaching expertise. "He was good-looking and he had charisma," she said. "He would rush onto the stage and everyone would clap. Then in the course of the meeting he would do a little religious stuff for the religious people, a little political stuff for the political people, for the real intellectuals he would become intellectual—at my first meeting, instead of reading the gospel he read the San Francisco newspaper—and for the common people without much education, he would make a very emotional appeal. Jim Jones had the ability to speak to a thousand people and 999 would get something out of it."

Jones's weekly prayer meetings in San Francisco and Los Angeles were aimed primarily at recruiting blacks who were already familiar with his religious format. At the People's Temple commune in Redwood Valley, however, Jones's fervid preaching and other spiritual pyrotechnics took a back seat to his interracial agricultural community. It was there, at the Ukiah commune in the late sixties and early seventies, that Jones had little trouble converting many of the white members who were to become his top temple executives.

"My husband had always been into social work and working with the underprivileged, and we had five kids of our own who we were concerned about," said Jeannie Mills who, with her husband, Al, served on the People's Temple Planning Commission until they left the group in late 1975. "So we went up to Redwood Valley to see this man who, we had been told, was helping young people get off drugs. What we found was a group of caring, loving, friendly, warm people who immediately accepted us just exactly as we were. These people didn't care what I had. They were more concerned with who I was. My children had instant acceptance; people loved them. The other kids came over to them and were surprisingly friendly. My kids loved it and my husband and I were really impressed with the social structure of the group, so we joined to be a part of a cause that was doing good."

Once they joined the temple, most of the people we interviewed told us, their first two or three months of communal life were rich with emotional rewards and inspiration. Toward the middle to late seventies, however, members began to notice gradual changes in the orchestration of their daily lives and the conduct of temple affairs. In the manner of almost every cult, members were soon cut off from their families. A black woman who never joined the temple recalled the break that took place within her family. "We used to be very, very close, but after they [her relatives] joined Jim Jones, they wouldn't talk to us. Anytime I wanted to see them I would have to go down to the church and ask them to please bring them out. Sometimes they would let me bring them back to my house, but they would always have this anglo girl accompany them so we were never alone."

Jeannie Mills explained to us how Jim Jones succeeded in dissolving family bonds. "He did it slowly. He would say, 'You should always spend Thanksgiving and Christmas with me,' and eventually we had to clear any visits to our relatives. Pretty soon he started saying, 'Your relatives don't care for you. We're the only ones who care for you.' Then he would say, 'If you have to go see them, just ask them for money.'—but that would cause them to cut *you* off! Eventually, he denounced the whole world outside People's Temple as unenlightened and uninformed. 'The only real caring people are in the group,' he said. 'If you really cared about society, you'd be in People's Temple.'"

Similarly, Jones's financial requests of his members grew in stages. Until the early seventies, the temple maintained a policy of not exacting forced offerings from its members. Then, citing the practices of other churches, Jones inaugurated a tithing policy of 10 percent, which soon increased to 25 percent of each member's income. Then additional funds were solicited, supposedly to build a senior citizens' center or a school for retarded boys, and the church started selling special healing oils and pictures of Jim Jones in ornate lockets. Finally, Jones ordered members to turn over everything they owned as a measure of loyalty and devotion to the temple. Also during this time, individual work loads were increased to the point of exhaustion. As in other cults, great physical stress was placed on each member in the name of increased service to the church and its urgent mission. Members were required to go on frequent church campaigns throughout the state and across the country, and they were regularly subjected to marathon sermons that kept up for six hours or more. The pressure of hard work, arduous travel schedules, and Jones's interminable indoctrination sessions succeeded in monopolizing most members' attention and energy, leaving them little opportunity to stray or even doubt. As temple life became more demanding, each member's capacity to choose or reject it became more clouded.

"Nothing was ever done drastically," recalled Grace Stoen, "that's how Jim Jones got away with so much. You slowly gave up things and slowly had to put up with more, but it was always done very gradually. It was amazing, because you would sit up sometimes and say, wow, I really have given up a lot. I really am putting up with a lot. But he did it so slowly that you figured, I've made it this far, what the hell is the difference?"

A most revealing example of Jones's gradual manipulation can be seen in his attitude toward the Bible. From the beginning, in typical cult style, he relied upon subtle distortions to soften and remold his converts' beliefs. Jeannie Mills recalled how this technique made her a firm believer in Jones:

"For the first four months we heard the same sermon about errors in the Bible," she said. "He cited Matthew 1:16 and Luke 3:23, which gave two different genealogies of Jesus. Then he handed out this whole long list of errors, and I went home and checked them out and it was just incredible. God wasn't the sweet, loving God I had always thought him to be. Here I saw he was murdering and commanding people to murder and to take young women for handmaidens and do other atrocious things. I was really disillusioned. When he destroyed my Bible, it was as if he had just pulled the rug out from under me. There I was with everything I had believed for thirty years gone. So I figured, yeah, he must be right. And I saw that he was doing all these very humanitarian, loving things, and I thought, well, by their fruits ye shall know them."

In 1976, as Jones's attacks on the bible grew more vicious, he prompted one woman to quit the temple. "I left when he denied God," she said. "At first he preached Christ just like anybody else would, but then he cursed God and called Mary a whore and he threw the Bible across the church. He said he was going to destroy the Bible, that it was nothing but a paper idol. Until then I had really believed in him. I thought he was a prophet come from God."

While the temple grew rapidly—accumulating wealth, membership, and political power—Jones's declarations and behavior became more extreme. He stepped up his preaching about imminent earthquakes and nuclear holocausts and of a coming race war between blacks and whites. He established a "relationship committee" to preside over his methodical splitting up of marriages and families, and, while he declared sex evil, he solicited temple members to engage in relations with him as a sign of their loyalty. Jones carried on impulsive affairs with white female members of his inner circle, and pursued illicit relationships with other members, both men and women, as well as with people outside the temple.

Yet, despite his own sexual profligacy, at one point Jones directed church members to swear off all sexual relations, even with their own spouses. According to Jeannie Mills, Jones's defense of abstention was based on ideological, not spiritual grounds.

"He considered sex to be counterrevolutionary," she told us. "He justified it by saying that when Mao Tse-Tung went on his Long March all of his soldiers gave up sex because you just can't have a revolution when your heads are filled with sexual desires. He said, 'We're in the middle of a revolution, and you should all be willing to put aside sex until we're able to live in our beautiful utopia.'"

Jones's prohibition against sex was heeded by much of the temple membership, but like so many of his arbitrary rules, it also gave rise to numerous acts of transgression and disobedience. Jones was deeply disturbed by any violations of his edicts, however minor. In the beginning, in Redwood Valley, discipline was mild and evenly meted out. Mischievous children were spanked, goldbricking members were chastised verbally. But in the early seventies, Jones's punishments became less evenhanded, and progressively more severe to the point of brutality. A young child who had stolen a cookie or two teenagers caught holding hands might be beaten repeatedly with a heavy wooden paddle known as the "Board of Education." Older members deemed slack in their duties might be compelled to fight in "boxing matches," sometimes for several hours, with up to three or four bigger, stronger opponents. Others, particularly the children, would be subjected to the "blue-eyed monster"—a secret disciplinary weapon that was said to be a kind of electric cattle prod that sent a severe shock through the child's body. Jones rarely administered these punishments himself. He required members of his choosing to carry out the beatings. The entire temple membership was called on to witness and be warned.

In 1973, Jeannie and Al Mills were forced to watch as their teenage daughter, Linda, was brought up before the commission. Linda's response, as well as their own, gives some insight into the extent of Jones's influence.

"She hugged a girl in the parking lot who hadn't been to church for several weeks, so Jones decided that Linda was a traitor," Jeannie Mills told us. "They beat her seventy-five times with the board, and she screamed bloody murder, but when they finished she said, 'Thank you, Father,' which was what everybody had to say after a beating. When we got home that night, Linda told us that it was the most positive experience she ever had, and I thought, as horrible as this seemed, as sick as it made us, this was the first time I had ever heard Linda say she had learned a lesson."

According to Mills, it was Jones's response that determined how the members would react to the various disciplinary measures. "We all watched Jim's cue. If Jones laughed, we laughed. If he got incensed, we got incensed. If you looked disapproving or if you even frowned, one of the ushers would turn your name in to Jones and you'd get called up for discipline yourself."

In addition to physical correction, Jones had other ways of keeping people in line. In Planning Commission meetings, he asked members to sign "loyalty oaths," in which they confessed to having committed criminal acts or to being homosexuals or lesbians. He made them sign statements swearing that they were willing to kill enemies of the temple and then commit suicide, and he instructed members that if they should ever leave the temple and attempt to expose him, he would release the documents to discredit them.

And always, from the beginning, Jones threatened the lives of potential defectors. "You know, after '73 we didn't stay in because we loved the group," said Jeannie Mills. "We stayed in because we knew we would be killed if we left. Jones had told us hundreds of times, privately, publicly, in Planning Commission meetings—it was common knowledge—that if you left the church you'd be killed."

Several years later, when the Millses finally did leave the church, Jones's henchmen seemed bent on carrying out his orders. "We lived in cold terror for about a year," said Jeannie Mills. "They put harassing letters on our porch. They called us in the middle of the night. We had cars tailing us. Jones used any tactic he could think of, figuring that if he could keep us scared, we would be quiet. And in most cases it worked. People who left him twenty years ago in Indianapolis are still afraid to speak out."

These acts of physical punishment, coercion, and, finally, repeated unconfirmed reports of murder underscore the failure of Jones's haphazard attempts at mind control. For the most part his methods were randomly selected and crude. He was less of a mind-bender than an arm-twister. Because he had no systematic technique for controlling his members' internal thought processes, Jones was constantly forced to control them from without.

"What was amazing was that he would beat these people, and it would hurt, really hurt," remembered Grace Stoen, "but they would still go ahead and disobey his rules. Then, as each form of punishment would lose its effect, he would introduce a new one that was more drastic. This really bothered Jim Jones, the fact that he could not obtain that control."

Ironically, Jones was losing control over his own members as he appeared to be gaining influence in the outside world. In 1975, Jones mobilized his followers to deliver a bloc of votes that helped liberal Democrat George Moscone become mayor of San Francisco, a favor that was returned when Jones was appointed chairman of the San Francisco Housing Authority. Flexing his newfound political muscle, Jones used his position to make other contacts, collecting a file of personal letters from such luminaries as First Lady Rosalynn Carter, Vice President Walter Mondale, H.E.W. Secretary Joseph Califano, Jr., and Senators Hubert Humphrey and Henry Jackson, which he later used as letters of entrée and endorsement in Guyana and elsewhere (although some of those letters now appear to have been forged).

With each social and political gain, the focus of Jones's attention shifted further away from his people and his temple. He became obsessed with himself, playing his role of "Dad" and "Father" to the point of irrationality. Eventually, Jones not only claimed to be God, but, at various times, the reincarnation of Christ and Lenin, and he came to demand from his followers total identification with his mushrooming self-image. "No matter what you did as an individual," recalled Grace Stoen, "everything had to be credited to Jim Jones. We had to constantly say that the only reason we were in the temple was because of Jim Jones, that the only reason we did something was because of Jim Jones. You had to, and if you didn't, you got confronted for not giving him credit. He was a megalomaniac. He was determined to go down in history."

If he was concerned with his place in history, Jones was also obsessed with his welfare and personal safety. He instituted unusually strict security measures in his temples, searching all incoming worshipers and eventually requiring all members to wear badges with photo-identification. He also endeavored to make "Father's" personal safety of paramount concern.

"He would say to people in meetings, 'What are we going to do if anyone ever tries to get Jim Jones?' And everyone would scream, 'Kill! Kill!' " recalled Grace Stoen. "A thousand people with their fists in the air screaming, 'Kill! Kill!' That was heavy."

In time, someone did try to get Jim Jones, not to harm him physically but to expose him. As early as 1972, *San Francisco Examiner* religion writer Lester Kinsolving attacked Jones in print for his claim to have brought more than forty persons back from the dead, also for his habit of surrounding himself with aides armed with pistols and guns. Jones was outraged. According to Grace Stoen, it was this first media criticism that confirmed his worst fears.

"The bad press totally blew him apart," said Stoen. "From that point on, Planning Commission meetings were stepped up to almost every night. Jones said we had to be prepared because these kinds of things were going to happen again. He became obsessed. That's when he began to believe there was a conspiracy out to get us."

Jones sustained other crushing blows during that period. In 1973, the People's Temple had its first large-scale defection. Eight young members of Jones's revolutionary guard quit in response to Jones's growing extremism. According to Jeannie Mills, it was this defection, as much as the Kinsolving articles, that pushed Jones to the edge.

"Those eight young people were a revolutionary group within the temple," she said. "They'd been hyped up with stories of Che Guevara and they had been doing some practice with weapons, and when they left, Jones got scared. He really thought they were going to come after him. Actually, all they wanted to do was get out of the temple so they could live their own lives. It was at that point, though, that Jones started taking ridiculous precautions to save his life, like instituting the guards and having us sign incriminating letters for his protection. That was also when he issued the order that if anything ever happened to him, every person who had ever left the temple was to be killed."

Jones's fear of defection was apparently linked to his fear of betrayal and exposure, and he soon introduced a new practice that would turn out to be his final solution to the problem. In January 1976, Jones tested his first suicide drill on Planning Commission members. He explained afterward that the drill was designed to test their loyalty. Grace Stoen recalled:

"Jim Jones said, 'Just to show you how much I love you, I'm going to give all of you some wine.' We couldn't drink or smoke so everybody was excited about this treat. We all drank it and Jim Jones asked, 'Is everybody finished?' And we said yes. Then he said, 'Okay, you've all just been poisoned and you have one hour to live.' When I first heard that I said no, I don't believe it; but Jones went so far as to have some people fake that they had dropped dead. Others pretended to be freaking out to encourage anybody on the border line to do the same. When the hour was up, Jim Jones said, 'Well, that was just a test. You did well.' "

The frequent suicide drills that followed were the most dramatic in a series of indignities Jones forced upon his flock, and throughout 1976 a steady trickle of defectors—including, to Jones's great dismay, Grace Stoen—caused a mounting wave of rumors and horror stories to begin cresting around the People's Temple. In early 1977, when Jones received word that a devastating exposé based on interviews with ten defectors was being prepared for publication in *New West* magazine, he did everything within his power to prevent its appearance, including eliciting prepublication protests from *New West*'s advertisers and representatives of the American Civil Liberties Union. Jones's move to censor *New West* failed, however, and as the publication date neared he began his crash move to Guyana.

Jones used his usual ploys to induce temple members to accompany him. He told his black followers that if they stayed in America they would be put in concentration camps. He warned white members that they were already on the CIA's enemies lists. As always, rebels and potential defectors were threatened with blackmail and death. From the outset, Jones spoke of the life they would find in Guyana in only the most glowing terms: everyone would live and work together in tropical splendor and interracial harmony. Only temple executives knew Jones's real intention of making Guyana the seat of his unbounded authoritarian rule.

"I remember once in San Francisco, Jim Jones said to me, 'Boy, when we get people down to Guyana we can do anything we want to them,' " said Grace Stoen. " 'There will be no more authorities and officials, no more police reports. We won't have to put up with any of that crap.' "

In the weeks before the *New West* article appeared, Jones made a hasty attempt to cover his tracks and prepare for his move to Guyana. Church administrators called upon rank-and-file members to turn in receipts they were given for donations to the temple as well as items of veneration such as the lockets with Jones's photograph. When *New West* hit the stands, the word was out. There were more defections of temple members who hadn't yet gone to Guyana, and the temple's San Francisco headquarters became primarily a supply and communications base for operations in Guyana. A shortwave radio link was set up between the two points as Jones proceeded to conduct his distant forces and his attending throng in the creation of his earthly paradise.

Life in Jonestown resembled not so much a paradise as a prison. According to survivors' reports, the commune was run like a concentration camp. Residents were required to work eleven-hour days in 120° heat with only a ten-minute break, constructing camp facilities and attempting to cultivate the land they had cleared of jungle growth. But farming proved to be a futile undertaking. Dense weeds would grow back and choke the crops within twenty-four hours. Before long, the commune's residents, who had visions of sharing their harvests with the Guyanese people, were themselves reduced to living on a diet of boiled rice with gravy.

On the surface, however, Jones had managed to build an impressive jungle community, complete with living quarters, a central meeting place, a school, and one of the best-equipped medical facilities in Guyana. But as his agricultural experiment foundered, Jones appeared to sink deeper into despair and madness. He ordered disciplinary measures more harsh and punishments more brutal than those he practiced in California. Members indicted by Jones for infractions were sentenced to "the box"—a kind of isolation and sensory deprivation cell. Young children were tied up and lowered down a well until they screamed for mercy. In nightly "business meetings" that often lasted until 3 A.M., which all commune members were required to attend, women who violated Jones's moral code were forced to have sex publicly with cult members selected at random by Jones. Those found guilty of other crimes were called on the floor before the assembly, then stripped naked and whipped, beaten unconscious by security guards, or pummeled bloody in boxing matches against opponents wearing weighted gloves.

For the boldest dissidents or those who could not be dissuaded from wanting to leave, Jones established a special "extended-care unit" of the Jonestown medical facility. There runaways and other unruly members were confined and given massive doses of mood-altering drugs. Published reports have established that huge supplies of psychoactive drugs were smuggled into Jonestown by temple officials, including Quaaludes, Demerol, Valium, morphine, and some 11,000 doses of Thorazine, a powerful tranquilizer used in mental hospitals to subdue violent patients. Many of these drugs also promote hallucinations, blurred vision, confusion, speech disturbances, euphoria, depression, and suicidal tendencies. After a few days in extended-care, survivors have reported, people seemed to lose any desire they might have had to leave Jonestown or disobey Jones. "When they came out a week later, they were changed," one observer reported. "They couldn't talk to you and they walked around with empty faces."

There seemed to be no end to the inhumanity at Jonestown. Mail to residents from relatives in the United States was never delivered, but those whose families expressed concern were forced to write letters home dictated by temple officials in which they would describe the fulfilling and idyllic lives they had found, express their unqualified joy and happiness, and reaffirm their commitment to make Jonestown their permanent home. Around the clock, Jones kept up his feverish ranting. In his nightly meetings and for up to six hours each day, temple loudspeakers broadcast to the farthest reaches of the Jonestown clearing. At night, after the exhausted, overloaded, and battered workers were finally permitted to go to sleep, Jones would turn on his loudspeakers again, screaming "Alert, alert, alert! Everyone to the pavilion!" and begin to rave anew about imminent attacks by the U.S. Army or CIA guerrillas. In these frequent "White Night" ceremonies, Jones would order commune members to drink from a fifty-gallon vat a fruit drink that was purported to contain lethal poisons. He declared that the commune was on the verge of being destroyed and that the only remaining course of action was "mass suicide for the glory of socialism." Afterward, when those who had fainted with fright or keeled over from suggestion alone had been revived, Jones announced that he had only been putting them through a loyalty test and now they could go back to sleep.

These tales of life in Jonestown first came to public attention in the spring of 1978, when Deborah Layton Blakey, once Jones's trusted aide and financial secretary of the People's Temple, escaped from Guyana and returned to the United States intent on notifying the media and authorities of the abuses taking place in Jonestown, and of the prospect of mass suicide as she witnessed it in Jones's White Night rehearsals. She submitted a detailed affidavit to the press, local officials, and the U.S. Justice Department; but even after her sworn testimony was printed in the *San Francisco Chronicle*, there was little public outcry and no widespread call for an investigation. When official inquiries were made, Jones responded with legal challenges and menacing warnings. In a letter Jones reportedly sent to all U.S. Senators and Congressmen when he heard of a possible government investigation, he spoke of his readiness to sacrifice himself and the members of his temple. "I can say without hesitation," stated Jones, "that we are devoted to a decision that it is better even to die than to be constantly harassed from one continent to the next."

When Representative Leo Ryan left for Guyana with the media and representatives of the Concerned Relatives group, there had been ample warning and demonstrated cause for concern, not only from sworn testimony and Jones's own mass suicide threats, but from reports that originated in San Francisco of illegal shipments of arms and ammunition to Guyana.

From the testimony of former members, we came to understand many aspects of the People's Temple experience, but, as we had suspected, they provided few hard clues to the states of mind of the nine hundred who died. The few survivors who returned to tell their stories have proved to be rare exceptions: an elderly woman who slept through the entire ritual, a young man who had an opportunity to escape when a nurse sent him to get a stethoscope. These individuals cannot tell us what went through the others' minds when they sipped the poison, but from their accounts, as well as those of other defectors, ex-members, and relatives, we can draw some preliminary conclusions about the degree to which People's Temple members were under mind control.

Former temple members confirmed for us that Jim Jones did impair his followers' ability to question and to make choices. In this his manner was straightforward. "When he would ask people to do something," one elderly woman told us, "he would say to them, 'Now don't ask me why, just do it.' He never gave anyone a reason." Jeannie Mills recalled how Jones explained his need for unquestioning obedience. "He told us that he was set up in a position of leadership and that in order to be an effective agent for change he had to have full power and we had to protect the office—which is what he called himself. He said that meant we could never criticize him or question him because to do so would be to weaken the effectiveness of the group."

Jones also relied upon group pressure to keep people from questioning and objecting. "I always had a nagging doubt in the back of my mind about whether or not his healings were for real," one woman recalled. "But I couldn't just say to someone, hey, that looks phony. You just didn't talk like that about Jim Jones. No one else was questioning. It seemed to me that I was the only person in the whole group questioning, so eventually I stopped questioning."

And, like every cult leader, Jones used his finely honed rhetorical skills to dissect his members' peace of mind. "He would talk for hours and hours about slavery and Fascists and Hitler killing the Jews," said another ex-member. "It would be like a bell ringing in your ears all the time. Then you would get to where you didn't listen to anything else. Your mind didn't have time to create anything on its own, and that was all you'd know."

Overwhelmed and exhausted, as in other cults, at some point many of Jones's followers seemed simply to switch off their own thought processes. Jeannie Mills told us that after she and her husband had quit the church, only to be coaxed back several months later by their children, they made a conscious decision to close their minds to the contradictions and "strange things" they had observed. She recalled how she—and no doubt many others—surrendered her will to Jim Jones. "You voluntarily chose not to question. You voluntarily chose to allow someone else to make your decisions. Then you kind of turned off this logical portion of your mind which people use to make everyday decisions. You stopped using it. And eventually you lost the capability of making decisions."

To relatives and other close observers of temple members, there is a virtual unanimity of opinion on our question of mind control. One elderly ex-member of the temple expressed the reigning opinion in less than clinical terms. "Toward the end, they looked like they were under some sort of spell. It seemed like they were helpless under him. They looked weary and worried and depressed, very depressed."

As with all cult members, however, the strongest evidence of mind control is to be found among those who left the temple. They report the kinds of aftereffects that commonly follow a cult experience, including the residual disturbances of thought and feeling that suggest some deeper alteration has occurred. "After I left, it took me five months to a year to come around," said Grace Stoen. "I moved as far away from the temple as I could, I got a job, but all I wanted to do was sleep. I would just sleep and sleep and sleep. I was very confused and mixed up and crying a lot. I couldn't talk to anyone because people couldn't relate to what I had to tell them. It was just too bizarre. I was very depressed, and I was having bad dreams. At one point, I said, I'm going back, I'm already a ruined person and I can't make it out here. And one of the people who had left earlier said not to worry, that I needed more time, that time alone would heal it. I said, yes, but what's wrong with me? She said, 'I don't know, but I went through the same thing.' "

More than a year later, Grace Stoen was still having difficulty making choices and acting on her own. "For a long time it was very hard to make decisions," she told us. "Up until just a little while ago I found myself calling people and saying, 'By the way, I was thinking of doing such and such, what do you think?' I was very unsure of myself and my judgments."

Massacre or mass suicide? The dilemma might be resolved either way. There is ample evidence—plus the weight of official and public opinion—to support the contention that the dead took their lives of their own free will. But it is equally possible to argue that Jim Jones was a mad, sadistic figure who presided over the execution of nine hundred helpless people—nearly three hundred of them children.

We believe it was a massacre. The Jonestown commune was a living hell. The people at Jonestown were subjected to extreme physical and emotional duress, then willfully deceived and confused beyond the point of self-responsibility. But there is a terrible irony to the tragedy at Jonestown, an irony that makes the massacre of 912 people so much sadder and more foreboding. With his wealth and power, Jones was free to pursue any course of action he desired. But his followers had no alternatives. They had indeed been charmed, coerced, exported, and imprisoned. Yet, despite the lies Jones told them, their twisted perceptions probably found their way to the truth: following the airport killings, there was no escape—either to freedom or from the inevitability of Jones's wrath.

Few who died in Guyana knew just how correct they were in that final belief that they had no other way out. For all they knew, most of those who had defected had already been murdered. Those members who were aware of the existence of the Concerned Relatives Committee and the Human Freedom Center knew only that all their missions to Guyana had ended in failure. Beyond that, however, most members had no idea that nearly every major government agency had been asked to investigate the People's Temple and had refused. The Treasury Department had been informed of illegal arms shipments to Guyana eighteen months earlier. The Federal Communications Commission had declined to press charges against the People's Temple for violations of shortwave radio broadcast regulations. Twice in the preceding year, the Social Security Administration had attempted to determine whether cult members were being forced to sign over to the temple more than $40,000 in government payments every month, only to be told by the State Department that they found no evidence that members had been forced to sign away their benefits. And the Justice Department, after receiving hundreds of reports alleging "brainwashing," coercion, and criminal activities in connection with numerous religious cults, had repeatedly refused to investigate such groups on the grounds that such an investigation would violate the group's constitutional guarantees of freedom of religion.

Even lacking that knowledge, in all likelihood the residents of Jonestown were overcome that afternoon by a profound sense of hopelessness. For the majority of them, born black and poor, life had always been an uphill struggle against insurmountable odds. For the rest, the young white college graduates and the earnest middle Americans, their ideals and values shaken by the cultural upheavals of the sixties and early seventies, Jonestown may have simply been the final letdown in a long series of disillusionments. For a time, unlike the other cults we have studied, the People's Temple offered them a real course of action for social change. "It was like you died and went to heaven and it was beautiful," said Jeannie Mills, "then suddenly God went crazy and everything went sour."

That may be the real tragedy of the People's Temple, that it was born of a sincere desire to make life better, but that its founder's notorious achievement was to undermine the very premise of our human existence. Grace Stoen offered a final thought on the fulfillment of the vision of the People's Temple. "When they first set things up in Guyana it was beautiful, it was fantastic, until Jim Jones came down and spoiled everything. It was so painful to watch. There was so much ability in the people. So much could have been accomplished, but Jim Jones ruined it. People's Temple could have been something. It could have been an example to the world."

We didn't investigate the People's Temple in the first edition of *Snapping*. Seven months ago, of the estimated 3,000 religious cults active in the United States in the seventies, the People's Temple didn't even bear mentioning among the ten largest, richest, or potentially most destructive. Our original investigation focused on the major groups currently operating on a national or international scale and those that employ identifiable techniques for stilling the mind. In that sense, as we have described it, Jim Jones's program of manipulation does not and never did fall within the scope of what we originally defined as *information disease*—the lasting alteration through intense experience of an individual's fundamental information-processing capacities, more commonly, his abilities to think and feel.

Since Jonestown, public concern over the cults has revolved around a single theme: their potential for violent, criminal, or self-destructive behavior. This was an issue we barely touched upon in *Snapping* because of its obvious sensationalism, the difficulties we encountered trying to verify reports, and on the unyielding advice of our lawyers. In recent months, however, a mass of new information has come to light, and the climate of discussion has changed enough to permit, if not demand, a full public airing of all evidence suggesting that other religious cults have a capacity for violence similar to that demonstrated by the People's Temple.

Our immediate concern is aroused by those cults that have expanded their operations into other countries and continents. In recent years, this tactic seems to have been chosen by a number of groups as a way to minimize the risk of exposure in the American media and to escape the scrutiny and jurisdiction of local, state, and federal government agencies. By 1973, after a number of legal clashes, Hannah Lowe's New Testament Missionary Fellowship, one of the first cults to proselytize on college campuses in the East, had moved most of its operations to Colombia. In 1974, following the publication of an unfavorable report by New York State's Charity Frauds Bureau, the Children of God moved about 90 percent of its nationwide membership overseas, where they have since touched down in England, Italy, France, Spain, the Canary Islands, Morocco, and Libya. In 1978, the cult changed its name to the Family of Love—an apt reflection of its recent turn to prostitution as a means of soliciting money and new members—and it now claims to have 829 colonies around the world.

All the major cults we investigated—the Unification Church, the Hare Krishna, the Divine Light Mission, and the Church of Scientology—have headquarters or primary operations in the United States, while maintaining active bases in other countries. Many may have branched out internationally to keep tabs on the large sums of cash they are reported to have deposited in foreign banks, just as the People's Temple stashed secret funds said to approach $10 million in secret bank accounts in Switzerland and Panama. Other cults undoubtedly find foreign outposts useful places to hide members who are being sought by their parents or law enforcement officials, and, like Jim Jones, some groups appear to be setting up remote hideouts in preparation for a mass exodus from the United States.

A number of controversial cults, shunning public attention, have withdrawn to the relative security of rural communes in the United States. Since 1975, several hundred members of the Tony and Susan Alamo Christian Foundation, which began in Hollywood in the late sixties, have lived in near-total seclusion in Dyer, Arkansas (Pop. 609). The Unification Church, which in addition to its vast religious and business operations in South Korea is reported to be expanding its operations in Europe and South America, maintains a number of farms and rural retreats in the United States to which it brings many new recruits in the initial stages of their conversion and indoctrination. Within the last few years, the Unification Church has also begun large-scale commercial fishing operations in the United States and has transferred significant resources in wealth and membership to out-of-the-way towns such as Gloucester, Massachusetts; Norfolk, Virginia; and Bayeu Le Batre, Alabama.

But perhaps the most lavish retreat of any major cult is that of the International Society for Krishna Consciousness near Moundsville, West Virginia. The retreat of more than two hundred acres, known as New Vrindaban, is home to nearly three hundred Krishna members. Many of them have been laboring since 1973 on the construction of the cult's ornate "Prabhupada Palace"—named after their late founder. Soon to be completed, the palace, which would cost millions if built commercially, will have a twenty-two karat gold-leaf dome, two terraces, moats, gardens, marble from forty countries, and gold and copper leaf everywhere.

New Vrindaban may also be the site of one of the largest stockpiles of weapons known to have been acquired by any domestic religious cult. Since 1973, the Krishnas have collected an arsenal that includes M-14 military-surplus semiautomatic rifles, handguns, and thousands of rounds of ammunition. Cult leader Kirtanananda Swami has claimed that the weapons are only for self-defense, citing instances when local vigilantes invaded the Krishna farm; and Krishnas declare themselves to be nonviolent, pointing out that their simple vegetarian diet shows their reluctance to kill another living thing. Their own teachings and codes, however, tend to undermine this argument.

As it turns out, many cults, while professing to be peace-loving and nonviolent, have doctrines sanctioning criminal or violent acts, and collections of weapons that might be used to carry them out. The seemingly passive Krishnas present cult researchers with what may be the most vivid ironies: former members have reported receiving identical instructions from their temple leaders on how to deal with deprogrammers and other "demons"—their word for outsiders—who are being "blasphemous." "The Krishna teachings offer three choices to devotees when they face blasphemy," said one. "The first is to leave the place, the second is to kill the person being blasphemous, and, if all else fails, the third is to kill yourself."

Although all profess simply to be taking defense precautions, other cults appear to be gearing up for armed confrontations. Investigators probing the operations of Synanon since that group's alleged rattlesnake attack on Paul Morantz report that the organization has purchased a total of 152 pistols, rifles, and shotguns and more than 660,000 rounds of ammunition. The Way

International, a Christian cult that has a college in Emporia, Kansas, enrolled students and faculty members in marksmanship and weapons-safety classes at a local National Guard Armory. An eyewitness reported that more than five hundred people attended the course with .22-caliber rifles, yet cult spokesmen say they were only seeking hunters' safety training.

The controversial Church of Scientology has allegedly been linked to a number of criminal or violent acts, in addition to its recent charge of having infiltrated and burglarized agencies of the U.S. government. The FBI's 1977 raid on Scientology headquarters yielded some startling paraphernalia: two pistols, a blackjack, electronic eavesdropping equipment, a lock-picking kit, plus vials of knockout drops and something labeled "vampire blood." It also uncovered files that appeared to confirm allegations that, throughout the seventies and before, Scientology has engaged in a systematic campaign of harassing its critics by legal and illegal means. Paulette Cooper, author of *The Scandal of Scientology,* has filed a $20 million suit against the cult, claiming that following publication of her book in 1971, church members stole her stationery, sent themselves a bomb threat, and then had her indicted on criminal charges. Two years later, after she had spent more than $20,000 in legal fees and $6,000 for psychiatric treatment, Cooper was cleared of all charges when she submitted to a court-supervised truth serum test. It wasn't until 1977 that the FBI uncovered a Scientology file marked "Operation Freakout" containing documents that concerned "getting PC incarcerated in a mental institution or jail."

But perhaps the most comprehensive threat of large-scale criminal or violent action is posed by the Unification Church, many of whose members have been told to prepare to become "heavenly bullets" in Reverend Moon's worldwide crusade against Communism. Moon's own speeches reveal his master plan to create a world theocracy under his rule. In 1973, he vowed, "I will conquer and subjugate the world." Later that year he said, "The present United Nations must be annihilated by our power." And in 1974, he told his followers, "So from this time, every people and organization that goes against the Unification Church will gradually come down or drastically come down and die. Many people will die—those who go against our movement." Moon's threats may sound idle or grandiose, but he has the materials and manpower to back them up. With his factories in Korea that manufacture ammunition and automatic rifles, his worldwide fleet of fishing boats, and his thousands of hard-core American followers and reported hundreds of thousands in South Korea, he has the means to initiate a major international skirmish; and he is said to be already drawing up plans for large-scale international campaigns—both spiritual and otherwise.

We enter the eighties with ample evidence of the cult threat in America and around the world, not only in the flagrancies of mass violence and destruction like that which took place in Guyana, but in the subtleties of mind control that have altered the lives of an estimated three million young Americans in this decade. Beyond the immediate crisis of the cults, the issue of mind control is a broadening one. Almost daily, the panoply of techniques for altering human awareness and personality reaches new levels of sophistication and popular acceptance. Following the trail first blazed in the sixties by the pioneers of America's consciousness explosion, in all likelihood Americans in the eighties will continue to pursue adventures in personal growth and spiritual fulfillment. They will be solicited in ever-increasing numbers and with ever more accomplished marketing schemes by groups offering some form of revelation, ecstasy, or psychic superpowers.

Our concern in this cultural trend is that it has already become a free-for-all. Under current laws, neither the techniques nor the technicians are subject to any form of government regulation or consumer protection. Behind the blazing shield of the First Amendment, it appears that a new generation of con men and megalomanics has grown to frightening maturity, in many instances assuming near-total power over their followers and customers. And now, as each group endeavors to expand its activities and scatter its personnel and resources, the threat of unchecked mind-control technology is spreading out from its cradle in America to the rest of the world.

In recent months we have come upon a number of spurious international blueprints being drawn up or carried out by cultlike organizations so large, so professional in their organization, and so socially acceptable that they appear to have become invulnerable. These groups now permeate the mainstream of American society, and in the current outcry over "the cults," their activities are being largely ignored. Perhaps the best known of these grand designs is the Hunger Project, an independent nonprofit organization created and funded by Werner Erhard's est. Its stated goal is to bring about "the end of hunger and starvation on our planet by 1997," but it has been reported that of the more than $883,000 it had raised by late 1978, less than 1 percent had been given to organizations that actually provide food for hungry people. Instead, most of the money was being used to sell the idea of the Hunger Project to the public.

Further down the mainstream, a number of evangelical Christian sects have inaugurated large-scale mass media campaigns of awesome scope and technical sophistication. To cite one example, the Campus Crusade for Christ, among the most visible and enterprising evangelical organizations, has launched a $1 billion crusade aimed at placing inexpensive radio and television sets in more than two million villages around the world. In 1978, the movement announced its new "Here's Life, World" program, complete with a "special task force on technology" headed by a former president of McDonnell Douglas Astronautics. Already claiming two million converts in Hong Kong, Mexico, and India, "Here's Life, World" aims to "share the gospel with every person on earth by 1982."

But undoubtedly the most ambitious international project of all is that of the Maharishi Mahesh Yogi's Transcendental Meditation organization, which recently established a "World Government for the Age of Enlightenment" at its American headquarters in South Fallsburg, New York. From there, according to multiple reports, the Maharishi has sent out advanced TM teams to areas of social and political turmoil in 108 countries, to "resolve outbreaks of conflict and violence" and to "create a dramatic and soothing influence in the atmosphere" through the practice of his TM technique. His most recent announcement was a plan "to bring invincibility to Israel," a direct appeal to American Jews to travel to Israel for a special two-month TM "Sidhis" course in levitation—at $2,500 per person. Many Sidhis graduates told us that they have "gained mastery of the laws of nature," and that they now have the ability to rise off the ground and "fly."

It is the promotion of this type of delusion and vulnerability to suggestion that we consider most alarming about groups such as these and the techniques they use, along with the possibility that large numbers of people in other countries may soon be laid open to mind control at the direction of self-appointed religious, social, and political leaders. The tragedy in Guyana has served to alert the American people and people around the world to these potentially destructive developments, but the public's dawning awareness has yet to grasp the havoc that may lie in store.

Seven months ago it was much easier to draw back from our work and take an objective look at the dangers we were foreshadowing. Our worst fears were largely hypothetical, based on long hours of travel, personal interviews, and poring over scholarly research and laboratory data. Back then, the only people who shared our concern were those whose lives had been touched by the phenomenon. On impact, Jonestown appears to have changed all that. The public seemed to sense some personal message in the photographs of 912 bloated bodies so peacefully laid out and colorfully clad.

In our initial inquiry, we confronted the emergence of a new software technology capable of producing, in our opinion, frightening new forms of mental illness. In *Snapping,* we described three forms of this new illness as varieties of *information disease,* and since introducing that term, we have observed new classes of information disease that we believe to be more subtle, yet equally dangerous. Initially, we concluded that the effects of cult techniques could be counteracted by direct intervention in the form of skilled deprogramming and rehabilitation. We believed that any individual could recover from these effects regardless of how long he had been under their control. In the many miles we have traveled since then, after talking with hundreds more parents, former cult members, and mental health and legal professionals, our findings have been confirmed in the majority of instances, but we have also seen troubling signs that some cult techniques may damage the brain and nervous system in ways that are permanent and irreversible.

Our original hope and optimism have been dampened in other respects. Over the years, we have watched a gathering storm of what borders on religious fanaticism spread across the United States and the world. In some arenas, religion in this country has given rise to a new form of mental illness. In others, it has given way to terrorism. Yet, because the strength of our country is so intimately bound to noble principles that seem to defy any attempt to safeguard against their exploitation, the United States is currently helping, inadvertently, to foster a wave of chaos that has grown to international proportions.

The question in our minds is whether America's people and politicians have the desire—and the nerve—to halt the trend, for ultimately it will be the citizens of this country who determine what happens. Will America abandon the principles and ethics of science and the technology that we as a people have looked to discover and have so tirelessly created? Or, as the problems of the eighties roll toward us, will we simply throw up a smokescreen of religious rhetoric? Religion has played and will continue to play a vital role in America's social development, but we question whether it can continue to do so standing on worn-out myths and arbitrary principles that deny basic human freedoms. Today, every nation and every religion is being called upon to reevaluate its premises, its doctrines, and its sacred rites to weed out those that are destructive to individuals, to their relationships with other people, and to society. Without this chastening introspection of our most fundamental attitudes and beliefs, we face only the terror of unmovable minds snapped shut with absolute answers.

The human mind afflicted in this manner has been the subject of our inquiry. Through it all, we hold fast to the optimism that has kept our own spirits from faltering. We say that each new report of cult abuses and criminal offenses will stir a major advance in public opinion and await the moment when policymakers in government become aroused to action. But, on reflection, it seems to us that even the carnage of the People's Temple may fail as a warning. Beyond Jonestown, staring at us in the eighties is a tyranny that may move people and nations over a precipice.

January 31, 1979

Acknowledgments

WE EXPRESS FIRST our gratitude to the many mass-therapy participants, former cult members, and concerned parents around the country who helped us in our research for this book, with the understanding that we would respect their privacy by not revealing their identities.

We also wish to thank William and Betty Rambur and James and Henrietta Crampton of the Citizens Freedom Foundation, Dr. and Mrs. Marvin Galper, Marjoe Gortner, Leslie Van Houten and Maxwell Keith, and Ted Patrick and Sondra Sacks.

We are indebted to several distinguished scientists and professional people who shared with us their thinking and, in many instances, their latest research. Concerning the human potential movement, its sources and outgrowths, and the position of American psychology and psychiatry in general, we thank Paul Brenner, Russ Denea, Gilla Prizant, Betty Meador, and Will Schutz; and we are especially grateful to Jack Gibb and Carl Rogers.

The so-called "hard" scientists we interviewed—the mathematicians and physicists, the neurophysiologists and bio-information scientists, and the interdisciplinary thinkers who fall at various points along the communication spectrum—have contributed immensely to both the research and the spirit of this book. We are grateful to John R. Pierce for helping us separate the engineering aspects of communication from the new science's human applications; to Fred Crowell, John Lyman, G. D. McCann, and David Rumelhart, for their views on the problems and promises of the human information-processing perspective; and to Hans Bremermann and Karl Pribram, for their willingness to speculate with us on their own developing theories and other recent and controversial scientific research.

Special thanks are in order as well to Dr. Alfred G. Smith, Director of the Center for Communication Research at the University of Texas, for his creative instruction and his thoughtful insight into some of the difficult questions we set out to explore in this book.

We thank a number of close friends, relatives, and new acquaintances around the country who sustained us in our travels and who, in many instances, made difficult times easier, and even fun: Bob Baker, Don Cameron, Holly Conway, Kacey Conway, Mike Conway, Robert and Virginia Conway, Lois and Larry Davis, Mary and Dick Deich, Debbi Dudziak, Judy and Michael Einbund, Grace Gianforte, Patrick Green, Paula Harrington, Bob and Birchie Henderson, Evie Juster, Marilyn, Judy, and Bill Kanoskie, Joe Marcella, B. Lynn Micale, Doris Peck, Davis Perkins, Eric Rayman, Roger Repohl, Don and Rene Ross, and Aaron Smith. We want to make grateful mention also of some of the many individuals with whom we made only brief personal or telephone contact: the Crudups, the DeBlassies, Milton Erickson, Bill Farr, Sam Farry, Thelma Moss, the Randalls, Steven Smale, and Irving Yalom.

The enthusiasm of Sallie T. Gouverneur gave our project the momentum it needed to get off the ground. The aid and counsel of Donald C. Farber, and his continuing belief in us both, have been not only a catalyst but quite possibly the decisive factor in this endeavor.

Our appreciation goes to the many people who encouraged, helped, and arranged for us to write *Snapping* for J. B. Lippincott Company: editor-in-chief Ed Burlingame, Beatrice Rosenfeld, Kathryn Frank, Katharine Kirkland, and Elaine Terranova; and, above all, we thank our editor, Peg Cameron.

Finally, we thank our parents, Bob and Helen Conway and Leonard and Arline Siegelman, for more material help, moral support, and love than we could ever fully acknowledge or repay.

FLO CONWAY and JIM SIEGELMAN
New York, N.Y.
New Year's Day, 1978

FOR MORE INFORMATION CONTACT:

CITIZEN'S FREEDOM FOUNDATION, P.O. Box 7000-89, 1719 Via el Prado, Redondo Beach, CA 90277.

AMERICAN FAMILY FOUNDATION, INC., P.O. Box 343, Lexington, Massachusetts 02173.

COMA (Council On Mind Abuse, Inc.), Box 575, Station Z, Toronto, Ontario M5N 2Z6 Canada.

Notes

Bracketed numbers refer to works listed in the accompanying Bibliography.

Page

Chapter 1: SNAPPING

11   . . . nearly eight thousand techniques for expanding human awareness: This figure appears in a *Newsweek* cover story, "Getting Your Head Together," September 6, 1976, p. 56.

   . . . six million alone had taken up some form of meditation: A Los Angeles *Times* article, "Meditation: Millions in U.S. in Pursuit of Inner Peace" (Sunday, February 13, 1977, Part II, p. 1), reports 6 million American meditators; according to recent Gallup poll findings, 4 percent of Americans are involved in Transcendental Meditation.

12   . . . three million young Americans had joined the one thousand religious cults active in the United States: These are the upper estimates, according to an article in *U.S. News & World Report*, "Religious Cults: Newest Magnet for Youth," June 14, 1976, p. 52.

15   "perfect knowledge": This phrase is used frequently by followers of the Guru Maharaj Ji, founder of the Divine Light Mission.

   The Children of God . . . the Attorney General of New York: See "Final Report on the Activities of the Children of God," submitted by the New York State Charitable Frauds Bureau to Hon. Louis J. Lefkowitz, State Attorney General, September 30, 1974.

16   . . . expanding into regional markets and spawning local imitators: Many of these local spin-offs are nearly exact copies of est and other mass therapies and bear vaguely similar names, such as the Training of New Mexico, for example, which operates a mass-group therapy enterprise in the Albuquerque–Santa Fe area.

Chapter 2: THE SEARCH

22   "sixty hours that transform your life": See Adelaide Bry's *est* [26].

25   Est is, without a doubt, the most controversial: All this information on est, along with many more details and personal accounts, can be found in Bry [26], Fenwick [28], Kornbluth [33], Litwak [35], and Marin [38].

26   . . . an article in the March, 1977, issue of *American Journal of Psychiatry:* by Leonard L. Glass, M.D., Michael A. Kirsch, M.D., and Frederick N. Parris, M.D. When their work was done, Dr. Glass was Director of the Emergency Service, Langley Porter

Page

Neuropsychiatric Institute, University of California, San Francisco, where Dr. Kirsch was Resident in Psychiatry and Dr. Parris was Clinical Instructor, Department of Psychiatry. At the time of publication, Dr. Glass was Assistant Psychiatrist at McLean Hospital, Belmont, Massachusetts.

Chapter 3: THE FALL

29   "deprogrammers": The subject of deprogramming will be dealt with in depth in chapter 6.

35   The Unification Church holds a special place among the cults: Our insight into the Unification Church, its doctrines, and its activities comes from personal interviews with a number of former members in addition to Lawrence and Cathy Gordon. Many talks with one-time Moonies, both rank-and-file members and higher-ups, supported and expanded on facts and views of the church presented in Patrick [40], Yamamoto [47], and the newspaper references that follow.

. . . the old New Yorker Hotel: In the *New York Times,* May 13, 1976.

The Washington *Post* . . . South Korean Central Intelligence Agency: On August 5, 1977, the Washington *Post* disclosed the findings of a report issued by the House of Representatives Subcommittee on International Organizations, which stated, "We have received reliable information that [Mr. Moon] and organizations connected with him maintained operational ties with the government of South Korea and specifically the Korean Central Intelligence Agency." An Associated Press article in early December, 1977, reported that Moon's chief aide and translator, Col. Bo Hi Pak, was once the Korean military attaché in Washington, and an earlier article in the Washington *Post* (reprinted in the New York *Post* November 8, 1976) reported that "according to U.S. Intelligence information Pak met in the 'Blue House' presidential mansion in Seoul with South Korean President Park Chung Hee, Washington-based South Korean businessman Tongsun Park, and KCIA officials in late 1970 to discuss plans for the Capitol Hill influence buying." The article also reports that according to "informed sources in the justice and state departments," the South Korean Central Intelligence Agency requested the massive demonstrations that followers of Moon staged on Capitol Hill in 1974 opposing the impeachment of then President Nixon. Pak and other Unification Church spokesmen have denied all connections to the KCIA."

Chapter 4: THE ROOTS OF SNAPPING

40   A recent Gallup poll reported that half of all adult Protestants . . . say they have been Born Again: This poll and other signs of America's mushrooming Evangelical movement were reported in a cover story in *Newsweek,* "Born Again!" October 25, 1976, pp. 68–78.

42   Christian Charismatic movement has spread . . . to an estimated fifteen million communities: This figure, attributed only to the Charismatic or Pentecostal branch of Evangelical Christianity, can be found in O'Connor [39].

45   The creation of a Harvard Business School graduate and former adman for Coca-Cola: These figures concerning the I Found It crusade were reported by CBS News correspondent Bill Moyers on *CBS Reports'* "Born Again," broadcast July 14, 1977, 10:00–11:00 EDT (used with permission).

One of its board members posted the bail money for Eldridge Cleaver: *Ibid.*

Jesus and the Intellectual: Bright [25].

". . . from all your filthiness": This quotation from Ezekiel 36:25–27 in the Old Testament, appears in the American Messianic Fellowship booklet [22], p. 22.

Born January 14, 1944: The biographical material in this section on Marjoe came from our interview and the extensive background provided in Gaines [29].

Chapter 5: SNAPPING AS SOMETHING NEW

The first steps in that direction: A thoughtful and comprehensive perspective on the early days of the human potential movement was presented by Tomkins in his *New Yorker* profile on Michael Murphy, co-founder of the Esalen Institute [20]. Two slightly different perspectives on the movement's beginnings, written during its heyday, can be found in the "History of Encounter" chapter of Schutz's *Elements of Encounter* [14], and in the new preface to Maslow's *Religions, Values, and Peak-Experiences* [8].

. . . the theory and practice of encounter edged closer to its revivalist forerunners: Although Jacob Moreno has been credited with using the term "encounter" in regard to group therapy and employing basic encounter methods in Vienna as far back as 1910, most early American groups bore closer resemblance to traditional Freudian group psychotherapy. Ruitenbeek reports in *The New Group Therapies* [13], p. 14, that around 1930 the American psychiatrist and former minister L. Cody Marsh began employing religious revival techniques in his group work with psychotics, a method he discussed in an article in *Mental Hygiene* (1931), "Group Treatment by the Psychological Equivalent of the Revival."

The Hare Krishna hired its own admen; . . . est gave a top position to a former Coca-Cola executive: Our personal conversation with an ex-Krishna higher-up revealed that cult's move to hire professionals and other laymen to market the cult's highly commercial incense products. With regard to est, Kornbluth [33] reports that the organization's president, Don Cox, had been Director of Planning for Coca-Cola, U.S.A., as well as a former instructor at Harvard Business School.

In the remote bush country of Australia . . . *The Crack in the Cosmic Egg:* Pearce's discussion can be found in [110] pp. 125–32.

Anthropologists point to . . . the longest unbroken line of cultural development: Pearce rallies an impressive array of supporting views for an argument with which few Americans today would disagree: that our Western mode of consciousness is not necessarily the ultimate in human capability. He cites Claude Levi-Strauss as a champion of the aborigine world-view, which, Pearce says, the French anthropologist considers to be "an intellectual refinement as well knit and coherent as any culture's in history" [110], p. 127.

. . . organization men: See Whyte's *The Organization Man* [114].

Journalist Sally Kempton, writing in *New York* magazine: Kempton's life-changing encounter with Muktananda is fully described in "Hanging Out with the Guru" [32], from which the excerpt has been drawn.

Chapter 6: BLACK LIGHTNING

In truth . . . exaggerations . . . about deprogramming . . . are part of a heavily financed and well-coordinated campaign: Sometime after we interviewed Patrick in Orange County, we received copies of two anti-deprogramming tracts that were reportedly being

Page

produced and distributed on an international scale by several large worldwide cult organizations. One booklet, titled "Deprogramming: The Constructive Destruction of Belief," appeared to us to be a parody of a manual of deprogramming techniques. Prepared in Great Britain "based upon techniques as they are practiced in the USA," the manual distorted every aspect of the deprogramming process as we had come to understand it, advocating the use of "food termination," "shame-inducement through nudity," and "physical correction" ("It goes without saying that in keeping with the above approach any physical correction should be administered with as little bruising as possible"). The subtlety of the attack can best be seen in the section on "Sex and the Deprog Tech": "There have been stories of subjects being hetero- or homo-sexually raped by Technicians. These would be laughable if they did not occur with such regularity. . . . Far from rape, what the subject has experienced is almost certainly the application of aggressive sex by the Technician (the beneficial aspects of which are dealt with above)."

70   Logic . . . the son of Steve Allen from television: Not long after Patrick attempted to recover several members of the Love Family, Steve Allen issued a statement to the press in which he said, "It's fine with me that my son and grandchildren are living in a religious commune. I decided that if it was reasonable and productive for him, it was fine by me." From Patrick [40], p. 131.

Chapter 7: WANTED: PROFESSIONAL HELP

80   CFF: Readers interested in contacting the CFF may write directly to: Citizen's Freedom Foundation, P.O. Box 7000-89, 1719 El Prado, Redondo Beach, CA 90277.

84   "the cult syndrome": This term was introduced in "Destructive Cultism" (*American Family Physician,* February, 1977, pp. 80–83) by Eli Shapiro, M.D.: "I have concluded that a distinct syndrome of *destructive cultism* can be defined. . . . Change in personality is the most prominent characteristic of this syndrome."

Chapter 8: THE CRISIS IN MENTAL HEALTH

89   . . . the "robot model" of man: Ludwig von Bertalanffy, the brilliant biologist and theorist, was an outspoken critic of the robot model, which he saw as "theoretically inadequate in view of empirical fact and . . . practically dangerous in its application to 'behavioral engineering.' " In his far-reaching book *General System Theory* [50], he discussed at length how the dominant schools of modern psychology come together in the image of man as robot: "One leading concept is the *stimulus-response scheme,* or S-R scheme for short. Behavior, animal and human, is considered to be response to stimuli coming from outside. . . . This may be classical conditioning by way of repetition of the sequence of conditional and unconditional stimuli according to Pavlov. It may be operant conditioning by reinforcement of successful responses according to Skinner. It may be early childhood experience according to Freud, beginning with toilet training" (pp. 188–89).

This so-called Third Force in psychology: See the Preface to Maslow's *Toward a Psychology of Being* [9].

92   At the end of the seventies: For a partial view of the current dilemmas confronting psychiatry and the mental health field in general, see "Psychiatry in Crisis," by James

Page

S. Eaton, Jr., M.D., and Leonard S. Goldstein, M.D., in the *American Journal of Psychiatry*, June, 1977.

Chapter 9: BEYOND BRAINWASHING

98 "At Panmunjon . . . a third world war": This quotation appears in Schein [44], p. 288. It was attributed to a "Commander Ding" of the North Korean Army by S. J. Davis in *In Spite of Dungeons* (London: Hodder & Stoughton, 1954).

Their tiny, loose-knit, fledgling organization: The work of Return to Personal Choice was described in an article in *Woman's Day*, "Why Kids Join Cults," by David Black [23]. Our own research included in-depth interviews with one member of RPC and a number of former cult members around the country who had worked with or been treated by various members of the group.

101 Verifiable links have been discovered: Again, see Black [23].

103 . . . animal response to the techniques of hypnosis is almost exactly opposite: See Estabrooks [27], p. 43. "The accepted way to hypnotize a sheep, for example, is suddenly to pull its legs out from under it, hold the animal firmly on the ground, then gradually relax the pressure. . . . [Man] simply does not respond to these methods. . . . For example, that sheep will show no 'practice effect.' It is just as easy to hypnotize him the first time as it is the fiftieth time. . . . This is directly contrary to what we would expect in human hypnotism."

The techniques employed by cult and group leaders bear no resemblance to the classical induction of hypnosis: An excellent example of the classical method of inducing hypnosis can be found in Marcuse [37], p. 52.

Chapter 10: INFORMATION

110 Cybernetics, succinctly defined as the study of "communication and control in the animal and the machine: See Wiener [85], p. 11, for the derivation and definition of the term.

. . . the vital element of "feedback" . . . he identified as "information": Wiener likened steering mechanisms, automatic antiaircraft guns, and human and animal reflexes to "This method of control, which we may call control by *informative feedback.*" In Wiener [85], p. 113.

. . . their British counterparts preferred . . . "variety": British engineer W. Ross Ashby, in *An Introduction to Cybernetics* [49], p. 126, defines "variety" in the same terms as Shannon defines "information" in *The Mathematical Theory of Communication* [79], p. 32. Both concepts leaned heavily upon earlier notions of information introduced in the 1920s by two Bell Labs scientists, H. Nyquist and R.V.L. Hartley.

. . . the simple on-off, heads-or-tails choice: It is important to note that Wiener's concept of information appeared to be much less discrete and more fluid than Shannon's. These varying views do not necessarily contradict each other, however, but represent a dualism which can be as helpful (and, at times, confusing) as the complementary wave and particle models of light. Wiener's approach, as described in his autobiography, has received little attention in the engineering world, but his concept may be more applicable than Shannon's as a model of information flow in living things. Wrote Wiener, "I approached information theory from the point of departure of the electric circuit carrying a continuous current, or at least something which could be interpreted as continuous current. At the same time, Claude Shannon . . . was developing a parallel and largely equivalent theory from the point of view of electrical switching systems. . . . As I have said before, Shannon loves the discrete and eschews the continuum." Wiener [89], p. 263.

111 Wiener himself repeatedly voiced his concern over the impact of this new technology on human beings: See Wiener's classic popular works, *The Human Use of Human Beings* [88] and *God & Golem, Inc.* [87], which received the National Book Award.

Even as the new sciences were developing: See *Embodiments of Mind* [70] by McCulloch, a pioneer in the application of communication principles to the workings of the nervous system. A concise discussion of the subject appears in *The Physical Foundation of Biology* [60] by Elsasser, beginning on p. 71.

112 "chunking": The notion of "chunks" of information (as opposed to single "bits") was introduced by George A. Miller in a now-famous article, "The Magical Number Seven, Plus or Minus Two: Some Limits on Our Capacity for Processing Information" (in *Psychological Review*, March, 1956, and reprinted in *The Psychology of Communication* [72]), which dealt with black box experiments in memory and learning.

. . . by the early sixties, cybernetics and information theory were no longer being acclaimed: See "Information Theory After Eighteen Years," in *Science* [62].

113 Human beings . . . are not electrical circuits: This remark was made to us in personal conversation with Dr. John R. Pierce, a former director of Bell Labs known for his work in the development of communication satellites.

114 . . . the brain's only known function is one of information processing: See Elsasser [60], p. 75, ". . . the only known function of the nervous system and brain is the transmission and circulation of messages containing information."

118 . . . the *hologram*. A recent invention of the science of optics: Basic principles and recent advances in holography are covered in Gabor [61], Leith and Upatnicks [68], and Pennington [73]. Pribram's application of the model is clearly explained in his articles in *Psychology Today* [75] and *Scientific American* [77].

121 In 700 operations, Dr. Paul Pietsch: See Pietsch's article in *Harper's*, "Shuffle Brain" (May, 1972).

122 . . . introduced . . . by a mathematician named Dennis Gabor: See Gabor, "Holography, 1948–1971" [61].

Chapter 11: THE LAW OF EXPERIENCE

126 . . . information mixes freely: See Pribram [76], p. 16, ". . . finer nerve fibers lack an insulating fatty coating (the myelin sheath) which in large fibers prevents interaction among impulses. The slow potentials which occur in fine fibers . . . find therefore no obstacle for actual local interaction."

127 . . . the brain can be said to *metabolize* experience: The concept of the metabolism of information, which we think of as a holographic process of distribution and reorganization, has been suggested previously in more technical terms by a number of important physicists and biologists. Perhaps the best known statement on the subject was made by

the eminent physicist Erwin Schrodinger in his historic 1943 lecture, "What Is Life?" [78]. "How does the living organism avoid decay?" asked Schrodinger (p. 75). "The obvious answer is: By eating, drinking, breathing. . . . The technical term is *metabolism* [his italics]. The Greek word . . . means change or exchange. Exchange of what? Originally the underlying idea is, no doubt, exchange of material. . . . That the exchange of material should be the essential thing is absurd. Any atom of nitrogen, oxygen, sulphur, etc., is as good as any other. . . . What then is that precious something contained in our food that keeps us from death? . . . What an organism feeds upon is negative entropy. [Authors' note: Shannon, Wiener, et al. equate information, i.e., *order,* with the *negative* of randomness—called "entropy" in physics.] . . . Thus the device by which an organism maintains itself stationary at a fairly high level of orderliness . . . really consists in continually sucking orderliness from its environment."

In sensory deprivation tests: Toffler discusses the recognized effects and dangers of sensory deprivation in *Future Shock* [113], pp. 513–16. A more positive view is taken by Lilly in *The Center of the Cyclone* [7] (chapter 3), although the duration of his separate isolation tank experiments is not stated. (More on sensory deprivation can be found in *A Study of Thinking* by Jerome Bruner, with Goodnow and Austin [New York: Science Editions, 1962]; in *Sensory Deprivation: A Symposium,* P. Solomon, ed. [Cambridge: Harvard University Press, 1965]; and in *Sensory Deprivation, 15 Years of Research,* John P. Zubek, ed. [New York: Appleton-Century-Crofts, 1969].)

128   The fundamental workings of the mind . . . are determined by experience: The precise role of experience in brain development is still being researched and debated within the scientific community. Many psychologists, among them Hebb [65], hold that experience is essential for the proper development of even the most elementary perceptual faculties. Our talks with a number of bio-information scientists revealed that much of the latest research in the field confirms and extends this point of view.

. . . genius has been shown to be as much as 90 percent a product of experience: This figure, highly controversial in the continuing "nature vs. nurture" debate, was established in a series of experiments conducted during World War II and has been roughly confirmed in more recent experiments involving identical twins raised under separate circumstances.

129   . . . fundamental patterns of thought and feeling . . . are forged in the intimate relationships between parent and child: See Piaget, *The Construction of Reality in the Child* [74]; also his *Psychology of Intelligence* (Totowa, N.J.: Littlefield, Adams & Co., 1966), p. 158: "During the sensori-motor period the infant is, of course, already subject to manifold social influences . . . people gather round him, smile at him, amuse him, calm him; they inculcate habits and regular courses of conduct."

. . . this organic . . . shaping process is ongoing throughout the lifelong course of personal growth: Most scientists agree that, up to the age of five, the brain is in a particularly fluid and adaptable state. In later years, however, significant portions of the brain are constantly reforming themselves. At a recent conference, even those scientists who hold that the brain is as much as 90 percent "prewired" agreed that the remaining part "never stays still but constantly changes its structure to meet new stimuli and new perceptions." (From "4,000 Scientists in California Find the Universe in the Brain," the *New York Times,* November 13, 1977.)

Page

131   "Perhaps something of this sort occurs . . . original individualities": Ashby [49], p. 139.

    . . . he acknowledged that consciousness was "the most fundamental fact of all": See *Design for a Brain* [48], p. 12, "Vivid though consciousness may be to its possessor, there is as yet no known method by which he can demonstrate his experience to another. And until such a method or its equivalent is found, the facts of consciousness cannot be used in scientific method."

132   Science has only begun to understand . . . memory molecules: A survey of the latest thinking on this subject can be found in Pribram [76], chapter 2, "Neural Modifiability and Memory Mechanisms." See also Shepherd [80], p. 57, "Within the brain itself, synapses are, of course, modifiable during the differentiation and growth of neurons in embryonic and early life; the processes concerned, however, remain among the most profound unsolved problems of biology. In the adult brain, there is more and more experimental evidence of the modifiability of synapses."

Chapter 12: THE SNAPPING MOMENT AND CATASTROPHE THEORY

136   . . . in the aftermath of this shattering break, the brain's information-processing capacities may literally become "disorganized": Although there is at present no scientific data available on the snapping moment, we know from studies of epilepsy and electroshock therapy that an intense electrical "experience" may cause the complete severing of synaptic connections in the brain. "When strong electric currents are sent through the brain, momentarily all neural activity is disrupted and disorganized. When the excess currents stop at the end of the convulsion, there is a tendency for the old and normal neuronal interconnections to be reestablished because of their greater stability" (Wooldridge [90], p. 111).

    . . . may become firmly convinced that he is a chicken: The annals of hypnosis abound with stories of the feats of imagination the mind can perform—and rationalize—in even ordinary states of vulnerability and suggestibility. "The operator hypnotized a subject and told him that when the cuckoo clock struck he was to walk up to Mr. White, put a lamp shade on his head, kneel on the floor in front of him and 'cuckoo' three times . . . when the cuckoo clock struck, the subject carried out the suggestion to the letter.

    " 'What in the world are you doing?' he was asked.

    " 'Well, I'll tell you. It sounds queer but it's just a little experiment in psychology. I've been reading on the psychology of humor and I thought I'd see how you reacted to a joke in very bad taste' " (Estabrooks [27], pp. 80–81).

143   The most ambitious and promising applications . . . have been made by Professor E. Christopher Zeeman: Some of Zeeman's other applications of catastrophe theory include models of stock market crashes, prison riots, barking-dog attacks, and buckling steel girders. In contrast to the application we present here, many of these catastrophe representations have come under heavy criticism from the mathematical community, particularly where they have been used as tools of prediction, as they have in some British prisons.

144   In an article in *Scientific American:* See Zeeman [91].

147   Thom's theory has come under heavy fire: See "Catastrophe Theory: The Emperor Has No Clothes" (*Science,* April 15, 1977), Kolata [67].

148   Bremermann . . . in his review of Thom's book: See Bremermann [54].

Page

Chapter 13: VARIETIES OF INFORMATION DISEASE

153   "Psychopathology has been rather a disappointment . . . secondary disturbances of traffic": Wiener [85], pp. 146–47.

156   . . . the Love Family or Love Israel: Ted Patrick discusses the Love Family at length in *Let Our Children Go!* [40], beginning on p. 127.

161   . . . the "applied philosophy". . . . It now claims to be the largest "self-betterment organization" in the world": See Hubbard [31], p. 165.

. . . an estimated 3.5 million followers: In *Time* magazine, April 5, 1976.

. . . Dianetics, employs a technique called "auditing" ostensibly to raise an individual to higher levels of being: The theory and practice of Dianetics and the auditing process have been fully expounded upon by Hubbard in his voluminous printed works, most of which have been published in the United States by the American Saint Hill Organization in Los Angeles. See Hubbard [30], *Dianetics Today;* also *Dianetics: The Modern Science of Mental Health* (1950); *Dianetics: The Original Thesis* (1970); *Handbook for Preclears,* 7th ed. (1974); *Introduction to Scientology Ethics* (1974); *Scientology 0–8: The Book of Basics* (1970); and *Advanced Procedure and Axioms,* 3rd ed. (1957).

168   Psychodrama takes the imagination one step further than fantasy: See Moreno [10] for the original thinking behind this technique.

There have been documented instances of est graduates . . . feats in defiance of nature: See the *New York Times,* April 24, 1977, and the article in *American Journal of Psychiatry,* March, 1977, cited earlier.

169   . . . the Jews of Europe wanted to die: Marin discusses this famous est claim in "The New Narcissism," *Harper's,* October, 1975 [38].

176   Perhaps most disturbing of all . . . TM called on alleged scientific facts to prove . . . "severely deleterious effects": See, for example, Harold H. Bloomfield, M.D., Michael P. Cain, Dennis T. Jaffe, Robert B. Kory, *TM: Discovering Inner Energy and Overcoming Stress* [24]. In chapter 2, "Transcendental Meditation: The Technique of Contacting Pure Awareness," on p. 19, the authors (two of whom are expressly connected with the TM organization) write that: "some self-styled 'experts' of relaxation or other meditative techniques have been indiscriminately advocating their own makeshift mantras, unaware that severely deleterious effects can be experienced by their unsuspecting practitioners."

Chapter 14: SNAPPING IN EVERYDAY LIFE

183   A great deal has already been written about how the accelerating rate of drastic change: See McLuhan's *Understanding Media* [108] for the classic perspective.

Physicians have identified the various health hazards: See *The Stress of Life,* by Hans Selye (New York: McGraw-Hill, 1956); also "What Stress Can Do to You," *Fortune,* January, 1972.

184   . . . the approaching menace of "future shock": See Toffler's *Future Shock* [113].

. . . another form of snapping . . . much less tangible . . . is clearly observable in America today: Psychiatrist J.A.M. Meerloo, author of *The Rape of the Mind,* reported the

Page

existence of this phenomenon years before *Future Shock*. In "Contributions of Psychiatry to the Study of Human Communication" (Dance [57], pp. 130–59), Meerloo wrote, "Indeed, there exists a positive communication explosion, a prelude to an avalanche. I have already observed in some patients the breakdown of their communication systems as a result of this overloading. We are in danger of being crushed under a mountain of information debris."

. . . the more confused he may be . . . and vulnerable to suggestion: Marcuse discusses the "confusional technique" of hypnosis [37], p. 57.

188   American business and advertising have . . . the latest . . . knowledge concerning the manner in which human behavior can be manipulated: See Packard's classic work, *The Hidden Persuaders* [109]; also "The Gilded Bough: Magic and Advertising," by Howard Luck Gossage, in *The Human Dialogue* [107], p. 363, and "The Folklore of Mass Persuasion," by Floyd W. Matson [107], p. 371.

190   . . . our society has begun to acknowledge . . . an entire generation of Americans has now been molded in the image of television: See "What TV Does to Kids," *Newsweek*, February 21, 1977; also "Television and the New Image of Man," by Ashley Montagu, in *The Human Dialogue* [107], p. 355.

Chapter 15: SNAPPING AND PUNISHMENT

195   "Burglar, car thief": Bugliosi [94], p. 199.

Manson "appears to have developed a certain amount of insight": Bugliosi [94], p. 196.

196   According to Bugliosi, the Process was founded by a former disciple of L. Ron Hubbard: Bugliosi [94], p. 636.

"Undoubtedly," wrote Bugliosi, "he . . .": Bugliosi [94], p. 635.

197   "He whispered into my left ear": From Atkins [92] as excerpted in the New York *Daily News*, September 21, 1977.

198   "These defendants are not human beings, ladies and gentlemen . . . mutation.": Bugliosi [94], p. 606.

In her recently published book, *Susan Atkins: Child of Satan—Child of God*. . . . Completely gone: From Atkins [92] as excerpted in the New York *Daily News*, September 23, 1977.

207   Dr. Joel Fort . . . a "maverick": The *New York Times*, March 1, 1976.

Fort . . . argued . . . Patty was a "willing participant": The *New York Times*, March 9, 1976.

Browning told the jury, "they wash each other out": The *New York Times*, March 21, 1976.

208   . . . one assistant prosecutor did succeed in suggesting . . . that Lifton had a vested professional interest: The *New York Times*, February 28, 1976.

209   In a half-hour interview granted to CBS News: The following quotes were taken from "Patty Hearst—Her Story" a CBS News "Special Report" broadcast December 16, 1976, 11:30 P.M.–12:00 M, EST (used with permission).

210   Dr. Martin Orne . . . stated that . . . "A totally helpless person would appear at that time": The *New York Times*, February 27, 1976.

Page

Another picture, drawn by *New York Times* reporter Lacey Fosburgh: See "Patty Today," The *New York Times Magazine*, April 3, 1977, p. 100.

. . . the opinion expressed by Ted Patrick: Patrick [40], p. 284.

211 . . . man in the street . . . "brainwashing can only be done by experts": The *New York Times*, March 21, 1976.

Berkowitz was said to have shown "no remorse": The New York *Post*, August 11, 1977.

212 . . . doctors ruled out the possibility . . . of physical brain damage: The New York *Post*, August 18, 1977.

. . . "emotionally dead": The New York *Daily News*, September 2, 1977.

214 "I said I didn't bring it to the field": These quotations from Berkowitz's letters to a woman described as a high school sweetheart were published in the New York *Daily News* on August 15, 1977, in a copyrighted article, "Sam Letters: From Here to Insanity?" by Richard Edmonds and Alton Slagle.

"There seemed to be a personality change": This description by an army friend of Berkowitz's appeared in another article in the New York *Daily News*, August 15, 1977, "The Saga of Sam," second of a series, "A Mind in Torment: Drugs, Dogs, Korea and Christ," by Alton Slagle.

"When I look in the mirror": From "Sam Letters: From Here to Insanity?", the New York *Daily News*, August 15, 1977.

215 "I must truly admitt": *Ibid.*

"I hope they let me go home": *Ibid.*

"I just asked him to go to church with me one day": From an Associated Press story in the New York *Post*, August 25, 1977.

Chapter 16: THE FUTURE OF PERSONALITY

218 . . . a new book on . . . the Unification Church: See Sontag [45].

The FBI recently conducted raids on Scientology headquarters: See *Time* magazine, July 25, 1977, p. 67.

The once-tiny Children of God: See *Time* magazine, August 22, 1977, p. 48.

Werner Erhard has launched a new campaign: See the *Village Voice*, "Werner Erhard Thinks He Can Feed the World," October 10, 1977, p. 1.

221 Jack Gibb: Gibb, a pioneer in encounter group theory, has been developing his own theory and method of encounter, called TORI, from principles he helped develop at the National Training Laboratories. See Gibb [3].

224 Researchers who for years have been questing after exotic "psi energies": Two physicists at the world-famous Stanford Research Institute offer an intriguing perspective along these lines in *Mind-Reach: Scientists Look at Psychic Ability* [112]. The authors' scientific methods have been widely criticized as unscientific, however (see the *New York Times Book Review*, March 13, 1977).

And slowly that framework appears to be taking shape . . . the new scientific languages of quantum physics, neuroscience, cybernetics and information theory: Extensive research in these areas has been going on in the Soviet Union for decades, where science

Page

and the socialist state have devoted considerable resources to the study of "biocommunication." One Russian scientist has gone so far as to quantify the information-carrying capacity of human extrasensory channels. In controlled experiments in intercity telepathic communication, he has measured the number of bits per second that may be transmitted between test subjects separated by distances of up to 1,000 kilometers. Current Russian findings suggest that extrasensory communication and perception function on the basis of extremely low-frequency electromagnetic radiation. In their view, these little "ELF" waves constitute a kind of low-energy mental radio that individuals may broadcast to one another. See [112], p. 43, and [104].

Postscript: Jonestown
The Face of the Eighties

227 . . . "the story of the decade": Jimmy Breslin in the New York *Daily News,* November 23, 1978.

227 The twenty-eight-count indictment . . . in history: For details on the government's charges, see the *Washington Post,* August 16, 1978.

228 After a three-year probe . . . M-16 rifles: See the *Washington Post,* November 2, 1978. The Unification Church has issued a 279-page denial of the charges.

228 . . . Synanon's self-styled "Imperial Marines": The *Los Angeles Times,* October 13, 1978.

229 "It is time to die with dignity" . . . "Mother. Mother. Mother. Mother.": This description of the death scene at Jonestown appeared in *Newsweek,* December 4, 1978.

229 . . . "one of the most shocking . . . outside of wartime": The *New York Times,* December 2, 1978.

229 . . . Jones no longer believed in religion: From a previously published interview with Jones's wife, Marceline, in the *New York Times,* November 20, 1978.

234 He "had a different faith . . . in an individual way": Statement by George Hunter, editor of the *Ukiah* (California) *Daily Journal,* in the *New York Times,* November 23, 1978.

237 Jones . . . pursued illicit relationships . . . outside the temple: "On December 12, 1973, Jones was arrested by Los Angeles police for allegedly making a lewd advance to an undercover officer in an adult theater." In *The Suicide Cult,* by Marshall Kilduff and Ron Javers (New York: Bantam Books, 1978), p. 56.

239 (although some of those letters now appear to have been forged): The *New York Times,* November 21, 1978.

241 . . . eliciting prepublication protests from . . . representatives of the American Civil Liberties Union: *Newsweek, op. cit.*

242 . . . huge supplies of psychoactive drugs were smuggled into Jonestown: The *New York Times,* December 29, 1978.

242 "When they came out a week later . . . empty faces": *Newsweek, op. cit.*

243 "I can say without hesitation . . . one continent to the next": The *New York Times,* November 21, 1978.

245 The Treasury Department . . . eighteen months earlier: The *New York Times,* December 3, 1978.

Page

245   The Federal Communications Commission . . . regulations: The *New York Times*, November 23, 1978.

246   . . . the Social Security Administration . . . sign away their benefits: The *New York Times*, November 22, 1978.

246   . . . the Justice Department . . . freedom of religion: The *New York Times*, November 24, 1978.

247   . . . the Children of God moved . . . 829 colonies around the world: The *Philadelphia Inquirer*, December 2, 1978.

248   . . . the Unification Church has . . . transferred significant resources: For a local view of the problem, see *The* (Massachusetts) *Magazine*, January 7, 1979, "The Moonies in Gloucester," by Gillisann Haroian.

248   The retreat . . . known as New Vrindaban: Information on New Vrindaban appeared in the *Philadelphia Inquirer*, December 31, 1978.

248   Their own teachings . . . undermine this argument: Krishna leader Kirtanananda quoted from the Krishna Code of Manu, which, he said, "teaches that it is a favor to kill someone who has committed an offense, because it absolves him from carrying the sin into his next life." In the *Philadelphia Inquirer*, December 31, 1978.

248   "The Krishna teachings offer three choices . . . to kill yourself": In Patrick [40], p. 197 and elsewhere.

248   Investigators probing the operations of Synanon . . . ammunition: The *New York Times*, January 20, 1979.

249   The Way International . . . only seeking hunters' safety training: The *New York Times*, January 22, 1979.

249   The FBI's 1977 raid on Scientology . . . "vampire blood": *Newsweek*, August 28, 1978.

249   "Operation Freakout": The *Los Angeles Times*, August 28, 1978. Other instances of Scientology harassment and criminal frame-ups have been alleged and, in some instances, proved in court, but the public is largely unaware of the cult's explicit sanction of such activities in its official doctrines. One such "Policy Order" issued in 1967 by Scientology founder L. Ron Hubbard concerns "SPs" or Suppressive Persons, also known as "enemies." Titled "Fair Game," the order states that such persons "may be deprived of property or injured by any means by any Scientologist. May be tricked, sued, lied to or destroyed." Cult spokesmen claim the order was rescinded years ago, but provide no conclusive evidence to that effect. Another little-known Scientology doctrine is labeled "R2-45: An enormously effective process for exteriorization but its use is frowned upon by this society at this time." Former Scientologists assert that R2-45 authorized the killing of church enemies with two .45-caliber bullets. There is no evidence that this order was ever carried out, however, and cult spokesmen claim "it was only a joke." Also in the *Los Angeles Times*, August 28, 1978.

249   "I will conquer and subjugate the world": In the New York *Daily News*, November 30, 1975.

249   "The present United Nations must be annihilated . . .": *Ibid.*

249   ". . . Many people will die—those who go against our movement": *Ibid.*

249   . . . he is said to be already drawing up plans for large-scale international campaigns: See

Page

      "The Dark Side of the Moon," by Alan MacRobert, *The Real Paper* (Boston), March 5, 1977.

250   The Hunger Project: See "Let Them Eat *est,*" by Suzanne Gordon, *Mother Jones,* December, 1978. Gordon claims that the Hunger Project's underlying purpose is to recruit customers for Erhard's mind-bending est training seminars. She and other investigators report that everyone who volunteers for the project is encouraged, even openly pressured, to sign up for the training. est vehemently disputes Gordon's charges and has announced its intention to sue *Mother Jones.*

251   . . . the Campus Crusade for Christ . . . "every person on earth by 1982": In the *Los Angeles Times,* August 12, 1978.

Selected Bibliography

THIS LISTING of books, magazine articles, and scholarly papers is not intended to be complete, but it will provide the reader with references to the main sources cited in this book, along with some of the key texts and seminal works used by the authors in the formulation of their perspective. Entries are grouped under headings that do not necessarily indicate the main subject matter of the work but rather the context in which it was found to be most valuable in this book. All newspaper articles and many other magazine articles are described in the accompanying Notes.

Topics in Modern Psychology and the Human Potential Movement
1. Freud, Sigmund, *Civilization and Its Discontents,* trans. by J. Strachey. New York: W. W. Norton, 1962.
2. _____, *New Introductory Lectures on Psychoanalysis,* trans. by J. Strachey. New York: W. W. Norton, 1965.
3. Gibb, Jack R., "Climate for Trust Formation," in L. Bradford, J. R. Gibb, and K. D. Benne, eds., *T-Group Theory and Laboratory Method.* New York: John Wiley & Sons, 1964.
4. Jung, Carl G., *Modern Man in Search of a Soul,* trans. by W. S. Dell and Cary F. Baynes. New York: Harcourt, Brace & World, 1933.
5. Koch, Sigmund, "The Image of Man Implicit in Encounter Group Theory." *Journal of Humanistic Psychology,* 11:109–27 (1971).
6. Lieberman, M. A., I. D. Yalom, and M. B. Miles, *Encounter Groups: First Facts.* New York: Basic Books, 1973.
7. Lilly, John C., *The Center of the Cyclone.* New York: Julian Press, 1972.
8. Maslow, Abraham H., *Religions, Values, and Peak-Experiences.* New York: Viking Press, 1970.
9. _____, *Toward a Psychology of Being.* New York: D. Van Nostrand, 1968.
10. Moreno, Jacob L., *Who Shall Survive? Foundations of Sociometry, Group Psychotherapy and Sociodrama,* 2d ed. Beacon, N.Y.: Beacon House, 1953.
11. Rogers, Carl R., *On Becoming a Person.* Boston: Houghton Mifflin, 1961.
12. _____, *Carl Rogers on Personal Power.* New York: Delacorte Press, 1977.
13. Ruitenbeek, Hendrik M., *The New Group Therapies.* New York: Avon Books, 1970.

14. Schutz, William C., *Elements of Encounter*. Big Sur, Cal.: Joy Press, 1973.
15. _____, *Joy: Expanding Human Awareness*. New York: Grove Press, 1967.
16. Siroka, R. W., E. K. Siroka, and G. A. Schloss, *Sensitivity Training and Group Encounter*. New York: Grosset & Dunlap, 1971.
17. Skinner, B. F., *Beyond Freedom and Dignity*. New York: Alfred A. Knopf, 1971.
18. _____, *Science and Human Behavior*. New York: Macmillan, 1953.
19. Solomon, Lawrence N., and Betty Berzon, *New Perspectives on Encounter Groups*. San Francisco: Jossey-Bass, 1972.
20. Tomkins, Calvin, "New Paradigms" (a profile on Michael Murphy). *The New Yorker*, January 5, 1976.
21. Wann, T. W. ed., *Behaviorism and Phenomenology: Contrasting Bases for Modern Psychology*. Chicago: University of Chicago Press, 1964.

Topics in Religion, Religious Cults, and Mass-Marketed Therapies
22. *There Are Some People Who Really Care About You!* Chicago: American Messianic Fellowship, 1974.
23. Black, David, "Why Kids Join CULTS." *Woman's Day*, February, 1977.
24. Bloomfield, H. H., M. P. Cain, and D. T. Jaffe, *TM: Discovering Inner Energy and Overcoming Stress*. New York: Delacorte Press, 1975.
25. Bright, Bill, *Jesus and the Intellectual*. San Bernardino, Cal.: Campus Crusade for Christ, Inc., 1968.
26. Bry, Adelaide, *est: 60 Hours That Transform Your Life*. New York: Harper & Row, 1976.
27. Estabrooks, G. H., *Hypnotism*, rev. ed. New York: E. P. Dutton, 1943, 1957.
28. Fenwick, Sheridan, *Getting It: The Psychology of est*. Philadelphia: J. B. Lippincott, 1976.
29. Gaines, Steven S., *Marjoe*. New York: Dell, 1973.
30. Hubbard, L. Ron, *Dianetics Today*. Los Angeles: American Saint Hill Organization, 1975.
31. Hubbard, L. Ron, *When in Doubt . . . Communicate*, Ruth Minshull and Edward M. Lefson, eds. Ann Arbor, Mich.: Scientology Ann Arbor, 1969.
32. Kempton, Sally, "Hanging Out with the Guru." *New York*, April 12, 1976.
33. Kornbluth, Jesse, "The Fuhrer Over est." *New Times*, March 19, 1976.
34. Lifton, Robert J., *Thought Reform and the Psychology of Totalism: A Study of "Brainwashing" in China*. New York: W. W. Norton, 1961.
35. Litwak, Leo, "Pay Attention, Turkeys!" *The New York Times Magazine*, March 2, 1976.
36. Malko, George, *Scientology: The Now Religion*. New York: Delacorte Press, 1970.
37. Marcuse, F. L., *Hypnosis, Fact and Fiction*. West Drayton, Middlesex: Penguin Books, 1959.
38. Marin, Peter, "The New Narcissism." *Harper's*, October, 1975.
39. O'Connor, E. D., "Pentecost and Catholicism." *The Ecumenist*, July–August, 1968.
40. Patrick, Ted, with Tom Dulack, *Let Our Children Go!* New York: Thomas Congdon Books/E. P. Dutton, 1976.

41. Prabhupada, His Divine Grace A. C. Bhaktivedanta Swami, *Bhagavad-Gita as It Is.* Los Angeles: International Society for Krishna Consciousness, 1970.

42. _____, *Easy Journey to Other Planets,* rev. ed. Los Angeles: International Society for Krishna Consciousness, 1972.

43. Sargant, William, *Battle for the Mind: A Physiology of Conversion and Brainwashing.* New York: Perennial Library/Harper & Row, 1957, 1959.

44. Schein, Edgar H., with Inge Schneier and Curtis H. Barker, *Coercive Persuasion.* New York: W. W. Norton, 1961.

45. Sontag, Frederick, *Sun Myung Moon and the Unification Church.* Nashville, Tenn.: Abingdon Press, 1977.

46. Wolfe, Tom, "The 'Me' Decade." *New York,* August 23, 1976.

47. Yamamoto, J. Isamu, *The Moon Doctrine.* Downers Grove, Ill.: Inter-Varsity Press (Inter-Varsity Christian Fellowship), 1976.

Topics in Communication Science

48. Ashby, W. Ross, *Design for a Brain: The Origin of Adaptive Behavior.* London: Chapman & Hall, 1952.

49. _____, *An Introduction to Cybernetics.* London: Chapman & Hall, 1956.

50. Bertalanffy, Ludwig von, *General System Theory: Foundations, Development, Applications,* rev. ed. New York: George Braziller, 1968.

51. Bohm, David, "Some Remarks on the Notion of Order," in C. H. Waddington, ed., *Towards a Theoretical Biology,* vol. 2, *Sketches.* An International Union of Biological Sciences symposium. Chicago: Aldine, 1969.

52. Bremermann, Hans, "Complexity of Automata, Brains, and Behavior," in M. Conrad, W. Guttinger, and M. Dal Cin, eds., *Physics and Mathematics of the Nervous System.* Berlin and New York: Springer-Verlag, 1974.

53. _____, "Limitations on Data Processing Arising from Quantum Theory, Part I," in M. C. Yovits, G. T. Jacobi, and G. D. Goldstein, eds., *Self-Organizing Systems 1962.* Washington, D.C.: Spartan Books, 1962.

54. _____, "A Universal Topology" (a review of René Thom's *Stabilité structurelle et morphogénèse*). *Science,* vol. 192 (August 10, 1973), pp. 536–38.

55. Brillouin, Leon, *Science and Information Theory,* 2nd ed. New York: Academic Press, 1962.

56. Cherry, Colin, *On Human Communication.* Cambridge, Mass: M.I.T. Press; New York: John Wiley & Sons, 1957.

57. Dance, Frank E. X. ed., *Human Communication Theory; Original Essays.* New York: Holt, Rinehart & Winston, 1967.

58. Dechert, Charles R., ed., *The Social Impact of Cybernetics.* New York: Simon & Schuster, 1967.

59. Elsasser, Walter M., *Atom and Organism: A New Approach to Theoretical Biology.* Princeton, N.J.: Princeton University Press, 1966.

60. _____, *The Physical Foundation of Biology.* New York: Pergamon Press, 1958.

61. Gabor, Dennis, "Holography, 1948–1971." *Science,* vol. 177 (July 28, 1972), pp. 299–313.

62. Gilbert, E. N., "Information Theory After Eighteen Years." *Science,* vol. 152 (April 15, 1966), pp. 320–26.

63. Hall, Edward T., *Beyond Culture.* New York: Anchor Press/Doubleday, 1976.

64. _____, *The Silent Language.* New York: Doubleday, 1959.

65. Hebb, Donald O., *The Organization of Behavior: A Neuropsychological Theory.* New York: John Wiley & Sons, 1949.

66. Helvey, L. C., *The Age of Information: An Interdisciplinary Survey of Cybernetics.* Englewood Cliffs, N.J.: Educational Technology Publications, 1971.

67. Kolata, Gina Bari, "Catastrophe Theory: The Emperor Has No Clothes." *Science,* vol. 196 (April 15, 1977), pp. 287, 350–51.

68. Leith, Emmett N., and Juris Upatnicks, "Photography by Laser." *Scientific American,* vol. 212, no. 6 (June, 1965).

69. MacKay, D. M., "Cerebral Organization and the Conscious Control of Action," in J. C. Eccles, ed., *Brain and Conscious Experience.* Berlin and New York: Springer-Verlag, 1966.

70. McCulloch, Warren S., *Embodiments of Mind.* Cambridge, Mass.: M.I.T. Press, 1965.

71. _____, "The Reliability of Biological Systems," in M. C. Yovits and C. Scott, eds., *Self-Organizing Systems: Proceedings of an Interdisciplinary Conference.* New York: Pergamon Press, 1960.

72. Miller, George A., *The Psychology of Communication.* New York: Basic Books, 1967.

73. Pennington, Keith S., "Advances in Holography." *Scientific American,* vol. 218, no. 2 (February, 1968).

74. Piaget, Jean, *The Construction of Reality in the Child.* New York: Basic Books, 1954.

75. Pribram, Karl H. "The Brain." *Psychology Today,* September, 1971.

76. _____, *Languages of the Brain; Experimental Paradoxes and Principles in Neuropsychology.* Englewood Cliffs, N.J.: Prentice-Hall, 1971.

77. _____, "The Neurophysiology of Remembering." *Scientific American,* vol. 220, no. 1 (January, 1969).

78. Schrodinger, Erwin, *What Is Life? and Mind & Matter.* Cambridge, England: Cambridge University Press, 1967.

79. Shannon, Claude E., and Warren Weaver, *The Mathematical Theory of Communication.* Urbana: University of Illinois Press, 1949.

80. Shepherd, Gordon M., *The Synaptic Organization of the Brain: An Introduction.* New York: Oxford University Press, 1974.

81. Sokolov, E. N., "Neuronal Models and the Orienting Reflex," in M.A.B. Brazier, ed., *The Central Nervous System and Behavior.* New York: Josiah Macy, Jr. Foundation, 1960.

82. Smith, Alfred G., ed., *Communication and Culture.* New York: Holt, Rinehart & Winston, 1966.

83. Waddington, C. H., ed., *Towards a Theoretical Biology,* vols. I–IV. An International Union of Biological Sciences symposium. Edinburgh, Scotland: Edinburgh University Press; Chicago: Aldine, 1968, 1969, 1970, 1972.

84. Walter, W. Grey, *The Living Brain.* New York: W. W. Norton, 1953.

85. Wiener, Norbert, *Cybernetics: or Control and Communication in the Animal and the Machine.* Cambridge, Mass.: M.I.T. Press, 1948.

86. _____, *Ex-Prodigy: My Childhood and Youth.* Cambridge, Mass.: M.I.T. Press, 1953.

87. _____, *God & Golem, Inc.: A Comment on Certain Points where Cybernetics Impinges on Religion.* Cambridge, Mass.: M.I.T. Press, 1964.

88. _____, *The Human Use of Human Beings.* Boston: Houghton Mifflin, 1950.

89. _____, *I Am a Mathematician: The Later Life of a Prodigy.* Cambridge, Mass.: M.I.T. Press, 1956.

90. Wooldridge, Dean E., *The Machinery of the Brain.* New York: McGraw-Hill, 1963.

91. Zeeman, E. Christopher, "Catastrophe Theory." *Scientific American,* vol. 234, no. 4 (April, 1976).

General and Miscellaneous References

92. Atkins, Susan, as told to Bob Slosser, *Susan Atkins: Child of Satan—Child of God.* Plainfield, N.J.: Logos International, 1977.

93. Bronowski, Jacob J., *The Ascent of Man.* Boston: Little, Brown, 1974.

94. Bugliosi, Vincent, with Curt Gentry, *Helter Skelter: The True Story of the Manson Murders.* New York: (W. W. Norton, 1974) Bantam, 1975.

95. Burgess, Anthony, *A Clockwork Orange.* New York: W. W. Norton, 1963.

96. Cassirer, Ernst, *An Essay on Man.* New Haven: Yale University Press, 1944.

97. Cummings, E. E., *73 Poems.* New York: Harcourt, Brace & World, 1963.

98. Dewey, John, *Experience and Education.* New York: Collier Books/Macmillan, 1938, 1963.

99. Drake, Stillman, trans., *Discoveries and Opinions of Galileo.* New York: Anchor Books, 1957.

100. Fosburgh, Lacey, "Patty Today." *The New York Times Magazine,* April 3, 1977.

101. Eliot, T. S., "The Rock," in *The Collected Poems of T. S. Eliot.* New York: Harcourt, Brace, & World, 1963.

102. Heisenberg, Werner, *Across the Frontiers,* Ruth Nanda Anshen, ed., *World Perspectives,* vol. 48. New York: Harper & Row, 1974.

103. Hoffer, Eric, *The Ordeal of Change.* New York: Harper & Row, 1963.

104. Kogan, I. M., "Information Theory Analysis of Telepathic Communication Experiments." *Radio Engineering and Electronic Physics,* vol. 23, March, 1968.

105. Kuhn, Thomas S., *The Structure of Scientific Revolutions,* 2nd ed., International Encyclopedia of Unified Science, vol 2., no. 2. Chicago: University of Chicago Press, 1962, 1970.

106. Langer, Susanne K., *Philosophical Sketches.* Baltimore, Md.: Johns Hopkins Press, 1962.

107. Matson, Floyd W., and Ashley Montagu, *The Human Dialogue: Perspectives on Communication.* New York: The Free Press, 1967.

108. McLuhan, H. Marshall, *Understanding Media: The Extensions of Man.* New York: McGraw-Hill, 1964.

109. Packard, Vance, *The Hidden Persuaders.* New York: David McKay, 1965.

110. Pearce, Joseph Chilton, *The Crack in the Cosmic Egg.* New York: Julian Press, 1971.

111. Riesman, David, with Nathan Glazer and Reuel Denney, *The Lonely Crowd,* abr. ed. New Haven: Yale University Press, 1961.

112. Targ, Russell, and Harold Puthoff. *Mind-Reach: Scientists Look at Psychic Ability.* New York: Delacorte Press/Eleanor Friede, 1977.

113. Toffler, Alvin, *Future Shock.* New York: Random House, 1970.

114. Whyte, William H., *The Organization Man.* New York: Simon & Schuster, 1956.

Index

DATE DUE

Please remember that this is a library book,
and that it belongs only temporarily to each
person who uses it. Be considerate. Do
not write in this, or any, library book.